GETTING RESULTS

A Guide for Federal Leaders and Managers

GETTING RESULTS
A Guide for Federal Leaders and Managers

Barry White
Kathryn E. Newcomer
Editors

A Project of The Government Performance Coalition

Co-sponsors

⦀ MANAGEMENTCONCEPTS

Center *for*
Innovation
in PUBLIC SERVICE
THE GEORGE WASHINGTON UNIVERSITY • *BearingPoint*

MANAGEMENTCONCEPTS

8230 Leesburg Pike, Suite 800
Vienna, VA 22182
(703) 790-9595
Fax: (703) 790-1371
www.managementconcepts.com

Printed in the United States of America

Library of Congress Cataloging-in-Publication Data

Getting results : a guide for Federal leaders and managers /
    editors, Barry White, Kathryn E. Newcomer.
        p. cm.
    "A project of the Government Performance Coalition."
    IBSN 1-56726-163-9 (pbk. : alk. paper)
    1. Administrative agencies—United States—Management.
2. Executive departments—United States—Management. 3. Organizational
effectiveness—United States—Evaluation. 4. Government productivity—
United States. 5. Performance—Measurement. I. White, Barry, 1944
(Nov. 18)– II. Newcomer, Kathryn E., 1949–

JK421.G48 2005
352.3'0973—dc22

                                                    2004061042

Table of Contents

Preface

Getting Results: A Guide for Federal Leaders and Managers presents an integrated compilation of expert views on how federal leaders and managers can improve the results of their agencies and programs, and how Congress can support and critique that performance. The perspectives shared are non-political and non-partisan; they present objectively the challenges, effects, and lessons of executive and legislative branch performance initiatives and the experiences of federal leaders and managers.

Getting Results is a collaborative product of the Government Performance Coalition, which is an alliance of diverse organizations united in their focus on continual improvement of the results the federal government delivers to the public. Representatives of virtually every organization in the Coalition provided input to this book, although the views presented are personal views and may not represent the entire membership of each organization.

Publication of this book was co-sponsored by Management Concepts and the Center for Innovation in Public Service in the School of Public Policy and Public Administration at The George Washington University (GWU).

Management Concepts is an integrated consulting, training, and publishing company with expertise in the "people" issues of government. The company focuses on the professional growth of individuals and the effectiveness of teams. For over 30 years Management Concepts has helped government organizations serve the public more effectively by improving workplace performance and creating measurable results.

The Center for Innovation in Public Service is a research center housed at GWU that is a unique collaboration between the School of Public Policy and Public Administration and Bearing-Point. By combining expertise and insight, the Center supports research and provides forums for researchers and practitioners from the public, nonprofit, and private sectors to promote effective leadership and management in government.

The contents of *Getting Results* are intended to provide practical guidance to two groups that are critical to ensuring that federal government programs produce their intended results:

- Current and prospective appointed and career government officials who lead and manage agencies and programs

- Members of Congress and their staffs, all of whom expect the executive branch to improve government results.

Additional audiences for this book include nonprofit, private sector, and academic individuals and organizations interested in government performance.

The co-sponsors and authors all hope that the contextual background and guidance offered in *Getting Results* are useful and effective in strengthening leadership and management in the federal government. We all seek to ensure that our government programs produce results valuable for—and valued by—the American people.

Barry White
Kathryn E. Newcomer
Editors

INTRODUCTION

The Results Challenge for Program Leaders and Managers

Barry White

"This administration is asking you to perform an unnatural act: we are asking you to be managers."
—OMB Director Mitch Daniels, to presidential appointees

Getting Results: A Guide for Federal Leaders and Managers will be of value to all appointed and career leaders in government, as well as to all those in Congress and elsewhere who care about improving the results of government. However, this book is intended especially for a large and rather neglected group of critically important federal government officials: the appointed and career program managers who are held directly accountable for achieving results.

When appointed by the President or agency head, the titles of these officials are typically "Deputy," "Assistant," or "Under" Secretary. The civil servant or career program managers who report to them are typically members of the Senior Executive Service who head program offices, bureaus, services, administrations, and divisions—the terms vary across the government.

Most other senior agency officials have an organized network of peers in Washington, some established in law, others administratively. These groups represent their interests, enhance their status and visibility, and most importantly, help them further

---

Barry White *is Director of Government Performance Projects at the Council for Excellence in Government and Coordinator at the Government Performance Coalition.*

their craft. Such groups include: the Chief Information Officers Council, the Chief Acquisition Officers Council, the Chief Financial Officers Council, the Chief Human Capital Officers Council, the Budget Officers Advisory Committee, the Budget and Performance Integration Leaders Group, and the President's Management Council. Each group is directly supported by and relates to a counterpart office or official in the Office of Management and Budget (OMB) of the Executive Office of the President. These organizations have become so prominent that the 2004 edition of the Council for Excellence in Government's quadrennial "Prune Book" for new appointees devotes much of its text to them.

While all this attention is directed to the officers who provide essential support and who collaborate with program managers, there is nothing comparable for those managers themselves. With this book, we begin to restore the balance by offering program leaders and managers practical guidance for success in meeting some of the most important challenges they face in their efforts to achieve better program results for the public, Congress, and the administration.

WHAT IS THE RESULTS CHALLENGE?

It has become so common in Washington to use the term "results" that we are in danger of losing a sense of its importance and urgency. Three implications of the word highlight the messages in this book.

First and foremost, the demand for results derives from government's responsibility to the people. There is good reason for calling government personnel of all kinds "public servants." Government exists to protect the nation and to provide the goods and services people need, as determined through the legislative process and the leadership of elected officials. Results are what government promises to deliver to the public. Results drive public trust in government. Unfortunately, as described in a recent report of the Council for Excellence in Government ("A Matter of Trust: Americans and Their Government: 1958–2004," www.excelgov.org.), there has been a disturbing decline in the level of trust over time.

Second, government never runs on autopilot; its frequent changes in leadership and policy direction also change the results demanded of it. Federal program structure and organization change in response to changes in the nation's priorities, the economy, international pressures, and the needs of the people. The creation of the Department of Homeland Security is the most recent and dramatic example.

Less than a century ago, the federal government had no broad-based income support program for retirees or the poor. Fewer than 50 years ago, there were no major programs to help meet medical needs or support improvement in elementary and secondary student achievement. The government had few programs to help cities, to improve housing, or to develop job skills. Every time a new function or structural reorganization occurs, it is in response to a change in national priorities and it promises results to the public that add to or modify the results promises already on the record.

Third, fiscal pressures generate greater intensity of focus on results. Clearly, every competent manager, in flush times or stringent, wants to get the best results from his or her people and programs as a matter of straightforward professional responsibility. In the first part of the 21st century, the government faces powerful forces that make competition for resources for all government functions especially tough. These forces include the costs of a ground war and the struggle to defeat terrorism. Perhaps most importantly for the long run, America's demographics increasingly impose enormous financial burdens. Our population is living longer and costs more to sustain with medical and income assistance, let alone other important services. Even a long-running boom economy cannot grow us faster than these claims on resources. Comptroller General David Walker makes this case succinctly in "The Nation's Growing Fiscal Imbalance" (www.gao.gov).

What do the fiscal pressures mean for you as a program manager? Essentially, they mean that as tough as it may have been to get the resources you believe you can justify, it is only going to get tougher. The ability to demonstrate that your program is increasingly achieving the great results demanded to meet an important national need in the most efficient manner possible has become a linchpin in the strategy for getting needed resources.

Of course, there are now, always have been, and always will be some programs that are so popular that they are heavily funded regardless of results. Managers of those programs may, for a time, relax a little. But unquestioned priority for resources rarely lasts, no matter how powerful the interests that support the program. For example, the multi-billion dollar subsidized public jobs programs of the 1970s disappeared in the early 1980s due only in part to some improvement in the unemployment rate, but more because of the program's inability to demonstrate adequate results, serious management problems, and changes in national priorities.

When the hard questions are asked—What important difference does the program make, and to whom? If it is making an important difference, is it run efficiently?—programs that cannot answer adequately or cannot demonstrate the best results begin to lose out to programs that can make their case better, even if there's a good argument for the need for the losing program. In each chapter of this book, you will find guidance focused directly on what you need to do to achieve important results and to make the case successfully for investment in those results.

DO APPOINTED AND CAREER MANAGERS COME TO THEIR JOBS WITH THE NEEDED SKILLS AND KNOWLEDGE?

Some of you come to your positions knowing how to manage large, complex enterprises; many of you do not.

Appointees

As the former OMB Director's quote at the beginning of this Introduction illustrates, emphasis is shifting gradually toward valuing relevant management experience in the appointment process, but it has a long way to go. Some of you come to appointed positions from congressional offices, think tanks, academia, or advocacy groups. All those backgrounds help you contribute to policy formulation, but less often help you cope with your management responsibilities.

Making policy is only the beginning; making policy work well is government's most difficult task. It requires effective program implementation, program management, organizational management, people management, and successful navigation through the maze of laws, policies, and institutions that affect your success. This book will help you master these aspects of your job.

Appointee tenure is also a key issue. Most appointees average 18 to 24 months in office—long enough to make an impact on policy but rarely long enough to see that policy through to implementation or to respond fully to evaluations of results. Those of you who are appointees need to peruse this book all the more carefully to identify the aspects of agency and program management you can hope to affect most positively. As importantly, you need to understand the changes already underway in your agency to decide which to support and which to redirect. Any major organizational change, in the public or private sector, can take perhaps seven years to complete, which is obviously outside the normal appointee time window.

Career Leaders and Managers

Change is also in the air for the career service. The Office of Personnel Management is improving its standards for the competencies of senior managers and is implementing recent law changes that connect career executive pay more directly to performance. You will also feel the pressure from OMB and congressional demands for improved results.

Many career managers come up through the ranks, with promotion still tied mainly to technical skills. There are many, many generic training programs in supervision and management, but few are mandatory and most senior managers still learn to manage mainly on the job. Some agencies, like the Food and Nutrition Service of the Department of Agriculture, the Office of Student Financial Assistance, and the military departments operate their own leadership development programs to enable them to link learning to the actual challenges in their agency.

The good news for career managers is the reverse of the situation for appointees: Your tenure is usually much longer. You can often expect to see the benefits of your long-range plans to improve the skills and abilities of your staff, of multi-year rigorous evaluations that will help you determine if your programs are successful, and of multi-year program implementation strategies.

There is, however, a threefold danger inherent in long tenure: complacency, resistance to change, and weariness.

You need to guard against all three. Take action to keep your subject matter knowledge and awareness of your organizational needs current. Be open to change, whether from the ideas your people offer, the views of outside program experts, research, or the frequent changes in policy direction that characterize our governance system. And if you become too tired or worn down to achieve the best results, take the initiative to take a break or move on.

WILL THIS BOOK TELL ME ALL I NEED TO KNOW TO BE A SUCCESSFUL MANAGER?

Getting Results offers a lot, but not everything.

Our goal is to enhance your understanding and insight into many of the most important tools and approaches for successful program management. Return to these chapters as you gain experience to get tips on success and to help you ask the right questions of experts in your agency and elsewhere. Paramount among the experts with whom you must have good working relationships are the people in your agency who support your organization with help on human capital management, information technology, communicating with Congress and the media, budgeting, and procurement. They join you as essential members of your leadership team.

A book this size cannot hope to be comprehensive in its coverage of topics or in its treatment of each topic. We have selected those topics we believe are most important to most government program leaders and managers, but we know that for some of you, a missing topic may be as or more important. For example, we do not discuss in detail the management of financial systems, even though several authors correctly observe that no program manager succeeds fully without timely, accurate financial information connected directly to program information. Still, we hope that what you find here helps you do a better job and helps you figure out where you need more help from other sources.

We also caution you that while each author is a noted expert or practitioner in the field, no expert or practitioner knows everything about any issue. Each author also has personal opinions (even biases) shaped by experience and learning. The authors are speaking for themselves, not necessarily for their organizations or for the Government Performance Coalition. Even if you disagree with an author's views, reading the chapter will help you frame your own views and get up to speed more quickly.

Finally, understanding and becoming expert in the tools and techniques of how to lead and manage programs is the foundation for success. It is the necessary—but not the completely sufficient—condition. No book or lecture or research can ensure that you have "the will to manage." Clearly, to succeed you must be prepared and able to do the hard work, lead your organization well, learn from setbacks as well as successes, stay flexible, and be patient but act when the time is right. You will also need to keep your eye on achieving long-term results goals despite the constant distractions and disputes that often characterize the Washington atmosphere. Along with all that, we hope that you will keep your focus on enjoying life and family.

WHAT IS IN THIS BOOK TO HELP ME?

Getting Results is presented in four parts.

Part One: Leading for Results

Chapter 1 opens with a personal statement of the importance of the focus on results by *Maurice McTigue*, currently head of the Government Accountability Project at the Mercatus Center and formerly a New Zealand Cabinet Minister who helped lead that country's results-based reforms in the 1980s and 1990s.

Chapter 2 offers perspectives of leaders. The first is by a former Cabinet-level chief operating officer, *Mortimer Downey*, who served as Deputy Secretary of the Department of Transportation in the Clinton administration. The title of chief operating officer was formalized in the Clinton administration and confirmed by the Bush administration as the designation of the top appointed official held responsible by the agency head and the President for achieving results. Downey also served the Bush administration as chair of OMB's Performance Measurement Advisory Council.

The career public servant's perspective is described by Vice Admiral *Thad Allen*, Chief of Staff of the U.S. Coast Guard, an agency where virtually all the lessons offered in this book are put into practice every day.

Chapter 3 surveys the most important among the maze of federal laws affecting results management that managers need to understand. It is written by *John Kamensky*, a senior official of the Clinton administration's National Performance Review.

Chapter 4 provides a similar service, putting in perspective executive branch results-management initiatives (nearly all of which have left some residue in agencies), highlighting continuities across 40 years and focusing on the two most recent initiatives. Its author is *Jonathan Breul*, a senior OMB career executive across three administrations who worked closely with the President's Management Council in both the Clinton and George W. Bush administrations.

Part Two: Achieving Results

Chapter 5 takes up the first-order issues of managing the workforce. The first section addresses acquiring the best workforce. It is presented by *Rosslyn Kleeman*, Director of the Coalition for Effective Change, an umbrella group of some 30 organizations representing government managers, and *Brent Bushey* of the

Center for Innovation in Public Service. *Robert Tobias*, former head of the National Treasury Employees International Union and member of the IRS Oversight Board, then addresses the tough issues around linking individual performance to results and to compensation. *Thomas Dungan*, President of Management Concepts, a major provider of a wide range of training opportunities for federal employees, follows with a focus on helping the workforce acquire and maintain the skills and knowledge needed to succeed.

Chapter 6 provides perspective on the exciting and important developments in federal uses of electronic government and information technology to improve agency results and communicate more effectively with the public. The first two authors are *Patricia McGinnis*, President and CEO of the Council for Excellence in Government, and *Dr. David McClure*, Vice President for E-government at the Council for Excellence in Government and formerly leader of the Government Accountability Office's work on federal IT. Then *Dr. Hugh Walkup*, Director of the Strategic Accountability Service of the Department of Education, offers a case study of a new practical application of IT to improve dramatically how government identifies the results achieved in the tens of thousands of entities that share responsibilities in one of the most complex program environments: the federal/state/local systems of elementary and secondary education.

Virtually every federal manager leads or is a key player in devising and implementing major change at least once, often multiple times in his or her career. In Chapter 7, *Mike Davis* of the Center for Innovation in Public Service, and *Pete Smith*, head of the Private Sector Council, join to identify successful approaches to leading and managing change.

One of the fastest growing aspects of federal activity is the partnership with state and local government entities to achieve program results—a partnership that comes with centuries of American traditions in our federal system that do not all contribute to smooth relationships. *Richard Keevey*, Director of the Performance Consortium at the National Academy of Public Administration and a former state budget officer, explores this relationship and offers guidance on how to make it work well.

In Chapter 9, *Carl DeMaio*, President of The Performance Institute, addresses important and often highly controversial issues that arise when government uses contractors to achieve results.

Part Three: Communicating Results

Chapter 10, by *Maurice McTigue*, describes how managers need to think about the results message to communicate it successfully.

Chapter 11 describes the major vehicle agencies have for systematically communicating their results to Congress, the media, and the public: the statutorily required Performance and Accountability Reports. The key officials of the two outside organizations that publicly assess the quality of these reports offer their views on the importance of the reports and how their organizations carry out their assessments: *Harold Steinberg*, Technical Director for the Certificate of Excellence in Accountability Reporting program of the Association of Government Accountants, and *Maurice McTigue* of the Mercatus Center's Government Accountability Project.

Chapter 12 helps managers negotiate the intricacies of using results in the essential resource allocation and internal management processes. It is written by *Dr. Philip Joyce*, Professor at The George Washington University School of Public Policy and Public Administration and former state and congressional budget official.

Chapter 13 closes Part Three with a discussion of how to get the results message out to Congress, the public, and the media. Here, *Carl DeMaio*, who previously served in several staff capacities in Congress, is joined by his associate at The Performance Institute, *Ian Koski*, Director of Public Policy and Communications, to offer a down-to-earth primer on best practices.

Part Four: Assessing Results

Chapter 14 takes up the many aspects and forms of program evaluation, explored by *Dr. Kathryn Newcomer*, Director of The

George Washington University School of Public Policy and Public Administration, and *Jonathan Baron*, Director of the Coalition for Evidence-Based Policy.

Chapter 15 brings you information about two very important autonomous offices that review your results and your management, one from inside your agency and the other from an agency of Congress. *George Grob*, Assistant Inspector General for Evaluation and Inspections at the Department of Health and Human Services, describes how each agency's Office of Inspector General interacts with and often can assist managers. *Dr. Nancy Kingsbury*, Managing Director for Applied Research and Methods at the Government Accountability Office, explains GAO, whose recent name change from the General Accounting Office reflects the widespread redirection occurring across Washington toward the focus on results.

In Chapter 16, *Barry White*, Director of Government Performance Projects for the Council for Excellence in Government and Coordinator of the Government Performance Coalition, which brings you this book, concludes Part Four by describing keys to how leaders and managers can work successfully on results issues with the Office of Management and Budget.

The final chapter, Closing Thoughts, is from co-editor *Dr. Kathryn Newcomer*, who asks you, "Will you find the time to measure up?"

At the end of the book you will find biographical information on all the authors and an annotated listing of the members of the Government Performance Coalition.

The editors, sponsors, authors, and all the members of the Government Performance Coalition hope this book is helpful to you, and we wish every career and appointed manager a successful tenure delivering results for the American people.

Leading for Results

When you are the head of any organization, you consider yourself a leader and you believe that under your leadership, your organization will succeed in achieving great results. You believe you have the personal attributes essential for successful leadership or you would not have accepted your position.

Part One helps you supplement those personal attributes by learning how other leaders have successfully managed for results in government. It will also help you grasp the essentials of the statutory and executive branch frameworks that overlay the program laws for your particular organization—and within which you are expected to lead.

Chapter 1 is a personal statement about leading for results by *Maurice McTigue,* currently the head of the Government Accountability Project at the Mercatus Center and formerly a Cabinet Minister in New Zealand, leading that country's results-based reforms. McTigue shows you that you are not alone: Many countries are engaged in similar results-based governing initiatives.

Chapter 2 brings you back to the American experience with perspectives on leading for results from a presidential appointee and a career public servant. *Mortimer Downey* was Deputy Secretary for the Department of Transportation and also held the position of chief operating officer, the senior officer designated as accountable for results to the President and the Secretary. Vice Admiral *Thad Allen* is Coast Guard Chief of Staff, with a record of ever-increasing leadership and management responsibilities for more than 30 years.

Chapters 3 and 4 shift focus to the framework for leadership. Chapter 3 outlines the statutory framework put in place by Congress over several decades, highlighting the most important aspects of the laws that have a direct impact on what you are expected to do, regardless of your program area. The author, *John Kamensky,* now at the IBM Center for The Business of Government, has been both observer and direct participant in shaping these laws for several decades.

Chapter 4 turns to executive branch initiatives around managing for results. Political rhetoric in every administration can sometimes give the impression that managing for results was just discovered. In this chapter, *Jonathan Breul* of the IBM Center for The Business of Government explains how successive administrations for over 40 years have addressed the issues, noting the continuities throughout this uneven evolution. Breul has the perspective gained from his involvement in the development of several of the important management laws as well as his service as the top career official working with the President's Management Council in both the Clinton and George W. Bush administrations.

CHAPTER 1

Why Managing for Results Matters to Appointed and Career Leaders

Maurice McTigue

Whether you are there by reason of political appointment, as a career choice, or both, there is only one acceptable reason for being a leader in public service: You believe your country, your community, or society will be better off because you worked in public service. If this is not the reason you are in public service, then please leave now; you do not belong here. Once you accept your role as a leader in government, you must agree to be held accountable for getting the results our country deserves.

While for many this will seem self-evident, there is often wide disparity between this truth and the reasons some actually come to leadership positions in government. There are those who choose public service solely for the pay, benefits, credential for the next job, spotlight, retirement, etc. While these reasons might be in the best interests of the individual, they are not necessarily in the best interests of the government agency or the public. That is not to say that personal agendas are inappropriate; rather, self-serving self-interest alone is inappropriate.

It is no accident that governments around the world are grappling with the implementation of accountability systems based on results. Nor is it accidental that results are being defined as the public benefit achieved rather than the quantity of activity accomplished. At the 5th Global Forum on Reinventing Govern-

Maurice McTigue is Director of the Government Accountability Project at the Mercatus Center, George Mason University.

ment, held November 3–6, 2003, in Mexico City, Mexico, countries that presented on their efforts toward a results-based government included the United Kingdom, New Zealand, Mexico, Mongolia, Canada, Italy, South Africa, and the United States.

This drive for a results focus in government accountability is a response to a deep-seated public unease that government is not succeeding at solving the societal problems the public is concerned about. Classic examples are the incidence of hunger, poverty, and homelessness in affluent countries and the dependence of major industries on government subsidies (e.g., agricultural subsidies) to remain viable.

Leaders in the public arena are increasingly being judged according to the results they produce in terms of public benefits. As a leader, you must lead, not follow. Those who make decisions based upon the most recent opinion poll are not leaders, and they are indeed slaves to public opinion. If they succeed, it will be by accident. Set forth your own course, as you and your organization know best, following a few key doctrines.

Tips for Leaders and Managers

- Know what you're here to accomplish; government service is intentional.

- Keep in mind that results are the benefits achieved, not the number of activities completed.

- Know what is "do-able."

- Be sure you have "clarity of mission" and that mission drives action.

- Create realistic expectations of your organization.

- Choose management tools strategically, for results.

DOCTRINE OF "DO-ABILITY"

Success is the result of carefully identifying the causes of a problem and then designing and implementing solutions that will systematically eliminate those causes. That, of course, presumes the wisdom to know that the problem is real and can be remedied. This is the "doctrine of do-ability."

Success is equal parts (1) understanding the problem, and (2) knowing exactly what it takes to solve the problem. Every organization in government is intended to affect the nation positively in some way, and the leaders in that organization must understand what it will take to achieve success.

DOCTRINE OF CLARITY OF MISSION

When taking a leadership role at a government organization, or in any organization, the most important questions to ask are, "What are we trying to accomplish?" and "What benefit can the public reasonably expect from this organization?" If you don't get the same answer from everyone, then you have a problem. Until that problem is solved, it is unlikely that you will succeed in maximizing the public benefit generated by the organization.

Clarity of mission is the most critical factor in achieving success. If that mission is expressed as quantities of activity like "feeding hungry people," then it will never fully meet public expectations. It must be expressed as an outcome like "eliminating or diminishing hunger." Success under this mission will certainly meet public expectations.

Defining, clarifying, and communicating your mission will allow you to identify what to measure to determine achievement. "What gets measured is what gets done," but clarifying your mission is the essential first step in determining what will get measured.

The following examples help show that process. If the organization was the Environmental Protection Agency (EPA), for example, and the answer to the question "What do we do here?" comes back as "We fight or catch polluters," then the focus will be on prosecuting polluters. While this approach focuses attention on identifying and prosecuting the bad players, it also confines activity to a relatively small segment of the total cause of pollution. If bad or ill-informed practices represent, say, 3 percent of the total picture, then that limits achievement to no more than 3 percent. In contrast, changing practices across the whole field may give potential gains of 10–25 percent elimination of pollution or even higher.

If the answer given is "We diminish pollution," then a whole new scenario opens up. EPA starts evaluating the current status of the environment, looking at ways to diminish the bad effects on the environment while enhancing the good. Questions arise like "How do we prevent the pollution from occurring in the first place?" Maybe the agency expands its range of available tools by adding a strong education and best practices component to its prosecution activity. If the intended public good is less pollution, then the additional tool of education has improved the outcome success well beyond what the original primary focus on prosecution could achieve. Clearly the public seeks less pollution.

Another useful example comes from the Federal Emergency Management Agency (FEMA), which executed a significant turnaround in its performance during the 1990s. Part of the problem was that prior to 1993, FEMA had never enunciated its overriding mission. When the National Academy of Public Administration (NAPA) conducted a study of FEMA in 1992, "One interviewee described FEMA as 'a check-writing agency, an intelligence agency, a social service agency and insurance agency, with a fire administration thrown in.'"[1]

The mission adopted in 1993 was to "Reduce the loss of life and property and protect our institutions from all hazards by leading and supporting the Nation in a comprehensive, risk-based emergency management program of mitigation, preparedness, response, and recovery." This mission suggests a comprehen-

---

[1]*Coping with Catastrophe*, National Academy of Public Administration, 1993, pp. 42–43.

sive approach aimed at finding the highest benefit, lowest cost, and most effective ways of preventing loss of life and property, and the four means of accomplishing the mission were used to guide a reorganization of the agency.

DOCTRINE OF REALISTIC EXPECTATIONS

As the FEMA example illustrates, agencies may use multiple tools to advance their missions; similarly, the ideal approach for EPA is likely a blend of education, technological advances, best practices, and enforcement. But which approach gets priority and which approach creates the greatest public benefit are now issues central to the debate.

The crucial role for the leader is to create realistic expectations of what can be achieved by the organization and in what time frame. That expectation can influence, realistically, how the tools of success can be used. Managing the balance between all the activities available to the leader to produce the best possible result for the organization is a hard discipline to perfect. Leading this search for continuous improvement in results is the hallmark of the true leader.

The best leaders are exemplary at controlling expectations among all the parties interested in an organization's performance. The challenge for the leader is to set those expectations high enough to satisfy stakeholders but always at a level that the organization can achieve.

Caution

Leaders must manage themselves as a resource. They must discipline themselves to spend time on the most appropriate activities, to deliver the highest value for the organization. Allowing other demands on the leader's time to minimize the leader's attention to both the highest priority issues and the management-of-expectations issues will be highly prejudicial to the ultimate success of both the leader and the organization.

There will of course be other legitimate calls on the leader's time, but it is the leader's responsibility to see that his or her priorities are appropriate. The other two big calls on the leader's time are administrative management issues and the management of political expectations outside of the organization. Both of these are legitimate uses of the leader's time and failures in these areas can greatly affect the interests of the organization.

DOCTRINE OF STRATEGIC MANAGEMENT FOR RESULTS

To achieve the mission of the organization, a leader already has a variety of tools. The strategic use of these tools will greatly influence the organization's ability to achieve results. Programs are tools: They are a means to an end, not an end in their own right. As the focus on results becomes more intense, program effectiveness will receive greater scrutiny. That is a good thing. The best managers will develop internal procedures for continuously reviewing the effectiveness of programs and doing repairs, maintenance, and upgrades.

Virtually every administration launches some kind of initiative to demonstrate their commitment to societal problems and the effectiveness of current programs. Congress dramatically shifted the basis of these initiatives by codifying the principle of results management into law with passage of the Government Performance and Results Act in 1993. (See Chapters 3 and 4 for discussion of how administration and legislative initiatives have fared to date.)

This process of external and internal scrutiny of program effectiveness should increasingly create competition between programs addressing the same goal. This competition will ultimately encompass all activities by all organizations addressing a particular outcome. Program managers and their supervisors must understand clearly what outcomes their programs produce, at what cost, and what their shortfalls are. To be able to lead effectively in an environment where there is competition among government programs for funding and public support, they will also need to understand the performance of programs outside their organization.

These competitive pressures will serve to produce continuous improvement in the effectiveness of programs. The best leaders will adroitly choose from among the tools available to guarantee the best result. Hence, the "doctrine of strategic management for results."

Accountability can be expected to move more and more to a quantifiable measure of the benefit to citizens through diminished societal problems, so that the public and stakeholders will no longer accept that more money equals more results. They will require a means to measure outcomes against other programs able to deliver the same or similar outcomes at the same or lesser cost.

This accountability shift will not fall exclusively on those whose career is in public service; it will also affect elected politicians and the entire political process. Politicians are going to be taken to task more frequently for failure to cure endemic problems in our society. That accountability will focus on whether the problem was diminished or eliminated. The expenditure of more monies will not be viewed as a reasonable solution unless it is accompanied by a rational assessment of how—and by how much—the problem will be diminished.

In an ideal world, how will that work? The government organization will have to account for its performance in terms of the public benefit produced. The politician will have to account for what was purchased and what was delivered—and whether the desired result was achieved. If the desired result was not achieved, blame will fall to the politician for purchasing the wrong goods and services. Civil service leaders of today and the future will be willing to hold their own feet to the fire, before anyone else has the chance to do it for them.

CHAPTER 2

Perspectives of Leaders

The two essays in this chapter offer an appointee and a careerist perspective on managing for results. The first is from Clinton administration Deputy Secretary and Chief Operating Officer (COO) *Mortimer Downey.* The Clinton administration established and the Bush administration confirmed that each large agency must have a chief operating officer, whose primary focus is on achieving agency results. There are no rules for how a COO should function nor has the role been around long enough to develop a body of experience to guide new COOs. This makes it all the more important that those who have held the position share their perspectives. Downey's success in his tenure was recognized by the Bush administration, which asked him to chair its Performance Measurement Advisory Council.

The second essay is by Vice Admiral *Thad Allen,* Chief of Staff of the U.S. Coast Guard. During more then three decades of public service at ever-increasing levels of responsibility, plus an MPA from The George Washington University and an MS from the Sloan School of Management at MIT, he has developed a practical approach to managing for results from a career leader's perspective that is readily transferable to any agency, civilian or military.

A Chief Operating Officer's View

Mortimer L. Downey

Some take the view that managing for results is a process for long-term improvement of agency performance, but that it is somehow unconnected to the day-to-day challenges of managing the agency's work. To the contrary, while the long-term opportunities for improvement are significant, the process can be an important component of the agency executive's style—a way to connect the mission of the agency and its senior staff in a positive way.

Tips for Leaders and Managers

- Recognize the potential of managing for results as a useful tool for day-to-day management in the federal agency.

- Use managing for results to focus multi-level management on common goals and understand that it is outcomes that matter.

- Maximize the value of using objective measures for resource allocation and strategy formulation.

- Commit to frequent and personal involvement, and make sure the agency accepts the notion that measuring progress means keeping score.

- Work to develop the concept of managing for results in partnership situations—whether the partnerships involve delivery agents, those who share outcome goals but have competing program agendas, or those who provide the resources and oversight.

Mortimer L. Downey is Chairman of PB Consult and former Deputy Secretary of Transportation in the Clinton administration.

RELATING ACTIVITIES TO GOALS

The daily routine of the federal agency, especially at the level of a department, has more than its share of crises—programmatic or political—and the process of managing for results can draw the executive and the agency back toward the purposes and goals the agency has committed to achieve. Whether at the level of the agency itself or at the level of programs within the agency, managing for results forces people to look at what they are trying to accomplish and how their activities relate to that goal.

In the Department of Transportation's implementation of performance management, a key factor was the designation of safety as the overriding mission of the agency: protecting the lives of the American public as they use every mode of transportation. Recognizing this as the highest agency-wide priority—one that was measurable and reportable—brought an alignment to activities as diverse as life jacket use by recreational boaters and launch precautions for commercial spacecraft. Recognition that progress was indeed measurable—and would be measured—brought a focus to all departmental thinking.

Similar measures were applied to other broad departmental goals such as mobility, economic growth, security, and environmental protection. Knitting these together in both strategic and performance plans adds coherence to the agency and a sense of purpose to the executive's activities. The goals, as well as the agency's progress in meeting them, are constant themes in all communications within and outside the department, and are the basis for celebrating those whose actions and commitment have contributed to their achievement.

At the executive level, the existence of a performance plan with measurable results becomes the basis for interaction and oversight with administrators and program managers. A regular and formal process of discussion around goals, and particularly around performance, is the basis for setting and adjusting strategies: "What is the agency or program doing to achieve the goals?" rather than simply "What activities is it engaged in?"

ALLOCATING RESOURCES TO PRODUCE RESULTS

Among the most useful contributions of the results-oriented approach is its ability to make the resource allocation process a rational one. The resource allocation process, notably through the development of the annual budget, is the single most effective tool for organizational change available to the executive. In every agency, program advocates tend to seek additional resources for whatever they do. If simply doing more—an output measure—is the basis for budget decisions, it's very hard to say "no" to anyone.

If the measure is results, and if the performance measures have some degree of comparability across agencies and programs, a new dimension emerges: attempting to maximize results and incentivize the program managers to show how their programs really contribute. Carefully used, the budget-making decision process not only rewards those who are achieving results but can provide the basis for significant changes in resources where a lack of people or program funds is the reason why results are not being achieved. In the Department of Transportation, this process continued throughout the budget cycle, even including adjustment of results targets upward or downward depending on the outcome of congressional appropriations.

The resource allocation example pointed up one reason why focusing on outcome goals rather than process or output is important. But the significance goes well beyond resource allocation to program design and execution. As the Department of Transportation's preeminent goal, safety progress was typically measured by reductions in fatalities and injuries.

Among the department's agencies was the United States Coast Guard (until its move to Homeland Security in 2002), with responsibility for safety improvement in the commercial shipping industry, including barges and towboats. Traditionally, the Coast Guard had focused on outputs like number of inspections, number of citations, and number of violations. With focus shifted to how many lives could be saved, the Coast Guard redirected its efforts to education and training of the workforce, in conjunction with barge line operators, whose economic interests were served through accident reduction. The results were startling: Accident rates that had seemed to be stuck at inevitably high levels dropped dramatically.

PLANNING TO MANAGE, MANAGING TO YOUR PLAN

Where the performance plan is integral to the agency's management process, it is much more likely to be used and useful. The plan that is "bolted on" to the department's budget is likely to go on the shelf until it is time to put next year's package together, and any connection between the plan and its results is likely coincidental. In the Department of Transportation, the performance plans included the agency-specific strategies for achieving departmental goals and provided the measures of whether these strategies were succeeding. Both the strategies and the goals were translated into performance agreements between the Secretary and the agency leadership, monitored and measured regularly through performance reviews with the Deputy Secretary.

These frequent interactions meant that performance stayed on the radar screen for agency management, but also provided the opportunity to revisit and revise strategies where results were disappointing. For example, setting a strategy for automobile fatality reduction through greater seat-belt use—both of which were measurable quantities—provided the basis for emphasizing enactment of enforceable laws for mandatory use as the primary strategy, targeting the states with the greatest room for improvement.

The ability to measure improvements and adjust strategies isn't always easy, particularly where the implementation period is long and the outcomes seem distant. In a grant program that funds construction of new light rail lines to achieve mobility and environmental goals, for example, you can't wait decades to measure all the implications, nor can you reverse the capital investment. But the focus on outcomes can be reflected in the analysis that supports the investment decision, supported by an ongoing effort to calibrate and improve the planning models according to real-world results achieved through prior investments.

WORKING WITH YOUR PARTNERS

Of course, the process of managing for results doesn't stay within the four walls of the agency, or simply reflect the interaction among senior officials. Many stakeholders have an interest in its elements, and they need to be brought into the process in a variety of ways. Agency employees are in fact the ones who have to deliver if performance goals are to be met. Wide participation in the development of plans will build confidence and support for department management as plans are implemented. In the Department of Transportation, the planning process began with a cadre of senior officials but deliberately expanded to include literally hundreds of employees—headquarters and field, military and civilian, represented and non-represented.

In addition to including the planning process as an ongoing agenda item for the department's Labor-Management Council, union leaders were invited to participate in the department-wide planning meetings. Widespread participation was supported by an ongoing communications effort, taking every opportunity to emphasize the idea of "One DOT" that had one set of goals and celebrated together as they were achieved.

External stakeholders also need to be included in the development and execution of performance management, although this is easier with some participants than others. Partners, such as state departments of transportation or local transit agencies, are critical in effective implementation, but their interest is much more in efficient program operations than in what they might perceive as federally dictated goals. A careful process of diplomacy was needed to build awareness that goals such as safety and mobility were common interests of state and federal officials, and that the intent was to achieve these goals effectively without intruding into state and local prerogatives of project selection and plan development. Ultimately, federal investment must be justified on the basis of performance, and the states recognized that simply speeding up the flow of funds without a basis to measure their effective use was not in their long-term interest.

Whatever the program or agency in Washington, its proponents have likely formed their trade association or lobbying institution to further their mutual interests. Like the states, these groups tend toward the "ATM" view of their programs—their goal is often more money with less red tape. But again like the states, they can be brought to the view that measures of success are valuable in making their case.

At one stage in the development of the Department of Transportation's plan, representatives of all the interest groups surrounding the departmental programs were invited to a single workshop to provide input into goal development. Having all those groups at the same table led to some valuable insight into how the goals would be developed and used, as well as how the various groups might adopt the goals as a basis for their work in support of their individual interests.

Within the community of stakeholders, Congress is a special case. Clearly, Congress' control over program design and resources through the adoption of authorization and appropriation legislation is a critical element in success. Yet, Congress has bought into the process in only the most limited way, with the impetus for performance and results coming more from the oversight committees than from the authorizers and appropriators. Recent report language from a key subcommittee seems to forbid the inclusion of performance data in the traditional budget justification documents. No magic wand is going to change the ways of Congress, but like other stakeholders, Congress does generally have an interest in success; anything that moves toward measurement of that success might help.

KEEPING SCORE MATTERS

Keeping score is part of the process, and the simpler the presentation the better. The Bush administration's traffic light scorecard for the President's Management Agenda was questioned by some as overly simplistic, but it has served to keep both the White House and the departments focused on the process and its results. The fact that the Department of Transportation was the first to achieve four green lights is perhaps a reflection of its long-time commitment to performance management.

Where might managing for results go next? If it works well for individual agencies and departments, can it be applied across the government? Not an easy task, given the complexity of these agencies and their ties to a variety of interests and congressional committees. Efforts at rationalization and coordination within departments have a mixed record of success, but show some promise. At the Department of Transportation, it proved impossible to reorganize into what might have been a more rational structure, but alignment of programs across agencies met with more success. Even Congress was willing to allow greater flexibility; for example, its acceptance of flexible use of highway and transit money made it possible to gain the cooperation of the responsible agencies to create common regulations, forms, and procedures that simplified the execution of that flexibility.

Can a similar process of rationalization occur across government? Without question, it will take leadership from the top as well as a spirit of cooperation among departmental leadership. With processes like the Program Assessment Rating Tool and its effort to develop common measures, and with institutions like the President's Management Council to encourage interagency cooperation among officials who have learned how to work together, the potential is there. Certainly, the results will be worth the effort.

A Career Leader's View

Thad W. Allen, Vice Admiral

Managing for results enables career leaders to understand the process by which an agency provides the unique services that improve the lives of our citizens. The Coast Guard offers an example of how managing for results can focus an agency's mission and enhance its outcomes.

> ### *Tips for Leaders and Managers*
>
> - Foster a "systems" perspective in integrating the agency's organic legislative authorities, authorization and appropriation direction, and other mandates
>
> - Require the integration of activity measures with financial information and link resource allocation to performance
>
> - Use risk-based decision-making where resource constraints require tradeoffs between goals
>
> - Build an organizational framework and focus for improved information and knowledge management, human capital development, and investment decisions
>
> - Create a better, more effective balance between the "tyranny of the present" and the need to act with strategic intent in executing agency missions.

FOSTERING A SYSTEMS PERSPECTIVE

While managing for results provides leaders with day-to-day indicators of performance, its strength lies in the creation of clear, explicit linkages between strategic goals, performance

---

Thad W. Allen, *Vice Admiral, is Chief of Staff of the U.S. Coast Guard.*

goals, performance measures, and activities. The organization can be viewed as a system of activities that support agency missions.

The Coast Guard has long regarded its many statutory missions as a collection of mandates that are brought to bear in the maritime environment against a broad spectrum of threats, vulnerabilities, and demands for services. That maritime environment includes living marine resources, the world's maritime transportation system, the territorial waters of the United States, waters subject to both U.S. and international law, and, in some cases, the air space above and the seabed below. For that reason, the Coast Guard's strategic goals are defined at the systems level: maritime homeland security, maritime safety, protection of natural resources, maritime mobility, and national defense.

Coast Guard operating programs and activities are defined and tracked in relation to these overarching goals. They are intended to be synergistic and mutually reinforcing. For example, the maritime safety goal includes search and rescue, which is a response activity. Passenger vessel safety, maritime worker fatality prevention, and recreational boating fatality prevention also fall within the maritime safety goal.

While we are always prepared to respond to a distress call, the most effective way to reduce the risk to mariners is through safety and prevention programs. Response and prevention form the complementary component parts of the maritime safety "system." Further, these goals are aligned with the higher level goals of the Department of Homeland Security: awareness, protection, prevention, response, recovery, excellence, and service. In each case the overarching strategy is a systemic, layered approach to addressing threats.

It is well worth the investment in time for new and ascending leaders to review the agency's strategic plan and performance goals as a basis for creating the context and relevance of managing for results. Moreover, the plan should be challenged periodically to ensure that it accurately reflects the strategic intent of the organization.

LINKING RESOURCE ALLOCATION TO PERFORMANCE

A good deal of current management effort is focused on creating broadly visible indicators of agency activities and the results achieved. The "balanced scorecard" and "dashboard gauges" are two popular means to achieve this visibility. In structuring measures intended to focus on results, activity measures alone are insufficient to ensure that agency resources are being allocated to the best purpose or outcome. To that end, it is critical that the agency's system for managing for results include the integration of activity measures and financial information.

In the past, federal managers were pressed to expend funds under fiscal deadlines and government financial systems focused on providing fund balances. While the balance sheet and financial statements remain important, activity-based costing and managerial accounting information is now critical in developing the cost of results. The Coast Guard has made great strides in the last 10 years toward developing activity-based costing models that enable the organization to know the hourly cost of employing a cutter, aircraft, or rescue boat.

The resulting mission cost model, together with activity data such as lives saved, drugs interdicted, or the amount of oil spilled into the environment, permits an assessment of the cost of a program in relation to the results achieved. This model is now employed in all facets of planning, programming, budgeting, mission execution, and program evaluation. However, challenges remain, specifically in those mission areas where services are provided by individuals or teams that are not deployed on a cutter or aircraft (e.g., safety inspectors, law enforcement personnel on Navy ships).

USING RISK-BASED DECISION-MAKING

Solid strategic goals with attendant measures and the ability to cost out increments of effort that produce results are powerful tools. However, resource constraints dominate the world of federal managers who are pressed daily to make choices and tradeoffs among equally deserving programs or projects.

Risk-based decision-making can improve the quality of those decisions. It makes explicit the inherent risks of competing choices—in both quantitative and qualitative terms. Shortly after the attacks of September 11, 2001, for example, the Coast Guard developed a port security risk assessment tool that allowed field commanders to compare and contrast the relative differences in terms of expected outcomes (results) between actions they might take in a port to reduce vulnerabilities, mitigate threats, or reduce the consequences of an event. This risk model has been expanded recently to include the cost of resources associated with a particular action or intervention.

As a result, field commanders will not only be able to assess the impact of their choices in terms of results, but will be aware of the resource expenditure associated with that decision. Risk-based decision-making is an expansion of systems thinking that allows for the optimization of outcomes in relation to available resources. Risk can be further mitigated by the development of modeling and simulation tools that allow managers to ask, "What if. . . ."

BUILDING ORGANIZATIONAL CAPACITY

No organizational activity, whether it is external service delivery or internal support, is separate and distinct from the collective organizational effort that provides the American public effective mission execution. If you start with the end in mind, in this case managing for results, it becomes clear that basic decisions regarding the acquisition and management of knowledge, the development of human capital, and investment in technology and information systems must build the organizational capacity to support performance management.

The Coast Guard's mission cost model allocates operating costs and proposed investment cost to benefiting operating programs to create a linkage between the acquisition of capacity, competency, and capabilities to execute missions. The notion is that mission performance (i.e., reduction of risk in the maritime environment) is a function of specific inputs: authorities, capabilities, competencies, capacity, and partnerships. If you start with the intended results in mind, you will make better choices regarding factors such as human capital and investment.

ACTING WITH STRATEGIC INTENT

When managing for results, the gas gauge should not be confused with the direction the car is moving. Too often managers, particularly those working in Washington, become captives of the "tyranny of the present." Agendas, schedules, and the daily tempo of agency operations are dictated by annual budget cycles, congressional hearings, audits, and data calls. These features of life in government agencies are enduring and must be managed. Nonetheless, the shrewd federal manager will create the organizational and personal space needed in the day or week to look beyond the dashboard gauges.

The nexus between strategy and results—the ability to see the agency's mission and direction in everyday activities—is the essence of leading and acting with strategic intent. Managing for results is understanding the process by which an agency produces those goods or services unique to government and then providing the *outcomes* that improve the lives of our citizens.

CHAPTER 3

The Legislative Framework

John M. Kamensky

The President ". . . shall take Care that the Laws be faithfully executed . . ."
— Article II, Section 3, U.S. Constitution

"There are so many reporting requirements! I can't do justice to them all. Which ones do I really need to pay attention to, and which ones do I just make sure we check the box on?"
— Defense agency official

Most political appointees and new career managers are familiar with the laws related to policy areas of interest to them, but few are as familiar with the laws related to the administration and management of the agencies in which they may find themselves appointed to serve. The sheer number of these laws can be overwhelming to new appointees. Fortunately, you will not be expected to know the details of all these laws. But you do need to know enough to ask questions and be sure you are comfortable with the answers.

A new leader will need to interact with various congressional and institutional policy players during his or her time in office. In addition, a handful of results-oriented general management laws that apply to all agencies will have some influence on how a leader approaches his or her work. Forewarned is forearmed!

John M. Kamensky is a Senior Fellow at the IBM Center for The Business of Government.

Tips for Leaders and Managers

- Be aware that, in addition to the many laws that create and influence your agency's programs, more than 90 management laws reach across all federal agencies. You may not know they exist, but the relevant congressional committees do.

- Recognize that while you work for the executive branch, you also have multiple masters in Congress, who will sometimes send confusing and contradictory messages.

- Understand that the various management laws were created over a period of years. They do not constitute a coherent management framework for your agency. Your challenge is to make them seem coherent.

- Make the most of the recent management laws that emphasize better performance and results from programs and agencies.

- Do not ignore these laws; some of them have criminal penalties, including jail time.

APPOINTEES HAVE MULTIPLE MASTERS

Many appointees assume they work for the President, and of course, the President can remove them at any time. In fact, our constitutionally divided system of government makes this an incomplete assumption. The three branches of the federal government are actually interdependent and share power in managing the executive branch. While appointees are expected to do the President's bidding, they are also required to obey the laws they implement, even when some of those laws may require them to carry out policies with which they and the President do not agree.

Senior political appointees are appointed by the President and confirmed by the Senate. The Senate confirmation process itself often creates certain performance expectations between the person being confirmed and selected congressional leaders and their staffs. This process is carried out publicly via confirmation hearings and "questions for the record" to which potential appointees must provide written responses regarding both policy and management practices that they may be responsible for acting upon. These performance expectations may circumvent executive branch priorities set by the President and his staff. For example, as a condition some senators placed on him before the Senate would act on his confirmation, the chief federal procurement official for the federal government under President Bush essentially had to retreat from a major presidential initiative on competitive sourcing that he was charged with implementing. While these congressional expectations cannot be legally enforced, violating them can lead to the appointee's future ineffectiveness in obtaining congressional support for his or her initiatives.

THE CONGRESSIONAL FRAMEWORK

Congress can be divided into four types of committees, many of which have overlapping jurisdictions for various agency functions. As a result, agencies (and leaders) have multiple masters within the legislative branch as well, and must deal with each of the four types of committees at varying points in the policy and budget processes. Some agencies, like the Environmental Protection Agency, must deal with up to 70 different committees and subcommittees because of the way the agency was created years ago. Understanding what the different kinds of committees do can help you understand the roles and expectations of the many members of Congress with whom you may have the opportunity to work.

Authorizing Committees

Most of the committees in Congress are authorizing committees. Authorizing committees have responsibility for agency creation and oversight, and these are the primary committees with which many agencies work. Authorizing committees have jurisdiction over an agency in terms of drafting policy changes as well as agency-specific management issues. They also have jurisdiction over the implementation of programs within an agency's responsibility as well as any regulatory functions an agency might perform.

Since most laws set a time limit on how long a program is authorized, once an agency or program is "on the books," the primary role of these committees is to review agency progress and periodically "reauthorize" the agency or program. Understanding the reauthorization schedule for programs within an agency is important to new policy initiatives, congressional (and their investigative arm, the Government Accountability Office—GAO) oversight schedules, and agency planning and budgeting efforts.

Budget Committees

The budget committees (one in each house) were created as a consequence of a 1974 law requiring Congress to have a "bottom line" with regard to how much it will appropriate in total each year. Most agencies will have little need to work with the budget committees; nonetheless, these committees draft "budget resolutions" agreed upon by the entire Congress that set broad limits that in turn are used to limit the various appropriating committees. If spending is projected to exceed the limits, the budget resolution can direct authorizing committees to change programs within their jurisdictions to achieve the level of spending, revenues, and debt limits agreed to in the resolution.

This process, known as "budget reconciliation," occurs infrequently, but can result in sudden changes to agency programs and spending levels. If a reconciliation bill seems imminent, leaders should carefully watch and, as appropriate, participate in the process to protect the administration's interests.

Appropriating Committees

The appropriating committees (one in each house) are divided into a series of subcommittees that have jurisdiction over the budgets of individual agencies. These subcommittees have significant power and sometimes run counter to their counterpart authorizing committees and the Office of Management and Budget (OMB). Agencies often have to serve as the broker among their many masters; failing this, they may serve as a convenient target for their wrath. The annual budget process generates extensive interaction between agencies and their appropriators.

Agencies know they must invest significant time in providing timely information to appropriators, even if doing so means shortchanging other efforts. Getting on the wrong side of an appropriator is generally not a good idea. One former head of the Export-Import Bank found his salary zeroed out when he ran crosswise with the chair of his appropriations subcommittee!

Oversight Committees

While each of the authorizing committees often has an oversight subcommittee, two committees in Congress—the Senate Committee on Governmental Affairs and the House Committee on Government Reform—have broad oversight over the management and operations of the government as a whole as well as individual agencies and programs. These laws are the congressional counterparts (or in some cases, the driver) of an administration's results-focused efforts.

These committees attempt to define the management framework within which all agencies must work, so understanding what they do helps new leaders understand a set of important influences on their agency's operations—over which the agency often has little control. Also, because these laws are outside the authorizing and appropriating processes, many new leaders are often not briefed on them when they begin their new agency assignments. While their primary attention needs to be on the congressional actions affecting their specific programs, leaders do need to understand these "general management laws."

KEY MANAGEMENT LAWS

With such a daunting introduction, how does a leader begin to understand the framework of management laws? The Congressional Research Service (CRS) has cataloged over 90 entries that

describe general management laws in categories such as information technology, strategic planning, performance measurement, program evaluation, financial management, budgeting,
accounting, procurement, real property management, human
capital management, and ethics.[1] There is no overarching or integrated framework for these scores of laws, so it is difficult to
summarize them. In fact, some of them tend to work at cross-
purposes, at least philosophically. For example, the Paperwork
Reduction Act sets limits on how much information the government can collect from the private and non-profit sectors, yet
the Government Performance and Results Act requires agencies
to collect information regarding the performance of their programs, many of which affect the private and non-profit sectors.

To be effective, every leader needs to be familiar with four general management laws (with the caveat that there are many
more).

The Chief Financial Officers Act

The Chief Financial Officers Act of 1990 (CFO Act) and its subsequent amendments (see www.cfo.gov) strengthen financial accountability in the federal government by creating a focal point
in OMB to provide leadership; specifically, the act requires the
23 major agencies to prepare annual, audited financial statements. The law also created a governmentwide management
focal point by establishing a new position in OMB, the Deputy
Director for Management. Key points of the law include:

- The new OMB Deputy, appointed by the President and confirmed by the Senate, is the chief financial officer for the federal government and is responsible for governmentwide policy and leadership. The law also created the Office of Federal
  Financial Management within OMB, headed by a Controller
  who is responsible for providing advice and staff support to
  the Deputy.

---

[1]Clinton T. Brass, editor, "General Management Laws: A Compendium," Report RL 30795, Congressional Research Service, updated May 19, 2004.

- Each of the 23 major agencies must appoint CFOs and deputy CFOs who meet statutory qualifications for their jobs. The CFOs must prepare annual management reports for their agencies, including a financial statement and audit report, an assessment of the financial management status of their agencies, and a summary of material weaknesses (pursuant to a separate law, the Federal Managers' Financial Integrity Act of 1982). They must also implement and maintain financial systems that comply with governmentwide accounting standards. By fiscal year 2003, 20 of the 23 major agencies had achieved a clean audit opinion. A subsequent statute calls for combining the annual financial report with the program performance report.

- The Secretary of the Treasury is responsible for preparing an annual audited financial statement covering the entire executive branch. The first statement was released in 1998. To date, the federal government has yet to achieve a clean audit opinion on its statement.

- OMB is required to develop a five-year financial management plan for the federal government and provide periodic status reports. Agencies are required to conform their own financial management plans to the governmentwide plan. The CFO Act also creates a governmentwide CFO Council, chaired by the OMB Deputy Director for Management, which coordinates governmentwide financial management activities.

The CFO Act creates a management framework and the opportunity to create a critical mass of talent in each agency to collect and report financial information. The challenge to new leaders is to ensure that this talent is focused on creating timely information that is useful for managing and making decisions, not just for complying with statutory reporting requirements.

Investments in better financial management often lead to better program management decisions as well as increased congressional confidence that an agency is being well-managed. This, in turn, can lead to congressional committees granting an agency greater discretion to manage using common business practices rather than in response to detailed statutory requirements. This law is closely related to several others that are intended to create a broader framework to manage for results more effectively.

Government Performance and Results Act

The Government Performance and Results Act of 1993 (GPRA, or simply the Results Act), P.L. 103-62, creates a performance planning and accountability framework within each agency by requiring major agencies to clarify their missions, set program goals, measure performance toward achieving those goals, and report progress on an annual basis. Specifically, the three basic elements of the law require agencies to:

- Submit a strategic plan to OMB and Congress and update it every three years

- Submit an annual performance plan to Congress along with their budget requests in February of each year, covering each program activity in the agency's budget

- Submit an annual performance report covering the performance elements in the plan from the previous fiscal year. This report is now required to be integrated with the annual financial report into a Performance and Accountability Report (see Chapter 11).

Appropriately, the law does not specify a single focal point in agencies for the implementation of its provisions, nor does it specify a format. As a result, different agencies place these functions in different parts of their administrative infrastructure. Many assign these requirements to the CFO because of their relation to the budget and to the reporting requirements under the CFO Act. Others place them in the Office of the Secretary.

OMB has used the Results Act as a lever to promote the use of performance-informed budgeting and has administratively created an assessment tool to guide its examiners in assessing the effectiveness of major government programs (see Chapter 4, which discusses OMB's Program Assessment Rating Tool). In

2004 Congress began the process of considering legislation that would rename and institutionalize the OMB process.[2]

The significance of the Results Act for new leaders is that it has created an administrative infrastructure by which they can artic-ulate their priorities for the agency as a whole, measure progress, and link those priorities to the budget decision-making process. The Bush administration was the first to enter office once GPRA had been fully implemented. Some departments and agencies, such as the Department of Education, used the law to craft an overarching strategic agenda and significantly reoriented their priorities in a fairly short timeframe. In the case of Education, GPRA reframed the department's priorities around the imple-mentation of the No Child Left Behind Act. Reviewing the OMB performance assessments conducted to date will also provide new appointees a baseline for understanding the performance status of major programs in their agency's jurisdiction.

"My Cabinet Secretary was finally confirmed and in office just two weeks when he was asked to certify the accuracy of the contents of a big, fat report on the financial condition and per-formance levels of the entire department for the previous year. The report had been under preparation by his predecessor probably for six months before he came into office. He had no idea what he was being asked to sign. Submitting the report on time was required by law."

—Observation of a 2001 Presidential
Transition Team advisor

Clinger-Cohen Act

The federal government spends about $60 billion a year on in-formation technology. In the 1990s, there was widespread con-cern that this investment was not being leveraged wisely. As

---

[2]H.R. 3826, "Program Assessment and Results Act," introduced by Todd Platt, March 4, 2004.

a result, in 1996 Congress adopted the "Clinger-Cohen Act,"[3] named after its chief sponsors. This law is intended to improve the effectiveness of federal programs by improving the planning, buying, use, and disposal of information technology resources. Specifically, the law:

- Requires OMB to issue directives to agencies regarding capital planning, investment, business process reengineering, and information technology security. Agency investments must have measures of how technology performance is tied to the performance goals and objectives detailed in the agency's GPRA annual performance plan.

- Creates the position of chief information officer (CIO) in the 23 largest federal agencies to oversee their implementation of the provisions of the act. Agency CIOs are responsible for "developing, maintaining, and facilitating the implementation of a sound and integrated information technology architecture."

- Encourages agencies to adopt best practices and to make their technology capital planning and investment decisions on the basis of costs, benefits, risks, and performance improvement.

Building on the work begun in the Clinton administration, the Bush administration and OMB have used the provisions in the Clinger-Cohen Act to influence how government agencies plan for and buy technology. Agencies must submit a business case to OMB for approval along with their budget requests for new technology investments. Business cases are rated against a set of criteria that require details about how these investments will improve the efficiency and effectiveness of agency operations; if they are found to be insufficient, these business cases can be rejected.

---

[3]National Defense Authorization Act for Fiscal Year 1996, P. L. 104-106 (S. 1124), Division E (Sec. 5001, et seq.); see also: www.cio.gov and www.feapmo.gov.

Later statutory revisions[4] created a Chief Information Officers Council to coordinate governmentwide initiatives and named the OMB Deputy Director for Management as its chair, created an Office of Electronic Government in OMB to coordinate governmentwide IT policy, and requires agencies to develop performance measures for e-government that are both citizen- and productivity-related and to link these measures to their strategic and annual performance plans.

The Clinger-Cohen Act is significant for new political appointees because OMB's aggressive implementation approach is strongly influencing how agencies approach their work. The law encourages agencies to reengineer their existing processes to use technology rather than to reengineer technology to conform to their existing processes. If an agency's business plan does not reflect this approach, OMB will reject it. Also, OMB is increasingly defining an agency's technology approaches to ensure cross-government interoperability and the sharing of technology resources.

In the past, agencies could obtain funding for customized, freestanding systems. No longer. OMB's mantras are "buy once, use many times" and "simplify and unify" systems. Both of these principles flow directly from the Clinger-Cohen Act. The law also requires that attention be directed to different social goals: privacy, security, and access (such as to the disabled). Agency business cases must address these issues as well.

Human Capital Reforms in the Homeland Security Act and the National Defense Reauthorization Act for FY 2004

Clearly, significant changes are occurring in the technology arena in most agencies; human capital issues are not far behind. President George W. Bush is the first President since Jimmy Carter to

---

[4]E-Government Act of 2002, P.L. 107-347 (signed December 17, 2002); see also OMB Memorandum, "Implementation Guidance for the E-Government Act of 2002," M-03-81, August 1, 2003. This new law is part of a broader statutory framework begun by Clinger-Cohen, which includes the Government Paperwork Elimination Act of 1998 (P.L. 105-277) and the Federal Information Security Management Act of 2002 (P.L. 107-347, Title III).

make the structure and effectiveness of the federal civil service a presidential priority. Many agencies face significant challenges in changing their skill mix to reflect the new work brought about by technology and greater reliance on service contracting. Accomplishing this, however, requires fundamental changes in how the government hires, rewards, and trains its staff.

While these two laws provide for personnel reforms specific to the Department of Homeland Security and the Department of Defense, the reforms may ultimately serve as a template for other agencies. These laws also include a number of provisions geared toward managing for results more effectively in all agencies. These provisions, which apply governmentwide, include:

- The Homeland Security Act of 2002 (P.L. 107-296), Title XIII:

  - Requires all agencies to name a chief human capital officer to serve as chief policy advisor on all human resources management issues. The act also establishes a Chief Human Capital Officers (CHCO) Council and names the OPM Director as chair of the council.

  - Amends GPRA to require agency CHCOs to prepare sections of the annual plan and report that show how agencies plan to use human capital strategies to achieve the performance goals and objectives set forth in the plan and then, in the report, tell how they did use them.

  - Allows a "category ranking" system that reforms the federal competitive hiring process so that employers are not constrained to choosing from only the top three ranked candidates but rather can choose from a larger pool of qualified candidates.

  - Allows agencies to raise the total compensation (which includes bonuses) of career senior executives to the level paid to the Vice President ($203,000) if they have been certified by the Office of Personnel Management (OPM) as having a performance appraisal system that "makes meaningful distinctions based on relative performance." Agencies must be recertified every two years.

- The National Defense Reauthorization Act for FY 2004 (P.L. 108-136), particularly Sections 1121–1129:

  - Revises the pay of senior executives by creating broad pay ranges and allowing placement within a range based on an individual's performance and his or her contribution to the agency's performance, using a "rigorous performance management system." The top pay level is increased to $158,100 if agencies' performance appraisal systems are certified by OPM as making performance distinctions.

  - Specifies the design elements for pay-for-performance demonstration projects, allowing agencies to waive existing personnel rules with OPM's permission.

  - Requires agencies to conduct annual employee surveys to assess both employee satisfaction and employee perceptions of leadership and management.

  - Authorizes a Human Capital Performance Fund of up to $500 million to be distributed to agencies on a pro-rata basis if agencies have an OPM-approved performance appraisal rating system that "makes meaningful distinctions" in performance. To date, Congress has appropriated minimal funding for this effort. When funded, good agency systems can be allocated more dollars. A portion of the dollars is to be set aside to train managers on how to administer appraisal processes that make distinctions in performance. Agencies can use the fund to reward up to 15 percent of their employees with bonuses of up to 10 percent of their salaries.

The cross-cutting theme of the new provisions is to increase emphasis on the shift in the personnel system from a system that often based pay largely on individual longevity and experience to a system that bases pay on levels of individual contribution to agency performance.

These provisions are important to all leaders because most agencies are still in the beginning stages of implementing them and, as with the Clinger-Cohen provisions, you will face a num-

ber of contentious issues. The emphasis in the governmentwide
revisions is on a stronger link between pay and performance for
senior executives; a similar emphasis is reflected for all employees in the new personnel systems being developed in Homeland Security and Defense.

Because the emphasis on pay-for-performance systems is increasing, new agency leaders have an opportunity to leverage
this trend in their agencies, even though they may not yet have
the legal authority to apply them. You can do this by putting the
key elements in place (such as linking executive performance
commitments to elements in agency annual performance plans)
so your agency can take advantage of additional resources that
may become available down the road, such as funding of the
Human Capital Performance Fund.

CONNECTING THE DOTS

Taken together, these four sets of laws form a statutory framework of sorts for making agencies more results-oriented. One
overarching challenge is that these laws are on a cyclical timetable that requires interaction between the different elements,
yet the statutory timetables are not linked to the actual policy
development and implementation cycles. Through the use of
statutory authority to combine congressional reporting requirements and revise reporting dates (Reports Consolidation Act of
2000, P.L. 106-531), OMB has integrated many of the governmentwide reporting requirements. Nevertheless, agency leaders may need to revise their agencies' performance appraisal
rating cycles to ensure that timely and relevant agency-wide
performance information is available in the assessment and rating process.

In addition, over the years, Congress has created a number of
statutory management officials in each agency—chief financial
officers, chief information officers, chief human capital officers,
chief acquisition officers—and more are being considered (such
as a chief real property officer). Congress has not, however, required an agency framework that governs what the duties of
each should be or how they all must work together. In fact,
in many cases Congress has created cross-agency councils of

these officers that have the effect of reinforcing their specialties. While the President has administratively created a cross-cutting President's Management Council comprising agency chief operating officers, neither the council nor OMB has yet provided a structure to connect these many councils.

This fragmentation makes conflicting directions with diffuse accountability more likely. To address this challenge, GAO has recommended that a statutory chief operating officer position be created in each major department to "elevate, integrate, and institutionalize attention on key management challenges."[5]

As a new leader you will often be overwhelmed by competing priorities for your time. Make time to understand some of the key laws that influence what you can or cannot do. You may be able to get some of these laws changed, but do not ignore them in the meantime.

You might inquire where your agency stands with regard to the implementation of these various laws before you find yourself testifying before a congressional committee about why the agency has made so little progress. Also, GAO and your agency's Inspector General have made recommendations on how to improve the management of your agency. The GAO recommendations are filed with your appropriations subcommittee (they might ask about progress). The Inspector General recommendations are reported in your agency's annual Performance and Accountability Report to Congress. Find out what your agency's progress is against these recommendations before Congress asks.

Fortunately, the variety of legislative requirements—and the sheer number of them—makes it impossible for all of them to receive the same emphasis in terms of their implementation. Most agencies turn to the White House and OMB, or to their relevant interagency councils, such as the CFO and the

---

[5]U.S. General Accounting Office, "The Chief Operating Officer Concept and Its Potential Use as a Strategy to Improve Management at the Department of Homeland Security," GAO-04-876R, June 28, 2004.

CIO councils, for guidance. Although OMB and the councils may have differences of opinion, they are nonetheless a leader's best hope of crafting a consolidated, integrated, coordinated approach to establishing a sensible set of management requirements that will help your agency manage for results more effectively.

CHAPTER 4

Presidential Management Reform Initiatives

Jonathan D. Breul

"Just as every President comes in with an agenda with some vision for the world order, social policy, economic policy, tax policy, you need to devote attention to the management side of the picture."
— George Nesterczuk, appointee, Reagan and
G.W. Bush administrations

"If I had to give one priority in terms of a management agenda for a new administration, it would be performance measurement and performance management."
— Steve Kelman, Administrator, Office of
Federal Procurement Policy, Clinton administration

"Almost every recent President eventually initiated numerous efforts to improve the management of the federal government. But few of these efforts have survived the particular administration during which the initiative was announced."
— Joseph Wright, Director, Office of Management
and Budget, Reagan administration

The transition from campaign to government requires that presidential policies be transformed from rhetoric into an actionable agenda and then into concrete results. Neither good policies nor good investments are likely to work, let alone succeed, if they are undermined by poor implementation.

Jonathan D. Breul is a Senior Fellow at the IBM Center for The Business of Government.

Presidential management reform initiatives are hardly a new phenomenon. The Bush administration's President's Management Agenda, like the Clinton administration's National Performance Review before it, is the most recent in a series of attempts to improve the management and performance of the federal government. Some Presidents have consciously assigned a high priority to management issues and provided leadership in that regard. Others have directed greater attention to policy development. Yet history reveals a persistent pattern of presidential efforts to improve the management and performance of government.

> *Tips for Leaders and Managers*
>
> 1. Start early.
>
> 2. Establish an overarching set of principles and values.
>
> 3. Secure and maintain top-level support within both the White House and OMB.
>
> 4. Link efforts to the budget.
>
> 5. Coordinate and collaborate effectively.
>
> 6. Obtain support from Congress.

WHAT IS MANAGEMENT?

Some people think of "management" solely in terms of reorganization or administrative functions such as procurement, accounting, personnel management, financial management, and information technology. Public management, however, goes far beyond the tools of administration. It also involves the way democratic governments function in a complex world economy and how they balance out the competing and contradictory demands of citizens. It includes leadership and oversight of how agencies devise, obtain enactment, implement, manage, evaluate, and then, if necessary, modify the statutory programs and policies for which they are responsible, consistent with the policies of the incumbent administration.

The challenge of improving the management and performance of the government is increasingly complex and wide-ranging. There is no neat way to separate management from policy or from program design. Moreover, management issues are closely intertwined with the budget process. In the real world, resource allocation and management are synonymous.

CLEAR AND COMPELLING LESSONS

Forty years of presidential efforts to improve the management and performance of government suggest a number of clear and compelling lessons:

1. *Start early.* The right time to devise and implement a President's responses to government management and performance challenges is at the start of the administration, at the time he (or she) is defining his legislative, budget, and policy strategies. While many of the President's appointees will not yet be confirmed, management and performance cannot wait. How soon the administration begins its management initiatives will likely determine how successful the initiatives will be. President Ford, for example, initiated his President's Management Initiatives seven months before the end of his term—too late to produce many results.

2. *Establish an overarching set of principles and values.* A clear agenda is essential to building and sustaining the support needed to further a President's program and agenda. It is incumbent on a President and his immediate White House team to articulate the direction they want to take. President Reagan, for example, is widely recognized for the clarity of his vision and how effectively he communicated it.

3. *Secure and maintain top-level support* throughout the White House and within the Office of Management and Budget (OMB). President Nixon, for example, did so until Watergate derailed his presidency. In the absence of strong leadership at the highest levels, management agendas will have limited impact. Indeed, a management initiative may well be counterproductive in the absence of support and unequivocal commitment at the level of senior White House officials and Cabinet officers.

4. *Link efforts to the budget.* Strong linkage with the budget formulation process is a key factor in gaining serious attention for management and performance initiatives throughout the government. While each recent President has tried to do so, President George W. Bush has made the most significant progress with his "budget and performance integration" effort.

5. *Coordinate and collaborate effectively with the agencies.* The real responsibility for addressing management and performance rests with the departments and agencies and the networks of third parties they rely on to deliver program services. Task forces and interagency councils have emerged as an important leadership strategy both in developing policies that are sensitive to implementation concerns and in gaining consensus and consistent follow-through within the executive branch. Vice President Gore's National Performance Review probably made the most extensive and sustained use of interagency collaboration and coordination.

6. *Obtain support from Congress.* Without support from Congress, agencies may become distracted by competing signals, or even worse, denied the funding or flexibility necessary to implement a President's agenda. No recent President has been able to garner much interest or support from Congress for his management initiatives. Indeed, lack of congressional support has been a chronic limitation to gaining full acceptance by the agencies or to maintaining continuity beyond a particular administration.

FORTY YEARS OF PRESIDENTIAL MANAGEMENT AGENDAS

The past 40 years have seen a succession of presidential management agendas:

Johnson: Planning Programming Budgeting System

Nixon: Ash Council; Federal Assistance Review; Policy Directives System; Performance Measurement System; Management by Objectives

Ford: President's Management Initiatives

Carter: President's Reorganization Project; Zero-Based Budgeting; Civil Service Reform

Reagan: Anti-Fraud and Waste; Grace Commission; Reform 88

G. H. W. Bush: Program Evaluation; "SWAT" Teams

Clinton: National Performance Review; Chief Operating Officers; President's Management Council; Priority Management Objectives

G. W. Bush: President's Management Agenda; "Traffic light" Scorecard; Program Assessment Rating Tool; Chief Operating Officers and President's Management Council

Each administration's initiatives have promised to do what the others before failed to do. Inevitably, each stalled out or ended when that particular President left office. Sustained and lasting improvement will occur only when succeeding administrations recognize and build upon the clear and compelling lessons of their predecessors' efforts.

President Johnson (1965 to 1969)

President Johnson's dominant concerns were new policies and programs, not implementation or the mechanics of government. Indeed, some critics contend that President Johnson devoted virtually no attention to the problems of managing the Great Society programs. Yet at least one significant management effort was undertaken during the Johnson administration: the Planning Programming Budgeting System (PPBS).

Undertaken in 1965, PPBS was the most ambitious and far-reaching management control initiative to that date. It emphasized goal-setting, formal and quantitative analysis of program results and agency operations, and multi-year planning. Elements still survive in modified form in the budget process used in the Department of Defense, but PPBS was quietly dropped as a government-wide program early in 1969.

President Nixon (1969 to 1974)

President Nixon is regarded by many as having launched some of the most comprehensive and determined efforts to manage the federal government. Second-term plans to manage the government vigorously, however, were derailed with the Watergate investigation and President Nixon's resignation in 1974.

Ash Council

The highly influential President's Advisory Council on Executive Organization, headed by Roy Ash, established a framework for a series of management control initiatives as well as a bold plan for creating four goal-oriented "super" departments. The Ash Council was concerned that the President lacked the institutional capacity to manage the increased scope and complexity of federal domestic policy initiatives. The council's first recommendations focused on the Executive Office of the President, based on its conclusion that "the increased pace, scope, and complexity of national affairs require improvement in the managerial capacity of the President's office." In adding the management "M" side to the Bureau of the Budget, the President said: "The Domestic Council will be primarily concerned with *what* we do; the Office of Management and Budget will be concerned with *how* we do it and *how well* we do it."

Federal Assistance Review

A second effort focused attention on federal field establishments and their relationships to state and local governments. Under the direction of OMB, the Federal Assistance Review (FAR) program established standard federal departmental regional boundaries and common regional headquarter cities. It also devoted significant attention to the simplification of federal grants administration, decentralization, and the establishment of federal regional councils.

Policy Directives System

Responding to presidential concern that there was no systematic follow-up by agencies on White House decisions, OMB initiated and operated a formal policy directives system, beginning late in 1971. The system quietly died when attention moved to the problem of tracking implementation.

Performance Measurement System

In 1972, the Performance Management System (PMS) was launched as a management information "feedback" device for the President, periodically indicating progress toward meeting specific presidential objectives (such as control of drug abuse). The system proved to be cumbersome and overly detailed in practice, was not used within the White House to force critical decisions, and was abandoned shortly.

Management by Objectives

The administration instituted a Management by Objectives (MBO) system in April 1973 as the culmination of its gradual development of agency performance monitoring systems. The system required agencies to specify their basic objectives, including new policy initiatives, with special but not exclusive attention to objectives of presidential-level importance. Even though the MBO process was formally integrated into OMB's budget preparation and submission requirements, the process did not uniformly take hold.

President Ford (1974 to 1976)

President Gerald Ford's seven-month effort to improve executive management was the briefest of any major presidential management reform in recent history.

President Ford launched his Presidential Management Initiatives (PMI) in July 1976. Like MBO, PMI attempted to integrate management issues into the annual budget cycle. PMI produced limited results, partly because it was undertaken so late in Ford's presidency and the administration's attention soon turned to the election. The Carter administration terminated the PMI less than six weeks after taking office in 1977.

President Carter (1977 to 1980)

While on the 1976 campaign trail, Jimmy Carter promised to reorganize the federal government. Once elected, President Carter's reform agenda had three major components: agency reorganization, conversion of federal executive budgeting to a zero-based format, and civil service reform.

President's Reorganization Project

Created in OMB, Carter's President's Reorganization Project (PRP) was a hybrid organization comprising several hundred political appointees, OMB career civil servants, and detailees from departments and agencies working on 30 reorganization projects. The PRP effort elevated both the Education and Energy agencies into new Cabinet-level departments. However, in 1983 the Government Accountability Office (GAO) (then known as the General Accounting Office) concluded that the Carter-era reorganizations "were either of minor importance or impact, resulted from Congressional initiative or were a subsidiary link to policy change."

Zero-Based Budgeting

Even before his inauguration, President Carter put the government on notice that the zero-based budgeting (ZBB) system he used in Georgia would be coming to Washington. ZBB was extraordinarily paper-intensive and ill-suited to the complexity of federal departments, burying the valuable concept of priority-setting under an avalanche of process and an inability to distinguish among items of expenditure on grounds other than dollars. ZBB did not receive sustained high-level support, quickly allowing appointees to assign responsibility to lower levels and gradually letting decision-making revert to the pre-ZBB norm.

Civil Service Reform

President Carter's Federal Personnel Management Project was a joint effort of the Civil Service Commission and OMB. After a year of study and extensive consultation with agencies, field offices, and federal employees, the reform proposals were approved by President Carter and sent to Congress. Congress enacted legislation to: form the Senior Executive Service out of the top three ranks of the career civil service; replace the Civil Service Commission, which had overseen the civil service since the 1890s, with the Office of Personnel Management (OPM); place senior supervisory managers in a merit pay system; and create the Federal Labor Relations Authority and turn labor rights into law.

President Reagan (1981 to 1989)

Like President Carter before him, President Reagan came to Washington vowing to "clean up the mess." His management of the executive branch stressed greater central control from the White House and OMB over administrative rules and regulations. To exercise that control, he placed more political appointees at lower levels in the departments and agencies to direct policy.

Anti Waste, Fraud, and Abuse

In one of his first acts as President, Ronald Reagan fired all of the Inspectors General (IGs). Within weeks he formed the President's Council on Integrity and Efficiency to lead the battle against waste, fraud, and mismanagement and over time increased the resources and independence of the newly appointed IGs.

Grace Commission

Early on, President Reagan appointed the flamboyant and hard-driving J. Peter Grace to chair the "Grace Commission," officially known as the President's Private Sector Survey on Cost Control. The Grace Commission was unprecedented in size, scope, and method, with some 2,000 business executives, managers, experts, and special consultants brought in to help.

Grace presented President Reagan with 2,478 findings and recommendations in a blueprint for more efficient, effective, less wasteful, and smaller government. The commission produced 47 reports comprising well over 12,000 pages of material, bound in 38 separate volumes. While the Grace Commission worked

hard and produced some good ideas, it also generated a bliz-
zard of paper and produced uneven analytical work and du-
bious savings estimates. Much of the reform failed, with commission members blaming Congress for failing to act on their
proposals.

Reform 88

President Reagan also initiated an effort known as Reform 88
to modernize government, reduce waste, and help agencies
improve services, including consolidation or elimination of
incompatible, redundant, and obsolete financial management
systems. Shortly before the end of his administration, he appointed the first government-wide chief financial officer.

While Reagan achieved some success in a number of these administrative areas, the broader issues of policy implementation
and program service delivery were not dealt with adequately.
At the conclusion of his term, many of his initiatives were dis-
continued, including a mandated annual management report
to Congress.

President George H. W. Bush (1989 to 1992)

The Bush administration's efforts to improve federal management and performance focused less on administrative matters
and more on the management and operation of government
programs.

Program Evaluation

Early on, the Director of OMB recognized that the new budgetary enforcement framework enacted in the Budget Enforcement
Act of 1990—the annual limits on discretionary appropriations
and the pay-as-you go (PAYGO) requirement for new mandatory spending and revenue laws—would compel hard choices,
providing an opportunity for extensive evaluation of federal
programs. Over a period of several years OMB tried unsuccess-
fully to make systematic and sustained use of program evaluation in the budget process, although individual budget analysis divisions (now called resource management offices) had for

many years made it their practice to press agencies to carry out or contract for evaluations and to incorporate evaluation findings in the budget decision-making process.

"SWAT" Teams

Over several years, the administration also created dozens of management "SWAT" teams to "fix" problems in the management and operation of the Student Loan program, the Railroad Retirement Board, Medicaid, the Department of Agriculture field structure, and other programs and functions. The SWAT concept was not sustained by succeeding administrations, which instead relied on IGs for this kind of intervention.

President Clinton (1993 to 2000)

The National Performance Review (NPR) (later renamed the National Partnership for Reinventing Government, or "REGO") was one of the most sustained and well-known efforts to improve the management and performance of the federal government.

National Performance Review

Six weeks into his new administration President Clinton asked Vice President Al Gore to lead a performance review of the federal government. Six months later, Gore presented the President a summary report highlighting 118 of the NPR's 1,250 recommendations. Supporting details were subsequently published in 38 reports totaling nearly 2,500 pages.

NPR proposed to cut the size of the federal civilian workforce by 100,000. Congress upped the ante, passing the Federal Workforce Restructuring Act of 1994, which mandated government-wide reductions of 272,000 full time equivalent (FTE) positions. NPR and OMB directed agencies to restructure their workforces by directing the cutback to "management control" positions, including budget, procurement, and personnel positions as well as managers and supervisors. While there may well have been 272,000 FTEs who were not needed, implementation of the reduction did not sufficiently distinguish among staff, resulting in the loss of some skills and institutional knowledge that agencies needed to be effective.

Some of NPR's notable achievements included 350 "reinvention laboratories" to test ways to improve performance, 4,000 customer service standards, and congressional enactment of the Federal Acquisition Streamlining Act and the Clinger-Cohen Act to simplify the process of buying commercial products and services. NPR claimed $137 billion in savings resulting from its efforts to reinvent government. In response to congressional requests to substantiate these figures, GAO found that the relationship between the NPR recommendations and the savings claims was not at all clear. Like the Grace Commission, the political need to claim substantial costs savings was not adequately supported by analytical rigor.

Chief Operating Officers

In October 1993, President Clinton directed Cabinet Secretaries and agency heads to designate a chief operating officer (COO) to have responsibility for day-to-day operations of departments and agencies. Ideally, COOs were to be political appointees—typically the department's No. 2 official—with agency-wide authority and reporting, primarily at the Deputy Secretary level, where policy and management meet. In the past, such responsibility had been assumed by career Assistant Secretaries for Administration, who tended to handle administrative functions and serve in a staff rather than line capacity, lacking supervisory authority over operations or program results. In contrast, COOs still had to share their boss' policy and political duties—a tension, and competition for attention, that was then and still remains unresolved.

President's Management Council

President Clinton also established a President's Management Council (PMC) to coordinate government-wide implementation of the NPR recommendations. The PMC was chaired by OMB's Deputy Director for Management and consisted of the COOs from the Cabinet departments and selected major agencies. The PMC led a government-wide effort to implement the

FirstGov.gov one-stop portal to the web, developed balanced performance measures for senior executives, worked with Congress to secure passage of employee buyout legislation, and coordinated quick responses to the year 2000 (Y2K) and government shutdown crises.

Priority Management Objectives

To establish a clear set of priorities for management efforts, the administration also selected 24 key issues to be priority management objectives (PMOs), including approximately 12 government-wide management issues such as "Manage the year 2000 (Y2K) computer problems" as well as a dozen more program-specific objectives such as "Modernize student aid delivery." While the impact of PMOs is unclear, some—such as the effort to move the IRS forward with its modernization blueprint—did certainly accelerate, if not improve, efforts that were underway.

President George W. Bush (2001 to 2004)

From the beginning of his administration, and as the first "MBA" President, President George W. Bush called for better management and performance of the federal government. He released his President's Management Agenda in August 2001 and the White House set up a website (Results.gov) as a resource for the President's team.

President's Management Agenda

Rather than pursue a lengthy array of initiatives, President Bush focused attention on five chronic core management problems: (1) strategic management of human capital, (2) competitive sourcing, (3) improved financial performance, (4) expanded e-government, and (5) budget and performance integration. The administration assigned political appointees (four in OMB and one in OPM) as government-wide "owners" of these initiatives. OMB program examiners tracked agency implementation, forging a stronger link between management and budget than had been present in prior reform initiatives.

The President's Management Agenda (PMA) did not overtly feature an agency-wide management improvement strategy that links together the five elements, which were designed to be mutually supporting. Nor did it begin with a clear demonstration of how it built on the statutory requirements of the Government Performance and Results Act (GPRA), causing some confusion and duplication of effort in agencies. Thus, at the outset, many agencies' efforts were not directly linked to achieving agency mission and goals. By the third year, however, the focus on program results was emerging more strongly.

"Traffic Light" Scorecard

To ensure accountability for performance and results, the Bush administration used an executive branch management scorecard. The scorecard employed a simple "traffic light" grading system: green for success, yellow for mixed results, and red for unsatisfactory. Not only did the Deputy Director for Management meet regularly with agency officials to review and critique their scorecard, but the President is reported to have discussed the scores with Cabinet members.

Program Assessment Rating Tool

The administration advanced its effort to link resources to program results by "breathing life into GPRA" using a Program Assessment Rating Tool (PART) to explicitly fuse performance information into the budget formulation process at a funding-decision level. PART took the form of a diagnostic questionnaire with 25–30 questions about: (1) program purpose and design, (2) strategic planning, (3) program management, and (4) program results (i.e., whether a program is achieving its long-term and annual goals).

Each year, in preparing the FY 2004 and 2005 budgets, OMB evaluated approximately 20 percent of agency programs. Beginning with their FY 2005 budgets, most departments and agencies submitted a performance budget justification to both OMB and Congress. In June 2004, the House Government Reform Committee approved a bill by Rep. Todd Platts (R-Pa) that requires OMB to make assessments of each federal program at least once every five years. The aim of this bill is to evaluate the purpose, design, strategic planning, and management and re-sults of each program, essentially codifying the PART approach in statute.

Chief Operating Officers and President's Management Council

President Bush also directed Cabinet Secretaries and agency heads to designate a chief operating officer to have responsibil-ity for day-to-day operations of departments and agencies. He reestablished the President's Management Council (PMC) as "his" council to coordinate government reform and implement his management agenda.

The challenges of the 21st century require efforts to build upon and learn from past management reforms to institutionalize real improvement in government performance. Both mov-ing from process-oriented to more results-oriented business practices and taking advantage of technological advances will require nothing less than a structural and cultural trans-formation of the federal government. History tells us that the persistent impulse to improve federal management and per-formance will continue, with each President putting his own stamp on the process.

PART TWO

Achieving Results

Part One brought you perspectives of experienced leaders and ways to get a working handle on the statutory and executive branch frameworks that provide structure to managing for results. Part Two tackles five of the most important aspects of actually achieving those results.

Chapter 5 looks at three sets of issues you face in working with your employees. In the first section, *Rosslyn Kleeman* of The George Washington University and the Coalition for Effective Change and *Brent Bushey* of the Center for Innovation in Public Service examine hiring and retaining the best employees.

In the second section of Chapter 5, *Robert Tobias* of American University and the Institute for the Study of Public Policy Implementation shares insights into what many consider the toughest set of human capital management issues today: working with employees to link their performance to the organization's goals and results targets, and then linking compensation to how well they succeed. These concepts are very much works in progress in nearly every agency and are the subject of sometimes intense debate.

Chapter 5 closes the human capital discussion with a deeper look at your responsibilities for improving and sustaining the skills and knowledge of your workforce in a dynamic environment. *Thomas Dungan* writes from his vantage point as President of Management Concepts, a major provider of training and knowledge development courses.

Chapter 6 looks at the many ways e-government and information technology are changing how leaders and managers do their work and relate to the public. The first section of Chapter 6 focuses on e-government and citizen engagement. *Patricia McGinnis*, President and CEO of the Council for Excellence in Government, and *Dr. David McClure*, Council Vice President, are leaders in this field. Dr. McClure formerly led the Government Accountability Office's e-government work, giving him a perspective on developments across the agencies.

The second section of Chapter 6 is a short case study of a practical application of information technology to gathering the results information agency leaders need. *Dr. Hugh Walkup,* Director of the Education Department's Strategic Accountability Service, shares his experience leading a dramatic change in how that department is working with the tens of thousands of state and local entities that make up the elementary and secondary education program structure. That effort aims to support the work of those entities and to track progress on student achievement, in which all levels of government are investing hundreds of billions of dollars annually.

Chapter 7 is a primer on leading and managing organizational change, one of the most important roles you may play. Its lessons, drawn from a wide array of experiences in the public and private sectors, are presented by *Mike Davis* of the Center for Innovation in Public Service and *Pete Smith,* President of the Private Sector Council.

Chapter 8 addresses achieving results with state and local partners. Not all federal leaders and managers have programs that work through other levels of government to achieve results, but the rapid expansion of this way of addressing national needs indicates that a great many of you need to understand this area. It has evolved haphazardly, with each agency developing its own approaches to our complex intergovernmental system without necessarily learning from the experiences of others. *Richard Keevey* directs the Performance Consortium of the National Academy of Public Administration, many of whose members are at the forefront of the federal role in this area. He also brings to bear his experience as a state budget officer and federal agency official.

Just as working with state and local governments presents special challenges to leaders, so does working with contractors. From the first days of our nation, government has contracted with outside entities to help it achieve its results and that method has never stopped expanding. Expansion brings with it both rapidly increasing management challenges and growing concerns from some federal employees. Whatever the challenges and concerns, there is no prospect of the practice declining. In Chapter 9, *Carl DeMaio* of The Performance Institute takes up contracting issues, focusing on how you can get the best out of your contractors by using competition and increasingly important performance contracting methods.

CHAPTER 5

The Results-Focused Workforce

No enterprise, public or private, can succeed for long without a high-quality workforce that is sharply focused on achieving results for the organization. Successful federal managers have always known this, but obtaining and sustaining such a workforce has not historically been a high government priority.

One driver of change was the declaration in 1990 by the General Accounting Office (recently renamed the Government Accountability Office) that the quality of the federal workforce is a "high risk" area meriting special attention. Another was the establishment in the George W. Bush administration of "strategic management of human capital" as one of the five elements of the President's Management Agenda. Congress also became involved by enacting a series of laws that include, as part of Department of Defense reforms, government-wide human capital management initiatives such as requiring every major agency to have a chief human capital officer.

Realizing the improvements that GAO, the administration, and Congress envision is not a one-time effort. Some of the strategies for doing so will take years to implement fully. A permanent commitment to a high-quality workforce is required from all leaders and managers at all levels.

The first section of this chapter offers you an overview of the pressing issues posed by an aging federal workforce and outdated hiring and retention practices. The second section takes a deeper look at arguably the most vexing issue for managers: establishing and sustaining the meaningful connections between staff performance, compensation, and agency results goals. The third section addresses the ways managers can successfully connect learning and performance.

Together, these sections offer a flavor of three of the most important human capital management challenges that you as a federal leader face, some ideas for how best to resolve them, and enough information that you can intelligently ask the right questions of your peers, human capital specialists, and employees.

"As we face the challenges of the 21st century, the federal government must strive to build high-performing organizations. Nothing less than a fundamental transformation in the people, processes, technology, and environment used by federal agencies to address public goals will be necessary to address public needs. . . .The federal government needs to change its culture to become more results-oriented, client- and customer-focused, and collaborative in nature."

—from the "Highlights" section of
GAO report GAO-04-342SP

"I believe government's highest calling is to empower people and galvanize their energy and resources to help solve our nation's problems, meet our challenges and seize our nation's opportunities. I also believe it's a leader's role to help every individual draw out the goodness that's inside and inspire people to use that goodness to help themselves, their families and their communities."

—Senator George V. Voinovich

Getting and Keeping the People You Need

Rosslyn Kleeman
Brent Bushey

The underlying principle of human capital management (HCM) is straightforward: Organizational improvement is best accomplished through strategically investing in and managing one's workforce in relation to the results the organization seeks to achieve. Applying this principle within organizations has proven difficult. A first step in meeting the challenge of "getting the right people in the right jobs" is identifying questions that agency leaders and managers must ask themselves when addressing how to improve human capital management within their agency.

Tips for Leaders and Managers

- Plan before acting.

- Learn to use the rules to your advantage, including the many flexible hiring and retention authorities now available

- Recognize that many young people do not view their first job as the start of a long career and make your workplace attractive to the best of them.

- Recruit the high-quality mid- and upper-level people you are likely to need in large numbers from all sources, not just from within.

Rosslyn Kleeman is Distinguished Executive in Residence, School of Public Policy and Public Administration, at The George Washington University and Director of the Coalition for Effective Change. Brent Bushey is a Research Assistant at the Center for Innovation in Public Service.

> • Keep as many of the best people in your organization as
>   possible by offering available incentives and ensuring that
>   the work is challenging and rewarding.

THE FRAMEWORK

Since 2001, executive branch action has resulted in a multitude
of changes in the management of human capital. The President's Management Agenda (PMA) provided a starting point,
requiring as one of its five primary elements that agencies respond to specific standards of quality in human capital management. Additional changes included the Office of Personnel
Management (OPM) revamping its structure and focus around
the PMA element and standards, restructuring its job listing
website (www.usajobs.gov), and overhauling the Presidential
Management Fellowship Program (formerly the Presidential
Management Intern Program).

Congress clearly signaled its involvement in HCM when it created a chief human capital officer (CHCO) position in each major agency, along with a corresponding Chief Human Capital
Officers Council. The CHCO Council's charter states that it is to
advise the Office of Management and Budget (OMB), OPM, and
agency leaders on human capital strategies and policies as well
as on the assessment of human capital management in federal
agencies. The council is also to inform and coordinate the activities of its member agencies on matters such as the modernization of human resource systems and to provide leadership in
identifying and addressing the needs of the government's human capital community.

The legislation creating the Department of Homeland Security
and amendments to the Department of Defense's personnel authorities permit these departments to develop their own personnel systems outside of many of the strictures of the government-wide system and to strengthen the connection between
compensation and performance. These systems, as well as the
processes used to develop them, are expected to serve as tem-
plates for more widespread agency reform efforts.

PLANNING: THE FIRST STEP TOWARD SUCCESS

The first challenge for all agency leaders is to determine the skills needed to accomplish their mission. Some questions to consider are:

- Given the current rules and context, what's the game plan for achieving winning results?

- What types of players does the team need to execute the game plan? Do we have them or do we need to acquire them?

- Can we train current staff to improve their performance or develop new skills?

- What's the best recruitment strategy?

Determining the answers to these questions is the first step toward creating a strategic human capital plan. The goal is to develop a plan aimed at identifying, attracting, developing, motivating, retaining, and managing employees to achieve your organization's objectives. This process is absolutely vital as it will identify challenges unique to each federal agency.

Through this planning phase, leaders should be able to identify skill gap areas that must be addressed. An obvious way to address such skill gaps is to hire new talent. Other options include redeploying the workforce, retraining employees, and contracting out specific functions. Each of these options can help address individual agency needs and should therefore also be considered during the planning phase.

A key component of any successful planning efforts is leadership's dedication to the entire planning process. For example, under the leadership of Comptroller General David Walker, the Government Accountability Office (GAO) implemented a long-term strategic plan that incorporates human capital reforms aimed at leveraging employee talent. Walker emphasized the importance of conducting annual reviews of the plans to ensure that human capital reforms are implemented successfully and that any potential barriers to success are addressed in a timely fashion. While Walker professes that much work remains to ensure the continued success of GAO, his leadership has resulted in GAO being regarded as a model organization for government reform efforts.[1]

THE "HUMAN CAPITAL CRISIS" AND EFFECTIVE HIRING STRATEGIES

The retirement of baby boomer age employees has been dubbed by many a "human capital crisis." The Office of Personnel Management estimates that over 30 percent of the federal workforce will be eligible for retirement by the year 2008. This scenario poses a number of significant challenges, including revamping recruitment efforts.

By and large, traditional federal hiring practices were aimed at attracting entry-level employees who expected to spend their entire career within one organization or at least within government. In today's economy, however, many entry-level employees no longer expect to remain with the same employer, public or private sector, for their entire career. They look instead for employers who will afford them the opportunity to do meaningful work while also building their skills for advancement or employment elsewhere. Exemplifying this new mindset, a current student in a Masters in Public Administration course recently remarked, "I like my work in the Environmental Protection Agency because I feel I'm doing important research, but I don't expect to stay for my whole career like my dad did."

As a leader, you also need to determine the best methods for dealing with upper level openings. OPM's government-wide projections indicate that 44.5 percent of GS-14 level employees and 54.4 percent of GS-15 level employees will be eligible for retirement by 2008. In addition, GAO has projected that 55 percent of the Senior Executive Service (SES) will retire by 2008.[2]

---

[1]Partnership for Public Service, "GAO: People are the Strategy," November 5, 2003.
[2]U.S. General Accounting Office, "Human Capital: Status of Efforts to Improve Federal Hiring," GAO-04-796T, June 7, 2004.

Immediate replacement is not always the right response to a vacancy. Consider whether your organization still needs that position or could benefit from an internal restructure to become more effective. If the answer is that you still need that job filled, you can move to hiring strategies.

Historically, agencies have filled upper level openings primarily by promoting internal candidates. This practice that does not necessarily ensure the best candidate and, furthermore, may not even be feasible given the large percentage of upper level employees eligible for retirement. As agencies determine how they can best meet the need to attract future candidates for these positions, they should consider the suggestions set forth in "Mid-Career Hiring: Revisiting the Search for Seasoned Talent in the Federal Government."[3] This report by the Partnership for Public Service underscores the importance of attracting experienced mid-career professionals to the civil service and provides best practices and suggestions for agencies in addressing this important challenge.

THE CHALLENGE OF HIRING WELL

The first step in "hiring well" at any level is to ensure that the hiring process isn't overly cumbersome. Many reports have highlighted that application and screening periods for most federal jobs are unnecessarily long, often many months, resulting in many high-quality candidates deciding not to apply at all; some of those who do apply get discouraged by the delays compared to the speed with which many private sector positions are filled. Some agencies have taken effective steps to decrease this unproductive waiting period (for specific examples, see OPM's website, www.opm.gov or www.results.gov). Lengthy application processes can and should be dramatically shortened to ensure that agencies are able to compete for the very best talent.

---

[3]Partnership for Public Service, "Mid-Career Hiring: Revisiting the Search for Seasoned Talent in the Federal Government," September 2004. Available at www.ourpublicservice.org.

While the timeliness of hiring has received a great deal of attention, it is perhaps even more important that agencies ensure that their selection methods are effective at identifying highly qualified individuals. In "Asking the Wrong Questions: A Look at How the Federal Government Assesses and Selects Its Workforce,"[4] the Partnership for Public Service highlights common problems with federal hiring practices and provides helpful suggestions for improving hiring procedures.

You should also ensure that your agency is leveraging all the flexibilities and tools available in your quest for talent. Over the past four years, Congress has granted numerous flexibilities to improve federal hiring practices. These include those in the Federal Workforce Flexibility Act, signed into law October 30, 2004, which include significantly enhanced recruitment, relocation, and retention bonus authorities.

Some of the more popular flexibilities include student loan repayment options, signing bonuses, and other financial incentives for recruitment and retention. Although some of these flexibilities have been in place for some time, many agencies have failed to incorporate them into their hiring strategies.[5] OPM has taken steps to increase the use of such flexibilities; you or your staff should consult with OPM on how to take advantage of these options.

IMPROVEMENT IS VITAL BUT ALSO FEASIBLE

Agencies have made significant human capital management improvements in the past four years. Examples such as the Social Security Administration (SSA) should serve as models for others. In 2002, faced with prospect of half of its workforce retiring in the next ten years, SSA began to implement a number of hiring initiatives, including an outstanding scholar program,

---

[4]Partnership for Public Service, "Asking the Wrong Questions: A Look at How the Federal Government Assesses and Selects Its Workforce," October 12, 2004.
[5]U.S. General Accounting Office, "Human Capital: Increasing Agencies' Use of New Hiring Flexibilities," GAO-04-959T, July 13, 2004.

a federal career intern program, and temporary and term appointments. These hiring reforms have greatly improved SSA's hiring and retention of talented employees at all levels and have led to SSA being one of the first agencies promoted to "green" (the highest level) on the Bush administration's human capital management scorecard.[6]

Additional evidence supporting the feasibility of improving recruitment practices is found in a study released by the Brookings Institution indicating that a large percentage of job seekers would prefer a position focused on public service. Unfortunately, these same civic-minded individuals for the most part did not see the federal government as the place where they can make an impact.[7] This perception is all the more disappointing as many current civil servants feel that their work is vital to the nation and cite this as the main source of their occupational motivation. As an example, one State Department employee stated: "As a civil servant, I constantly battle the public's perception of the civil service as a place for lazy bureaucrats to work. At the same time, I go to work and negotiate international treaties on a daily basis and I simply wouldn't get such an opportunity anywhere else. That's why I love my job." This sentiment should be kept in mind as efforts continue to improve human capital management in the federal government.

The federal government faces many difficult challenges in improving its hiring and retention practices. Nonetheless, improvements have been made in recent years and the potential exists for much greater reforms and much wider agency use of those currently available. Attracting and keeping the most qualified employees is the first step toward building a culture focused upon achieving results.

---

[6]Partnership for Public Service, "SSA: Recruiting for Careers Not Jobs," August 2004.
[7]Paul C. Light, *In Search of Public Service,* Center For Public Service, Brookings Institution and Wagner School of Public Service, New York University, June 2003.

Building a High-Performing Workplace

Robert M. Tobias

To build a high-performing organization, every appointed and career manager has to take responsibility for creating a workplace where results are obtained on a sustained basis. There is no question that it is possible to do this by creating a meaningful connection between staff performance, skill development, rewards for good performance, and sanctions for failure to perform. Although many agencies have been working to achieve this connection, few have actually achieved it. Learning where your agency stands in this effort is an essential task for new leaders.

Designing a performance management system that creates such a connection requires the attention and support of top-level political and career federal executives. The task cannot be delegated solely to human resources specialists. An agency leadership team that is truly focused on improving agency productivity has a chance of being successful. An agency leadership team that is focused solely on creating new public policy rather than more effective public policy implementation has virtually no chance of success.

Tips for Leaders and Managers

- Create and sustain a strong link between organizational and individual performance through skill development, rewards for good performance, and sanctions for failure.

- Find out what flexibility your agency has to create performance management systems.

Robert M. Tobias is Director of the Institute for the Study of Public Policy Implementation at American University.

- Identify clearly your agency's mission, vision, goals, and objectives.

- Work hard to create trust between those who supervise or appraise work and those who do the work. Without trust, no matter how elegant the system design, neither individual nor agency performance will improve.

- Learn what tools you have at your disposal for dealing with poor performance.

THE CURRENT FEDERAL PERFORMANCE MANAGEMENT SYSTEM

The existing performance management system—classification, pay, evaluation, rewards, and discharge for poor performance—is rooted in statute and regulation. It was designed with a "one employer" view of the federal government. The system has been widely criticized as not giving departments and agencies sufficient flexibility to create individualized performance management systems tailored to their unique missions, visions, and goals.

Congress first began responding to these criticisms in 1979 with the Civil Service Reform Act, which gave the Office of Personnel Management (OPM) the authority to establish demonstration projects to test new approaches to more effective personnel management. In response, OPM has given several agencies the authority to experiment with different performance management systems that link pay and performance more closely. In 1995 Congress gave the Federal Aviation Administration (FAA) the authority to create a new pay-for-performance system. This action was followed by a similar grant of authority to the Internal Revenue Service (IRS) in 1998.

The most significant change in the "one employer" view came when Congress mandated the Department of Homeland Security (DHS) in 2002 and the Department of Defense (DOD) in 2003 to create unique performance management systems. As a result, more than half of the federal civilian workforce will soon be subject to new performance management systems.

Congress is expected to enact legislation giving the same flexibilities, perhaps with OPM review or approval, to all other federal agencies. Every federal agency may soon have the opportunity to create a new performance management system unique to its needs.

TOP AGENCY INVOLVEMENT AND COMMITMENT

Of course, having the authority to create a new performance management system is a far cry from actually implementing a system that increases agency performance. The existing performance management system has been in place for more than 50 years. It is bounded by statute, government-wide regulations issued by OPM, and departmental regulations implementing the OPM regulations. The statute and multiple levels of regulations have been supplemented with oral explanations and translated over time into actual use.

The system is proving difficult to change. Although employees may not like it, they are familiar with its benefits and arbitrariness and they know how to manage it to the maximum possible extent. A new system inevitably creates anxiety: The devil employees know is often preferred to the devil of the unknown future. (See Chapter 7 on leading and managing change.)

The commitment of an agency's political leadership to lead the organizational change effort necessary is critical to implementing a new performance management system. Because of the cost of design, the cost of training every employee affected by the change several times over the course of the implementation phase, the need to learn and adjust based on experience, and the significant risk that performance will not increase, career executives will not willingly risk implementing a new system without the support of the agency's political leadership.

CONNECTING MISSION, VISION, AND GOALS TO AGENCY PERFORMANCE

If political and career executives have a true commitment to the organizational change necessary to implement a performance management system that actually improves agency performance, the first step is to define a clear agency mission, vision, and goals. Every agency employee must understand how his or her effort contributes to achieving agency goals and objectives, and that starts with a clear definition of where the agency is headed.

This is no easy task. Every administration espouses some type of performance improvement initiative (see Chapter 4). In 1993, Congress enacted the Government Performance and Results Act, which requires agencies to create five-year strategic plans (updated every three years) and annual operating plans that link agency budgets to specific agency goals. Despite these efforts, few agencies have successfully made the sustained connection between individual employee performance and agency mission and goals. This sustained connection should be a key goal of every agency leader.

This is also an important goal from the perspective of federal employees. A recent analysis of government-wide employee responses to an OPM survey, conducted by American University's Institute for the Study of Public Policy Implementation and the Partnership for Public Service, showed that the number two issue (after effective leadership) in improving employee commitment to achieving agency goals and objectives is more effective utilization of existing employees' "talents and abilities." Employees want their skills to be aligned with their agency's mission, vision, and goals. They want to know that they are contributing directly to the agency's success.

INVOLVING EMPLOYEES

The broader and deeper the effort that agency leaders make to include employees in the process of defining an agency's mission, vision, and goals, the greater the chance for acceptance and engagement rather than resistance. An inclusive process enables participants to understand the issues, suggest alternatives, evaluate options as they are developed, and then understand the final decision. Such a process initiates employee understanding of the link between their actions and agency results.

In contrast, some agency heads consult only with a small coterie of top-level political appointees and etch a new agency mission on stone tablets for later distribution to the "followers." No matter how brilliant the insights contained in the newly inscribed tablets, and no matter how clearly the insights are articulated, they will not be incorporated in employees' mindsets when they are announced. The natural resistance to change, the resistance to change that is not understood, and the anger over not being included in significant matters about which employees have knowledge, expertise, and feelings will coalesce and make change ever more difficult.

The next step is to include employees in determining how to align their actions with the agency mission, vision, and defined goals. Every employee needs to know with clarity how his or her efforts contribute to achieving organizational results. An employee can't care if the agency achieves its goals if he or she is unclear how their contributions matter, or even whether they matter at all.

The goal is to unleash the discretionary energy of every employee—the energy that can only be given voluntarily. If an employee clearly understands the agency's goals and how his or her work supports achieving those goals, agency productivity will likely be improved. You cannot start too soon. It takes time, persuasion, and participation to gain understanding, create commitment, and generate action.

Once employees have a "clear line of sight" between the work they do and the agency's goals, the next step is to create the performance management system. Similar to creating the mission, vision, and goals, an agency head must decide whether to include career executives, managers, and employees in creating this new system.

The FAA and IRS legislation required those agencies to consult with career executives and managers and to negotiate with employee representatives before implementing a new system. The DHS and DOD legislation requires consultation but does not require negotiation with employee representatives before implementation. Nevertheless, DHS, in conjunction with OPM, embarked on an effort to listen to employee views through a number of different formats, created a committee comprising representatives from OPM, DHS, and unions representing DHS employees which created 56 options to be considered, conducted a public hearing on the 56 options generated, issued draft regulations for comment, and will soon be issuing final regulations.

At this stage, it is unclear what impact this process will have on employee acceptance and ease of implementation. But it is clear that DHS managers made the effort to listen to employees and employee representatives.

In contrast, DOD originally included only a few career and political appointee leaders in designing a new system. In response to very strong criticism from employee representatives and Congress, DOD subsequently reversed course and has begun anew, pledging to use the DHS process as the basis for developing its new system.

ELEMENTS OF A NEW PERFORMANCE MANAGEMENT SYSTEM

The existing performance management system has been criticized for years because many managers reward employees for time in service rather than for doing the hard work of defining and measuring relative performance. The goal of Congress in granting authority to FAA, IRS, DHS, and DOD to create new performance management systems was to require agencies to create a link between performance and pay.[1]

Before spending the energy and effort involved in designing a new performance management system, agency leaders must verify whether agency employees have the discretion to work harder, smarter, and with better quality. Employees must have sufficient discretion to improve their performance in response to the carrot of more pay. If the workplace is hierarchical and they are closely controlled, employees may have no option for

---

[1]For a discussion of pay for performance presented by a coalition of groups representing managers, see "Linking the Pay of Federal Employees to their Performance" at www.effectivechange.org/publications/.

changing their methods or sequence of work to improve performance. Employees must have the power to change their work patterns, improve the quantity or quality of their performance, and grab the carrot.

For example, in the IRS, revenue officers are assigned taxpayers who have failed to pay their taxes on time. It is the revenue officers' job to collect the overdue payments. Strict statutory and regulatory time periods for processing the cases are specified, and the revenue officers have no control over the number and timing of the cases assigned. If the IRS assigns too many cases, a revenue officer cannot meet the statutory and regulatory time periods; if too few cases are assigned, the revenue officer is inefficient.

If agency leaders are satisfied that employees have sufficient discretion to make real choices about the quality and quantity of their work, then it makes sense to begin designing a performance management system. Several key elements should be addressed.

Classification for Pay Purposes

Consensus has emerged that instead of the current classification system that puts employees in one of 15 grades with 10 steps in each grade, a "broad banding" classification system should be used. There is no consensus, however, on what type of broad banding system will achieve the goal of improving individual and agency productivity.

Broad banding has many permutations and combinations. For example, agencies might define "job families" based on occupational similarities and labor market factors. Each job family would have a pay range for entry/developmental, journey, senior expert, and manager bands. The agency would then define the criteria for placement in the band, progression through the band, differences between the adjacent job families, and links to private sector pay.

This approach eliminates the rigidity of the classification system, maximizes supervisors' and managers' discretion in determining an employee's success or failure in an agency, and links job families to market factors better.

Pay

The current Title 5 system provides for Congress to determine the base pay of federal employees by using the annual increase in the employment cost index plus an amount that reflects a comparison of federal employee pay and local private sector labor markets.

To enable the federal government to attract and retain individuals with the skills and abilities needed to meet ever more complex challenges, Congress enacted the federal employee pay-setting process in the Federal Employees Pay Comparability Act of 1990. This process provides a method for paying federal employees at a rate comparable to the private sector.

However, the system has not worked, largely because of disagreement over whether the system used to compare federal and private sector jobs is accurate. For example, it is often difficult to find comparable jobs and it is difficult to apply the "average" comparable salaries fairly and accurately to such a large, diverse federal employee population. In addition, the President can propose pay increases based on policy considerations other than pay comparability (e.g., the federal deficit). Finally, some critics believe that more federal employee pay should be "at risk" based on performance.

In response to these criticisms, to encourage higher performance, and based on prior experiments conducted by OPM, Congress has now given DHS and DOD the authority to put employee base pay increases authorized by Congress "at risk" based on performance. Employee anxiety will increase in direct proportion to the amount of pay at risk. The question is whether that anxiety can be translated into improved agency performance. Will employees have confidence in the fairness and accuracy of the pay for performance system? Will a sufficient number of individuals who are not already highly motivated become motivated by the new system to offset those who are discouraged by the new system?

Evaluation and Feedback

Key to success in a pay-for-performance system is creating trust between every supervisor and every person he or she manages that (1) the individual's performance evaluation will accurately reflect the work performed, and (2) the evaluation will be accurate in comparison to the evaluations of colleagues.

Supervisors must have the discretion and ability to assign tasks consistent with the agency mission and goals, define satisfactory employee output, measure results, and evaluate success. In addition, supervisors must have the skill to conduct conversations with employees that reinforce excellent behavior and change unsatisfactory behavior. The historical reluctance or inability of supervisors and managers to focus on performance will make the transition to a system that relies on these conversations challenging.

The managerial need for supervisors and managers to make subjective decisions concerning the performance of those they manage conflicts with employees' need for objectivity. Employees want clear output measures. Managers and supervisors want to measure not only output, but also such factors as attitude, creativity, and judgment—more subjective measures.

For employees to accept subjective evaluations, trust must be developed based on regular conversations between the manager and the employee. If employees do not believe that their evaluation—or their evaluation compared to others—is accurate, they will not be stimulated to perform better in a new system. Thus, creating trust between each manager/supervisor and those he or she manages/supervises will have a great impact on whether a new system will improve employee performance.

It is important that the evaluation process include an accurate definition of the competencies needed for success—and that a supervisor make clear at the beginning of the rating period what is expected at each success level. Nonetheless, regular conversations between employee and supervisor have the greatest impact on creating trust.

In *First, Break All the Rules: What the World's Greatest Managers Do Differently*, Buckingham and Coffman point out that the more employees in an organization who can say they "have received recognition or praise for doing good work" in "the last seven days," the greater the chance that the organization will be high-performing.[2] The element of creating trust between employees and their supervisors/managers as they discuss performance is critical to stimulating improved performance.

Currently, little if any systematically required training for federal supervisors and managers addresses the relationship that must be established between a supervisor and an employee to ensure that the supervisor has a performance message to deliver, the message is delivered, the message is heard, and behavior is changed. Training on why it is important to deliver bad news, good news, and just news on a regular basis, as well as training on techniques for delivering "news," is not routinely and regularly required. Supervisors and managers have little incentive to acquire these skills because most are not evaluated on how well the employees they manage develop.

Additional methods for creating trust and developing employees include providing relevant learning, empowering team members to achieve team and individual goals, building an atmosphere of collaboration, and improving professional expertise. To give supervisors and managers the confidence to have performance conversations, they need to understand their role and responsibilities in establishing trust, credibility, and receptivity.

Few federal sector managers meet this test. Leaders need to create an environment where trust is developed through a constant dialogue between employee and supervisor concerning performance.

Rewards

Whether or not there is a direct link between base pay and performance, leaders and managers have multiple opportunities to distinguish among employees based on performance through both cash and non-cash awards. Currently, employees are eligi-

---

[2]Marcus Buckingham and Curt Coffman, *First, Break All the Rules: What the World's Greatest Managers Do Differently* (New York: Simon & Schuster, 1999).

ble to receive within-grade pay increases, quality step increases, special awards or bonuses based on performance, and awards based on performance as a member of a team. Managers and supervisors can also reward employees with a wide variety of non-cash awards for performance, including certificates and prizes, time off, or preferred rotational assignments. Leaders need to ensure that all award systems are linked overtly and fairly to employee and team performance.

A within-grade increase occurs when a supervisor finds that an employee is performing satisfactorily at the current grade and step and is eligible for such an increase. Eligibility occurs after one year in the first three steps of a grade level, after two years in the next three steps, and after three years in the next three steps. Since more than 98 percent of all federal employees receive a within-grade increase when they are eligible, critics argue that the granting of these increases has devolved to "time in grade" rather than "performance level achieved."

Congress enacted legislation that changed the rates of pay and bonus system for the Senior Executive Service (SES) effective January 1, 2004. For those SES employees in an agency with a Certified SES Performance Appraisal System that "makes meaningful distinctions based on relative performance," the maximum rate of pay is $158,100; for those in agencies without certification, the maximum rate of pay is $145,600.

Each year, the President recognizes SES winners of distinguished and meritorious rank awards. Distinguished rank recipients receive a lump-sum payment of 35 percent of their base pay and meritorious rank recipients receive 20 percent of base pay. Alternatively, SES members are eligible for bonuses from their agencies.

The federal award program has been criticized as not being part of an integrated pay-for-performance system. Supervisors may use different criteria for rewards, and some systems may reward too many employees with too few dollars, but there is nothing in the statute or regulations that forces this result. Managers have substantial authority to connect awards directly to individual and team performance. Many do, and all should.

Unfortunately no systemwide data are available on how agencies allocate awards, such as the percentages of total award dollars that go to executives, managers, and supervisors; the size of awards; and, most importantly, the impact awards have on creating incentives to improve performance.

DHS and DOD now have the opportunity to address the criticisms and begin to integrate a total pay-for-performance system. Leaders and managers in other agencies need to watch and learn from those efforts.

DEALING WITH POOR PERFORMERS

In 1999, OPM conducted a survey of managers in the federal sector to examine "the pervasive suspicion that there are too many poor performers in the Federal government."[3] OPM found that just 3.7 percent of the workforce fell into the poor performer category, which it defined as: "These are employees with whom you are seriously disappointed. You have little confidence that they will do their jobs right. You often have to redo their work, or you may have had to severely modify their assignments to give them only work that they can do, which is much less than you would otherwise want them to do. They are just not pulling their weight."

OPM was unable to find any comparable study determining the number of poor performers in the private sector. OPM did, however, find "references in business literature to annual 'dismissal' rates in the United States, Europe, and Japan of about four percent while comparable statistics for the Federal workforce for the last three full fiscal years [FY 1995–1998] hover around three percent." OPM pointed out that misperceptions about the number of poor performers in the federal government could be diverting attention "from developing a realistic approach to addressing poor performance."

In light of the fact and fiction, perceptions and misperceptions, what actions might agencies take to deal more effectively with poor performers? Here are a few for leaders for consider:

---

[3]Office of Personnel Management, *Poor Performers in the Federal Government: A Quest for the True Story*, 1999.

1. *Provide the training necessary to give supervisors and managers the confidence, tools and techniques, and incentives to confront poor performance.*

   Delivering bad news is often difficult and uncomfortable. Supervisors and managers must be trained in how to deliver the news in a manner that is understood and acted upon.

2. *Provide more support to managers who are dealing with poor performers.*

   Support can take many different forms.

   First, if the problem is diagnosed as a bad fit between employee and job and/or employee and supervisor, and the best option is reassignment, agency management support and understanding are needed to move an individual to a new job that fits his or her skill level and personality. In short, a move should be made that solves a problem rather than creates a problem for someone else.

   Second, supervisors and managers need a supportive human capital staff that (1) can assist supervisors in developing performance standards that actually distinguish one performance level from another, (2) understand the regulations and policy concerning poor performers, and (3) are able to deal with the myths and realities associated with dealing with poor performers. Supervisors report that this information is in short supply or is not available.

   For example, in a 1999 survey of managers conducted by the Merit Systems Protection Board (MSPB), 47 percent of managers indicated that the inability to define different levels of performance contributes to their inability to develop meaningful performance plans. Coupled with 30 percent of the managers who say that agency guidance is unclear, and 29 percent who say they lack training, it is not surprising that supervisors and managers have difficulty creating the clear performance plans needed to deal with poor performers.

   Third, supervisors and managers need upper level management support. In the MSPB survey, 26 percent of supervisors cited the lack of upper management support as a reason for their difficulties in dealing with unsatisfactory performance.

One of the reasons for lack of support is that upper level managers exhibit the same reluctance to deal with poor performers as first-line supervisors do. One survey respondent said: "On the one occasion that I found it necessary to dismiss a poor performer, the decision was reversed by my second-line supervisor. I believe the real reason this supervisor did not support the decision to terminate was that he had not come to terms emotionally with firing an employee."

A second reason is that many agencies demand formidable documentation before any action may be initiated out of fear of being reversed on appeal. When a supervisor takes the time to prepare the documentation and it is then rejected for what appears to be an arbitrary reason, it will be a long time before that supervisor initiates a second action. It does not take long for the agency culture to reflect an avoidance of dealing with poor performers.

3. *Provide incentives to supervisors who manage the individual performance of those they lead effectively and disincentives to those who do not.*

Few agencies have clear managerial requirements for the development of those they manage; of those that do, an even smaller percentage actually evaluate using the requirements. That should not be surprising: It is very difficult to define developmental responsibilities clearly and even more difficult for a second-level manager to spend the time and make the effort to determine if the first-level manager is actually doing what is required for those managed.

But without incentives, disincentives, and an agency culture that values the time spent managing effectively, the poor performer problem will continue.

4. *Select supervisors not only on the basis of their technical expertise, but also on the basis of their ability to manage effectively.*

It is well-documented in the federal sector that managers are selected primarily on the basis of their technical expertise. But technical expertise is not enough. They must have an interest in managing and the basic talents to learn the skills necessary to manage effectively. The federal government needs to do better at finding the balance of technical expertise and managerial capacity necessary for supervisors to be successful.

With all the tools and options available to deal with poor performers, agency leaders must ensure that managers and supervisors know how and when to choose which option—and that they know they will be judged on the results. Passively allowing poor performance at whatever level cannot persist. In addition to adjusting the requirements of the performance management system to be more proactive, training managers to develop the aptitude in personnel management required to confront personnel issues effectively is critical to making this happen.

Broad-based inclusion, experimentation, learning, and adjusting are at the heart of the effort to create a pay-for-performance system that actually improves agency performance. It is a difficult, time-consuming job and there is no silver bullet for implementing a well-accepted, proven product. Leaders willing to engage in hard, focused work have the best chance of improving agency performance.

Learning and Performance

Thomas F. Dungan

As a leader, you are in a position to build a bridge between where the organization stands today and where it must move in the future. Particularly in this era of inevitable budget cutbacks, the most essential component of getting the agency job done well is skillful employees.

When we train and develop our people, we make a powerful and practical statement. We say that only people can move the organization forward to where it must go. Training affirms our employees' ability and their dedication to our mutual work and demonstrates that we will offer the support, tools, and structures that employees need to reach their goals and help drive organization results. Strategic planning and strategic learning are mutually supportive; cutting training and learning budgets cannot be permitted to be—as has often been the case in the past—the first item to feel the weight of the budgetary ax.

Tips for Leaders and Managers

- Take advantage of human capital planning in your agency to date, but conform it to your goals and objectives for the organization.

- Get input on human capital learning and development needs for all levels of your organization.

- Pay particular attention to the quality of supervision and how to improve it.

- Use limited training and development resources strategically, to meet highest priorities first.

- Create a results-oriented learning culture.

Thomas F. Dungan *is President of Management Concepts.*

WHERE MOST AGENCIES STAND NOW

Most observers agree that President Bush's President's Management Agenda created a structure for mission-driven accountability in government. Collaboration among the Office of Management and Budget (OMB), the Office of Personnel Management (OPM), and the Government Accountability Office (GAO) has resulted in common standards for measuring the strategic management of human capital. As a result, most agencies have already identified mission-critical occupations, assessed and mapped the skills employees need to achieve agency goals, and identified competency gaps that need to be closed. Most agencies have also created a strategic human capital plan, aligned to the mission of the organization.

As a leader, the first thing you should do is take a look at the work your agency has done to identify employee skill gaps and explore how to close them. Training programs are one avenue. While all managers may not be fully acquainted with the agency's strategic human capital plan, all should study the sections of the plan that do or do not match up with their projected needs for the future. Check out this fundamental gap analysis and see if it makes sense. If it resonates with your vision, use it. If it does not, new research and analysis may be needed to supplement the previous work.

TOP-DOWN OR BOTTOM-UP ANALYSIS?

The best human capital analysis is both top-down and bottom-up. Top-down analysis links organizational strategy with human capital practices. Bottom-up analysis provides data on current training and development efforts as well as barriers to making effective use of resources (such as perceived and actual poor supervision). Such an analysis may prove difficult because training and development costs are frequently hidden so as to protect them, and it is always a challenge to unearth entrenched problems. The benefit of making this analysis a management priority is that it provides baseline data for your action plan. Part of your success in the organization will be achieved by ensuring that the baseline data are kept current.

For the most part, strategic human capital initiatives flow from agency mission and are non-partisan in nature. Most agencies will not see a radical shift in human capital goals in a new administration or as a result of the often frequent changes in new leadership in an incumbent administration. Baselines should still work.

Next, begin a dialogue with your managers and supervisors and interact with other employees to determine whether resources are being used effectively (or are viewed as being used effectively), are appropriate and adequate, and are directed at the agency's most pressing needs. This is an opportunity to identify current problems that need to be addressed.

SUPERVISORS ARE KEY TO IMPROVED PERFORMANCE

Many agencies have come to recognize that improving front-line supervision is one of their most significant needs. Supervisors represent the largest and most neglected group of federal employees entrusted with the performance of subordinates. When supervision is poor, the costs can be high. Significantly, performance suffers at the point where it is most noticeable: where agency programs connect with the American public. When this happens, the public loses confidence in government. Poor supervision also causes expensive turnover, which in turn increases agency recruitment and retraining costs. Finally, increases in grievances and complaints, another by-product of poor supervision, often prompt the need for another costly item—third party intervention, such as mediation, arbitration, and court cases.

The National Academy of Public Administration recently researched and wrote a five-volume series entitled, *The 21ˢᵗ Century Federal Manager* (Management Concepts, 2003/2004). This ground-breaking study by the nation's premier public service academy lays out the issues, places them in sharp focus, and offers practical guidance for public leaders dedicated to helping government work better.

The Academy devotes one volume to *First Line Supervisors in Federal Service: Selection, Development and Management.* In focus groups conducted as part of the Academy's research, federal supervisors were asked what they would do to improve the quality of front-line supervision. Most had participated in supervisory training once during their careers, they said, but once is not enough. They noted that they had been targeted for promotion to supervisory work based on their technical abilities; they readily admitted that these skills, though essential, were not what they needed to lead a work group, motivate or discipline employees, give constructive feedback, and develop and hold employees accountable for performance.

The federal supervisors asked to be involved in a system of career-long learning, in which concepts taught in the classroom could be reinforced through stretch or developmental assignments, mentoring, and on-the-job coaching. In this environment, core concepts taught in the classroom would be tested in real-world situations where learning is optimal. That way, supervisors, the people they supervise, and the agency would not be put at risk.

If you "fix" supervision, will productivity improve? You should be able to make the case that it will. Focusing on supervision, particularly in the context of leadership succession planning, helps employees see their roles and responsibilities in the big-picture context of agency mission. It makes transparent the competencies needed at every leadership level and should result in better performance.

Employees see the logic of planning their career to move up the ladder by getting results at every step along the way. When training and learning programs are tied to agency strategic mission and objectives, with cascading goals that flow into each employee's performance plan, you should be on the way to building an agency where the gears all mesh.

RESOURCES FOR HUMAN CAPITAL IMPROVEMENT

Understand that you will not have adequate resources to do everything. Your job is to make the either/or decision, and you should make it. Too often training officers make decisions by default; they may feel compelled to parcel out resources "equitably" rather than concentrate on a high-risk problem at the apparent expense of other areas.

One useful approach is to create a representative core group of six to eight managers and employee representatives to work with you and your organizational training director to examine and wrestle with these countervailing pressures. The executive's responsibility is also to ensure that after training resources are allocated, you have access to data that assess whether or not the training is accomplishing its intended purpose. Hold your managers, supervisors, and training officer accountable.

Most agencies use formal or informal individual development plans (IDPs) to guide resource allocation. Prepared seriously, these indicate where resources are needed most. Managers and supervisors should review employee IDPs regularly to determine whether resources are being allocated to the highest priorities first.

It is important to allocate your learning and training resources; the longer you hang on to them in the fiscal year, the more at-risk they become, as other agency high-priority issues arise and the leadership looks for pockets of available resources to shift to other areas. Training often has the unfortunate look of something that can be "put off."

SPECIFYING WHAT CONSTITUTES SUCCESS

When you are working with your managers, decide up front what will constitute success. You may need to perform a thorough return-on-investment analysis or simply to devise a system that tracks that the training has been conducted and employees have actually benefited from it.

For hard-skills training—gaining higher-level proficiency in Word, using Excel to track budget performance, or maintaining contracting officers' warrants, for example—the proof is in the use. Are employees using the training, and are they performing better as a result? In soft-skills training—such as communication skills, leading a work team, or briefing and presentation skills—look to link improvements in organization performance to the skills being developed.

Look at the agency five-year strategic plan and annual performance plan to find the goals and operational objectives for which you are being held responsible. Study the strategic human capital plan, which is supposed to be integrated with the strategic and operating plans. You should find a wealth of information here to guide your use of training and development resources. Succession planning strategies will be identified and will help provide a blueprint for leadership development. You will see how the agency has identified its mission-critical occupations up to this point, and the identified skill gaps will help you select appropriate training.

Thus, your ability to garner resources for training and development will be enhanced if you can demonstrate that you are (1) closing skill gaps; (2) aligning training with mission-critical occupations; and (3) enhancing implementation of the succession and leadership development plan for the agency.

THE RESULTS-ORIENTED PERFORMANCE CULTURE

Consider the ability of your managers to deliver a results-oriented performance culture. Do managers and supervisors know how to write performance standards that are results-based, rather than activity-based, and to link these results to agency objectives? If not, what training or coaching do they need to get there? In a results-oriented world it is critical that supervisors and managers are trained in performance management. Determine if this is a need in your agency.

If you are (or you plan to be) involved in a long-term change, you may need to step back from your assessment of training and development in support of today's strategies to examine strategic change initiatives that are coming into play. A major restructuring of an agency obviously opens up pressing learning needs, as you are redefining goals and objectives with the explicit need to be competent in new areas. Such massive change initiatives—such as the restructuring of OPM and the creation of the Department of Homeland Security—tend to be fairly rare at the departmental level but quite common at lower levels.

ESTABLISHING A LEARNING CULTURE

As you align practical tactics to your mission and human capital management goals, you also have an opportunity to look beyond specific learning goals to develop a learning culture. Establishing a learning culture within the agency begins with you.

Folklore has it that General Patton's driver, observing an imposing formation of German troops, said to the General: "Sir, there seems to be a hell of a lot more of them than there are of us." Patton reputedly responded, "Don't worry, son. I've got a plan." You might want to consider the following learning and demonstration process to teach employees about your own learning and leadership style and to win their support:

- *Jump-start your understanding of the organization.* Review the enabling legislation, mission, organization charts, budget, and appropriations history. Read Inspector General, GAO, and OMB reports, asking why they were written and what changes did, or did not, result. Talk through current programs and strategy with your managers, and get a handle on the strengths-weaknesses-opportunities-threats facing the agency.

- *Ask smart questions.* Let everyone in the organization know that you are in learning mode and that you want to know how the place works as quickly as possible. Get out of your office and ask questions. Tease out the mismatches between "what we say" and "what we do."

- *Defer judgment.* Look first for themes and implications, not solutions. Resist the temptation to act on your positional authority.

- *Find the leaders.* Every organization has natural leaders, people who draw others to them for their knowledge, wisdom, and personality. We can all point, in our careers, to these special people—whether they served in the mailroom, front-line supervision, or on the executive team. Title and position are not necessarily true measures of impact in an organization.

- *Build consensus, not unanimity.* Be clear about what you believe in, but don't expect complete support—there will always be opposition. As General Frank J. Anderson, Jr. (ret.), President of Defense Acquisition University, suggested: Let nay-sayers (like smokers!) say their nays out-of-doors—they don't have to pollute the entire culture.[1]

- *Good planning and proper timing are better than luck, but luck helps.* Luck just doesn't help for very long. Early leadership success builds confidence and respect among employees. Find small, easy wins, use coalitions and teams, and build momentum to tackle the important problems.

A learning culture exists in an organization where mechanisms are in place—like communities of practice and feedback loops—to share best practices, surface community-wide learning needs, and provide a forum for fresh ideas and creativity. Similarly, action learning groups move a learning culture forward by giving employees the tools, providing support, and reducing the risks associated with confronting and solving workplace problems. You, too, provide a model for a learning culture as you teach through your personal leadership style and involve everyone in learning to perform.

You can help establish a learning culture in your organization by providing opportunities to stretch the capabilities of individuals and teams, by doing things differently yourself, by practicing innovation, and by championing new ideas. You will not always be successful. But too often, not failing means not trying. A learning culture learns from mistakes. Employees learn how to keep on learning.

Most important, you can model a learning culture through your own approach to leading and learning within the agency, and you can demonstrate that the habits of learning support a results-driven organization.

---

[1]"Leading from Where You Are," Excellence in Government Conference, Washington, D.C., July 2004.

CHAPTER 6

Effective Uses of Technology

Few things are changing more dramatically how governments at all levels, the private sector, other organizations, and most of all, individuals conduct their business than the rapid growth and evolution of electronic government and information technology. This is particularly true for how the government interacts with the public and enhances its results.

While leaders and managers may not need to be technically adept at understanding or using the Internet, computers, hand-held communication devices, and other technologies, they surely must make the effort to appreciate how these advances can make their programs more effective. Fortunately, a variety of laws and executive branch initiatives have made that easier by providing the necessary leadership, ensuring that agencies have expertise on staff, and setting standards for the most effective ways to design, justify resources for, and manage technology. Few programs today function without a significant assist from technology.

The first part of this chapter explores how technology is changing government and offers specific advice on how best to make it work for your success and the success of your programs. The second part is an instructive case study of an emerging application to support results management in an especially complex environment: the tens of thousands of entities that form the federal/state/local elementary and secondary education enterprise.

The Practice and Promise of E-government to Transform Government and Engage Citizens

Patricia McGinnis
David McClure, Ph.D.

"Achieving results for citizens in this new environment requires a whole new management approach; new ways of using IT to connect partners, new ways of ensuring accountability, new ways of measuring and monitoring performance and new ways of thinking about human capital needs."
—Stephen Goldsmith and Bill Eggers in "Governing by Network"

"E-culture is not lipstick on a bulldog. It is a fundamentally different way of life. It is not just a new wardrobe. . .or a little redecoration. It presents a demanding set of requirements for change."
—Rosabeth Moss Kanter, in "Evolve! Succeeding in the Digital Culture of Tomorrow"

When leadership, imagination, and technology converge, powerful results follow. The digital revolution is changing the way we work, travel, communicate, learn, read, manage, and govern. From getting directions from interactive maps in our cars, to exchanging video images and greetings with friends and family, to having our medical diagnoses reviewed by specialists thousands of miles away, to managing a global supply chain

---

Patricia McGinnis is President of the Council for Excellence in Government. *David McClure, Ph.D.,* is Vice President for E-Gov/Technology at the Council for Excellence in Government.

online, the impact and potential of these ever-expanding connections are truly astounding.

Electronic government is dramatically recasting the way government operates and connects with the people it serves. Citizens can connect with their government at every level to get information, download documents, file their taxes, renew licenses, fill out applications online, or comment on a new regulation that matters to them. The e-government revolution is just beginning—offering strategic connections not only between government and citizens, but also between government employees and their partners, between levels of government and with businesses, small and large, anytime, anywhere. The opportunity to delight partners, colleagues, customers, and citizens—who, after all, are the owners of government—with better service, meaningful opportunities for participation, and increased accountability is enormous, through collaborative leadership, strategic investments, creative marketing, attention to privacy and security, and evaluation of the costs and benefits of new approaches.

In other words, e-government must mean more than electronic government. It must also mean effective, efficient, and ultimately excellent government.

Tips for Leaders and Managers

- Focus on meeting the public's needs, priorities, and preferences.

- Don't act before you have a well-developed "business case."

- Collaborate with partners and stakeholders; don't try to go it alone.

- Protect people's privacy.

- Have a strategic blueprint or roadmap that lays out the path to achieving greater results.

POWERFUL BEGINNINGS

The impetus for e-government began and gained momentum during the Clinton administration, as part of the effort to reinvent government led by Vice President Al Gore. The movement was also spurred by the goal of reducing paperwork by putting information and services online.

"E-government: The Next American Revolution," published in 2001 by the Council for Excellence in Government in collaboration with government, business, and civic partners, articulated an ambitious vision and guiding principles that helped shape the e-government strategy. The guiding principles called for e-government to be easy to use, available to everyone, private and secure, innovative and results-oriented, collaborative, cost-effective, and transformational. The E-government Act passed in late 2001 reflects these principles and includes many of the report's recommendations.

The principles were advanced further under the Bush administration as a major strategy of the President's Management Agenda. In 2001–2002, under the leadership of a new Administrator for E-government and Information Technology, the Office of Management and Budget (OMB) pushed forward 24 "quicksilver" e-government initiatives. Uniquely cross-agency in nature and focused on "business lines" of government (e.g., grants, regulations, loans, taxation, disaster management), these initiatives were designed to achieve results through cross-agency initiatives.

Many of the financial benefits so far, including the reduced costs of government operations, have been called the "low-hanging fruit" of e-government. These include programs that automate routine processes; eliminate paperwork, reducing printing and mailing costs; and reduce the time that personnel need to interact with citizens on the phone or in person.

But the benefits are not just to government. Citizens now have quick access to the application and fee payment processes that have been moved online, instead of the frustrations of long lines and inconvenient office hours. E-government approaches that integrate systems and databases allow government operations to be more responsive and work more efficiently. The bottom line for citizens is higher quality, multi-channel, user-friendly services.

E-GOVERNMENT INNOVATION AT WORK

While there are many examples of the progress e-government has made toward these goals, many challenges also lie ahead. As of September 2004, only eight of 26 agencies met all of OMB's e-government standards for success, although 22 demonstrated solid progress according to OMB's management scorecard.

The Office of Personnel Management's USAJOBS site receives an average of 200,000 visits per day from federal job seekers. Federal employees have taken more than 160,000 courses through the GOVLearn.gov website. And the e-payroll initiative is consolidating government agencies' payroll services into just four service providers.[1]

Created in September 2000, Firstgov.gov is the portal for citizens to connect with federal, state, and local governments, Congress, and the judiciary. The "official gateway" to government information and services online, Firstgov provides a common framework for exploring, searching, and interacting with government. In 2004, the site received more than 2,000,000 visitors; over 200,000 websites link to FirstGov.gov.

Firstgov.Gov has made continual infrastructure improvements and has been measuring its performance. Using the American Customer Satisfaction Index, it relies on customer feedback to improve performance. In 2003 it won the prestigious "Innovations in American Government Award" from the Kennedy School of Government, Harvard University—the first e-government site to win the government "Oscar" in the 16-year history of the award. Recently, FirstGov en Espanol, a Spanish-language website, was launched.

---

[1]Office of Management and Budget, "FY 2003 Report to Congress on Implementation of the E-government Act," March 2004.

The Firstgov.gov framework and gateway are well-established. The challenge now is to connect and integrate information, services, and opportunities for citizen interaction across agencies and functions to allow FirstGov to become "OurGov."

For example, FirstGov links to a new cross-agency initiative, govbenefits.gov, where citizens can fill out a pre-screening application to see which federal benefits programs they are eligible for; they are then taken to specific sites to get information about how to apply. Recent improvements to the site include state benefits programs (with a minimum of one benefit program per state), a customer satisfaction survey, and, behind the scenes, a cross-governmental standards working group and governance structure to identify data standards.

Next steps for the site include the publication of data standards for the initial scope of citizen benefit data and the implementation of a cross-agency content management system to streamline and automate the collection and publication of benefit data. The ultimate goal is to offer a gateway for individuals or caseworkers not only to see the range of benefits, but also to apply and receive the services online.

The E-grants initiative has fundamentally changed citizen/business/researcher access to the multitude of federal grant opportunities: more than $350 billion in federal grant opportunities across more than 900 programs in 26 agencies. E-Grants is a powerful tool for people and organizations to get information and submit applications in a much more efficient way. The E-grants initiative will benefit from a new analysis, being conducted by OMB, of the opportunities to address the systems supporting the work processes associated with grants management.

STRONG PROJECT MANAGEMENT: A KEY TO GOOD RESULTS

In projects involving sizeable technology investments, organizations must constantly evaluate cost, value, and risks. Generally addressed under an IT investment management approach, these elements are inherent in the good business planning practices that have been adopted by leading commercial and public sector entities.

Most technology investments are focused on three fundamental performance improvements (which can also serve as measures): timeliness of services, enhanced service quality, and cost reductions or productivity gains. These improvements are most powerful if linked to the strategic goals and outcomes of the organization. Other benefits of e-government investments include: enhanced economic development, reduced redundancies and increased systems consolidation, and a fostering of democratic principles made possible by the free flow of information as well as access to and participation in government. It is imperative that the benefits and results be tracked and assessed throughout the life of a project and not just to make the case for initial funding justification.

OMB's April 2003 E-government Strategy outlined the Bush administration's approach. Its goals call for agencies to focus their IT spending on high-priority modernization efforts, having all IT systems certified and accredited, ensuring the operational integrity of e-government initiatives, and ensuring that they yield benefits and reduce redundant IT spending in the six overlapping lines of business identified in the FY2004 budget.[2]

To achieve a "green" level of performance on the Bush administration's scorecard for electronic government, an agency's performance cannot vary from its cost, schedule, and goals by more than 10 percent. A "yellow" level indicates variation up to 30 percent. According to OMB, several factors reinforce an agency's green light status.[3] Of particular importance is whether actual cumulative performance measures up to approved cost and schedule baselines constructed in the business case.

---

[2]Office of Management and Budget, "FY 2003 Report to Congress on Implementation of the E-government Act," March 2004.
[3]Memorandum for Chief Information Officers from the Office of Management and Budget, Executive Office of the President, August 2004.

FOCUS ON THE PUBLIC

Several types of performance measures and accountability exercises have been used to assess the benefits of e-government programs. These include cost-benefit analyses, return on investment, customer satisfaction, customer adoption rates, and benchmarking.

Customer adoption rates (where customers consistently use the website as an accepted service delivery channel as opposed to "surfing") are of particular concern in the current evolution of government online service offerings. Adoption rates are receiving as much attention as problems associated with normal project cost overruns, cultural turf battles, and process or system integration issues.

Consider the cases of online drivers' license renewal programs in Utah and Texas.[4] Three years after rolling out the program in Utah, only 12 percent of the state's automobile registration renewals are conducted online. In Texas, only 2 percent of drivers renew their vehicle registrations online. Despite these low numbers, Utah's 12 percent ranks among the highest online auto registration renewal rates in the nation. Until higher adoption rates occur, government agencies will be hard-pressed to get the expected efficiencies and cost savings available from electronic government.

The problem has less to do with a "digital divide" (the roughly 75 percent[5] of Americans with Internet access versus those without) than with lack of effective outreach and marketing— and good understanding of the customer market before expansive initiatives are launched. To counter the trend of sluggish adoption, many state governments are actually requiring customers to use the Internet as an alternative for certain services.

---

[4]William D. Eggers, "Adoption Dilemma," *Public CIO Magazine*, February 2004.
[5]Nielsen//NetRatings, "Three Out of Four Americans Have Access to the Internet, According to Nielsen//NetRatings," March 2004. www.nielsen-netratings/com/pr/pr_040318.pdf.

In Michigan, for example, citizens can file for unemployment benefits only via the web or by phone. In Texas, businesses over $100,000 in revenue must pay sales taxes via electronic fund transfers to the state. At both the federal and state levels, government employees' training, payroll, and travel needs are all handled through web services.

Of course, making service delivery mandatory over the Internet is not a viable or desirable option for the vast majority of public services, so governments must do a better job building public and business awareness by marketing through direct mail, advertising, and public service announcements. The Council for Excellence in Government's 2003 e-government national public opinion poll found that the number one reason the public does not use e-government services is because they don't know about or can't find them.

MAKING E-GOVERNMENT MORE EFFECTIVE IN IMPROVING GOVERNMENT RESULTS

Technology is usually not the core problem with government performance. More often, the problem is the absence of collaborative and focused leadership, lack of management discipline, and resistance to change in core work flow processes. The infusion of new technology and use of the Internet are necessary, but they are not sufficient to transform government.

The federal government has decades of experience with tried and failed technology transformation projects. The phrase "over budget, over schedule, and not meeting expectations" has been used often in congressional oversight investigations and audits. To ensure greater degrees of success, public sector leaders need to embrace five approaches proven to be fundamental to successful industry e-commerce strategies and e-government approaches.

First, it is imperative that government leaders—both career and political—recognize the imperative to collaborate with partners and stakeholders, as well as the need to direct their own attention, participation, and ownership toward projects designed to modernize and transform government services and performance. Most large process change projects encompass varying degrees of risk and complexity that can affect expected benefit and value.

Perhaps the single most important element of technology-enabled business improvement projects is the demonstrated commitment of top leaders to change and collaboration. Leaders need to ensure organizational capability and readiness to tackle demanding projects. Top leadership involvement and clear lines of accountability are critical to overcoming organizations' natural resistance to change, marshalling the resources needed in many cases to improve management, and building and maintaining the enterprise-wide commitment to new ways of doing business.

A recent study on the status of e-government around the globe concluded that the rate of growth for e-government programs is much slower than originally predicted. One of the major reasons cited was agency turf war. "The problem is getting government agencies to work together. Most value their autonomy, and E-government forces them to merge their interests. It's one of the top complaints by government officials. . . ."[6] Collaboration is hard, but it is absolutely necessary to realize the potential of e-government.

Second, well-developed business cases should be used with fervent rigor to decide upon and manage e-government and technology investments. An explicit understanding of the costs and expected benefits up front provides the basis for a sound financial and strategic decisions and creates a baseline for managers and executives to measure progress. The business case provides assurance to agency executives, partners, and stakeholders that key factors have been adequately thought out and planned, including a clear identification of the risks (e.g., technical, resources and capabilities, timelines, political, cultural) and the risk mitigation approaches put in place.

---

[6]Darrell West, *Global E-government*, Public Policy Institute, September 2004.

Leaders should clearly understand the expected improvements in speed or quality of service delivery, the cost-effectiveness of the approach, and other anticipated improvements in operational effectiveness of the agency or specific program. Common sense, practical, and pragmatic questions about these issues can make a real difference.

Third, public sector leaders must embrace customer relationship management and citizen or business-centric service. As demonstrated in the *EGovernment Index Study* conducted in 2003 by the University of Michigan Business School and Forsee Results, Inc., quality, choice, and personalization are becoming key standards for rating e-government success. Rather than viewing government services from the inside out, smart organizations gather intelligent insights into citizens' needs, priorities, and preferences. This helps avoid building "a field of dreams" to which no one comes. In today's marketplace, that means providing seamless, interconnected channels of service delivery (web, phone, mail, in person) and directing citizens and businesses to the appropriate channel for their specific needs.

To be successful, agencies are finding that they must develop creative marketing strategies, regularly conduct customer information and feedback analyses, and build these into quality improvement activities. Customer satisfaction and performance scorecards are critically important in measuring the value being delivered by e-government.

Fourth, privacy protection has become a contentious issue surrounding the continued evolution of Internet-based services. Privacy assessments can become an integral part of understanding and responding to customer needs and concerns rather than inhibitors to effective service delivery. As technology expands, leaders and managers need to be aware of how privacy is affected. In the highly connected Internet world, information can be shared and disseminated easily and in seemingly harmless ways, but end up violating specific statutory-based protections on its use and access. Privacy protections, information assurance, and online authentication capabilities need to be addressed up front in e-government projects and not as add-ons or costly surprises prior to implementation.

The Internal Revenue Service and the U.S. Postal Service have been pioneers in recognizing and implementing best practices for privacy impact assessments associated with information collection and dissemination. Communication of privacy protections and effective computer security controls can build the public trust that is essential to the acceptance of e-government services.

Lastly, agencies need strategic blueprints that systematically define the current business, operational, and technology environments, as well as a dynamic roadmap that provides a path to a desired future state of performance. These blueprints and roadmaps are commonly referred to as "enterprise architectures." Although required by law and executive branch guidance of federal agencies, these plans are rarely understood by non-technology managers and executives. Everyone involved in a project must take the time to understand them and push for common sense explanations of what they are intended to do. Program leaders and managers cannot let technical experts alone dictate their strategies for using technology to enhance results.

If used effectively, enterprise architectures can be important frameworks for capturing facts about the core mission and functions of agencies (including overlapping and redundant processes and systems and their cost impacts on the organization) and for improving communication through a standardized vocabulary about existing levels of performance. Most importantly, an enterprise architecture serves to inform, guide, and constrain decisions about technology-based investments and can reduce the risk of buying and building systems and applications that are duplicative, incompatible, and unnecessarily costly to maintain and interface.

THE E-ROAD AHEAD

There is no doubt that e-government offers new and exciting possibilities for the reform of government processes and performance. But in the rush to electronic service delivery, it is important that public leaders remember the imperative of integrating people, processes, and technology upfront, rather than as an afterthought. This requires focus on building effective partnerships with other agency executives and fielding cross-jurisdictional project teams—neither of which comes naturally in the public sector where lines of authority, accountability, and budgets are traditionally fragmented by agency and program.

Accordingly, it is important that new funding approaches that are flexible and responsive to this kind of collaboration be considered. In particular, upfront capital investment strategies for long-term modernization and government transformation projects, coupled with a combining of public/private funding through "share-in-savings" contracting, can help provide flexible resources, particularly in a constrained budget environment. Accountability for results and demonstrated performance improvements must remain cornerstones of the return on investments in e-government.

As collaboration accelerates and government connects more seamlessly with citizens, longer term governance and organizational structure issues are bound to come to the center of public policy debate. Our vision of e-government—of, by, and for the people—means that the dialogue must remain focused on the needs, demands, expectations, and priorities of citizens.

Using IT to Enhance Results: The Performance-Based Data Management Initiative

Hugh Walkup, Ph.D.

"The Board of Directors of the Council of Chief State School Officers unanimously voted to support participation in the Performance-Based Data Management Initiative at their November 2003 meeting. The Council believes this initiative will ultimately reduce the federal data collection burden on the states and improve the quality of national education data. Member states are hopeful that the initiative will continue to move forward productively."
— Dr. G. Thomas Houlihan, Executive Director, CCSSO

The Department of Education (ED) has undertaken an IT-based initiative to transform current data collection and information management processes into an efficient system that supports 21st century accountability expectations. When fully implemented in 2005, the Performance-Based Data Management Initiative (PBDMI) will produce an Education Data Exchange Network (EDEN) that will:

- Improve the accuracy, timeliness, and utility of information collected to inform educational management, budget, and policy decisions

- Increase the focus on outcomes and accountability

Hugh Walkup, Ph.D., is Director of the Strategic Accountability Service at the U.S. Department of Education.

- Reduce the education data reporting burden by streamlining the data collection process and eliminating redundancy across ED programs

- Create a partnership between ED and state and local education agencies to improve data quality and management through common data standards and collaborative system planning.

NEED FOR AN EDUCATION DATA EXCHANGE NETWORK

The No Child Left Behind Act of 2002 dramatically increased the focus of elementary and secondary education programs on accountability for student performance. Implementation depends on accurate and timely data to inform accountability decisions. Consequently, performance-based information became much more important with passage of this act and its predecessor, the Improving America's Schools Act of 1994.

Unfortunately, the diffuse governance structure of education has made data on education performance historically late, inaccurate, unreliable, and incomplete. Since education is not expressly identified as a federal responsibility in the Constitution, education has generally been managed at the state and local levels. Federal education programs account for only approximately 8 percent of total national funding on education. As a result, responsibility for education data quality is dispersed across 163 different federal programs, 52 states and territories, 16,000 school districts, and more than 90,000 schools.

The trail of a single data point often runs from a school secretary's desk (after hours) to a school district staff person through a state program official to a federal program official working on one (or more) of 163 programs to a subcontractor who compiles all the data points for that program and sends them back to the federal program officer (usually a year or more after the initial event recorded by the data.) Those data points are then compiled, together with data points from the other 162 programs, into individual performance reports by multiple administrative and program offices in the Department of Education and submitted to Congress the following year.

This data trail does not support the kind of accountability for performance anticipated in the No Child Left Behind Act, the Government Performance and Accountability Act of 1993, the Paperwork Reduction Act of 1995, or modern management practice. The Department of Education set out to reengineer its elementary and secondary program performance accountability system in 2003. The result in 2005 will be EDEN (the Education Data Exchange Network.)

CHALLENGES IN DESIGNING EDEN

The first challenge involved in designing EDEN was that 18 different ED offices had some level of responsibility for or interest in P–12 (pre-school through 12th grade) data. Representatives from those offices became the initiative's steering committee. They also facilitated the initial step of inventorying each P–12 program's information needs and resolving conflicting definitions among offices.

The second challenge was that each state has its own unique methods for defining, capturing, and storing education data. Once ED had established a common P–12 data set for its formula grant programs, teams visited each state education agency to inventory the state's available data sources against the common ED data requirements. These visits also documented each state's technology profile in order to design efficient data transmission methods. ED piloted an electronic transmission system for the consensus data with 49 states plus the District of Columbia and Puerto Rico to test design assumptions.

Pilot data were used to demonstrate to program offices and program officials the potential of the initiative to meet program performance information and monitoring needs and to address the strategic policy needs of senior officials. Seven strategic priority questions were identified as the result of these reviews:

- Is each child meeting state standards in reading and math?

- What measurable value is added by federal P–12 programs?

- How are federal P–12 program funds geographically distributed?

- Which schools, districts, or states exceed expectations?

- Which grantees are potential high risks?

- Do higher performing states or districts share common characteristics?

- Do higher performing programs share common characteristics?

The initiative also worked with the software vendor community to establish common standards through the Schools Interoperability Framework (SIF), a private non-profit spinoff of the Software Information Industry Association (the author currently serves on the SIF Board of Directors.) Composed of more than 100 software development firms, including Microsoft, Apple, and Sun, SIF is adopting common definitions and standards for software used by P–12 schools. This will allow data entered in one software package to be easily transferred to another vendor's software. For instance, student information in an enrollment system could be used to generate library cards, bus routes, or state and federal reports. SIF has adopted ED's common definitions.

The final design of EDEN is fairly straightforward: Common definitions negotiated with states, approved by the Office of Management and Budget, and adopted by the software industry form the data architecture for the electronic transfer of data between states and the federal government. States can choose among four file formats based on their technological sophistication; the target format is XML (eXtensible Markup Language). Only about 20 percent of project resources were required to implement the SQL (Structured Query Language) database platform and associated transmission system in ED; aligning the diverse stakeholders represented 80 percent of the investment (see Figure 6-1).

Figure 6-1. Education Data Exchange Network

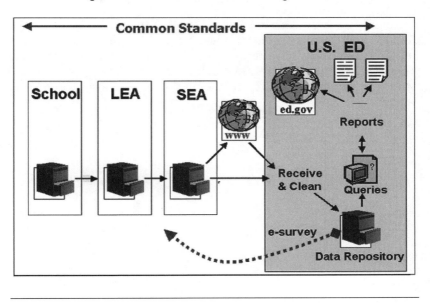

In November and December 2004 each state will transmit its 2003–2004 P–12 performance data to ED. Many states will use multiple files and systems to compile their data for their transmissions, as many have stovepipe systems that don't connect. All states, however, are developing or have recently implemented electronic systems to gather data from their school districts and store them in a central database; all are aligning their systems with EDEN. The files the states submit will be verified, validated, and stored in a central ED repository for access by ED offices and officials through standard reports and data analysis tools.

In subsequent years, the states will transmit data as they become available rather than wait for an annual transmission of all data from the prior school year. State-provided data will be supplemented by electronic survey data gathered from a targeted subset of schools or districts to gather information on a particular population, program, or issue. The first electronic survey will gather civil rights compliance data from a sample of school districts; survey data will be supplemented with data from the shared data repository.

In 2005 EDEN will replace the large annual data collections currently conducted by federal P–12 programs for program management, monitoring, and performance reporting. The data will subsequently be formatted for public access through the ed.gov website.

CHAPTER 7

Leading and Managing Change

Mike Davis
Pete Smith

Organizations change for a variety of reasons. In the private sector, factors such as fluctuating markets and consumer demand, new competition, and new technologies often drive change. New leaders sometimes want to move organizations in different directions and new opportunities for growth can provide the impetus for considerable transformation. In the best organizations today, change is a given: The concept of continuous improvement is embedded in the culture and is well-accepted by employees.

Conditions change in governments too. Perhaps the best recent example is the enormous change the growing incidence of terrorism around the world is creating in the way our society is governed. Witness the vast reorganization that created the Department of Homeland Security (DHS) and the related changes in congressional oversight of intelligence operations.

Whatever the sector, substantial organizational change is always a difficult process. Many people naturally resist change, either because they are comfortable with the status quo or because they are not convinced that the new processes or structures chosen by those leading the change are the right ones. In any case, the reality in government is that merely enacting legislation or announcing a program or management change does not actually accomplish change. Public service leaders must recognize that major project, program, or legislative change often requires changing the work and the perspectives of the implementing agency.

Mike Davis is Executive Director of the Center for Innovation in Public Service. **Pete Smith** is President of the Private Sector Council.

Recent efforts to initiate wide-scale change in DHS, for example, have been successful in many cases because of their focus on addressing the importance of change through communication, collaborative planning, and employee involvement. On the other hand, the Department of Defense's realignment of civilian employee pay systems initially proceeded without involving all stakeholders and addressing change resistance; as a result, the initiative suffered implementation setbacks. Government change leaders bear a tremendous responsibility to understand and communicate the potential impacts of changes on the public servants who will implement them.

Tips for Leaders and Managers

- Understand the current organization's history, capabilities, leverage points, and potential obstacles to change.

- Define the intended outcome to include recognition of the changed behavior, roles, and perspectives necessary to achieve it.

- Identify key stakeholders, engage them in dialogue, and involve them in the key decisions/considerations.

- Develop a detailed implementation plan that considers and addresses the direct and indirect impacts of change across people, processes, and structures.

- Communicate frequently—addressing both "what will change" and "how it impacts you"—while incorporating multiple feedback channels.

- Train key players in the change process, focusing on problem-solving skills that stress removing obstacles rather than merely enforcing/expecting compliance.

- Review progress against metrics, communicate results, and focus on long-term sustainment and growth.

EMPOWERING THE GOVERNMENT LEADER

So what are the requisite awareness, skills, and abilities for empowering the government leader to meet the particular challenges of public sector change? The first step is to understand the factors involved:

- *Rotating leadership.* Organizational transformation requires consistent leadership and direction from senior management. The short tenure of the average agency head—just over two years—precludes this, and many change resisters just wait things out.

- *Dual roles of policy and management/administration.* It's typical and reasonable for politically appointed agency leaders to focus more on policy than operational matters such as organizational structures or processes. But these are important factors in making or breaking policy success.

- *Risk aversion.* No matter how successful, almost any significant transformation involves some failures along the way. In the private sector, these are more readily tolerated and corrected; in the public sector, they may result in a congressional hearing and adverse publicity.

- *External management/administration agency actors.* The process of change within an agency often is impacted by interactions with the White House, the Office of Management and Budget (OMB), the Office of Personnel Management (OPM), and the General Services Administration (GSA). In the private sector, management is an internal function.

- *Distrust of management.* Partly for reasons of politics and partly because of inadequate training in leadership and change management, managers in many agencies do not have the trust of the people working for them. (This is clearly reflected in OPM's biennial employee attitude surveys.)

- *Congressional involvement.* Because of their ability to impose legislative criteria on policy and administration as well as to inquire into agency practices, Congress adds a stakeholder community with diverse interests and influences that is not present in the private sector.

- *Labor unions.* Lacking the rights to bargain on pay and benefits, federal labor unions are often extraordinarily involved in workplace rules. This can have a numbing effect on even routine changes, unless the unions and employees work cooperatively with management and their views are respected throughout the process.

Given the normal resistance to change and these additional challenges, how can government leaders create successful transformations?

SEVEN STEPS TOWARD SUCCESSFUL CHANGE

Seven steps can guide federal leaders and managers toward successful change:

1. *Assess the status quo.* Why is this change being considered? What systems or processes are failing? Are there clear metrics that support the need for change? Is there significant dissatisfaction with the status quo? If not, how difficult will it be to make a case for change? If there is not a clear rationale for the change, why make it?

2. *Define the desired outcome.* Articulate how the proposed change will improve the organization, its process, or results. In addition to an overall vision for the future, indicate the metrics that will be used to measure the effectiveness of the change.

3. *Identify key stakeholders and involve them in the decision.* Changes frequently fail because key stakeholders are left out of the early stages of the process. Before a decision is made, identify key stakeholders and make them part of the decision process. This includes key leaders and employee groups most likely to be affected by the change, congressional staffers, OMB, and OPM. For major changes, it is sometimes advisable to involve all employees in the process.

Take special care to ensure a strong, valid consensus among the leadership team about the need for the change. Nothing undercuts change more seriously than senior executives who publicly support the change but privately deride it.

4. *Develop a detailed implementation plan.* Change works more smoothly when work assignments, authority levels, timetables, and decision-making processes are clear. The implementation plan should be defined at the outset and kept up to date throughout the project.

   A key step that is often overlooked in change efforts is assessing the impact of the change on work processes, systems, and organizational structures. Thorough evaluation of the primary and secondary impacts of proposed change enables leaders to understand, address, and communicate the specific changes that will occur—and helps leaders avoid being blindsided by unintended or unexpected consequences.

5. *Communicate.* It would be difficult to overemphasize the importance of clear and consistent communications. Too often, change leaders communicate effectively at the outset of a change but then assume that these early communications are sufficient. They are not. Throughout the process, change leaders should regularly update those affected on how things are progressing. Mechanisms should be put in place to get feedback from employees on the change as well as their concerns and suggestions.

   Keep in mind the distinction between passive and active communications. Passive communications inform stakeholders about change in a general sense: "We're doing x because y, and it will involve z. . . ." Active communications involve addressing how stakeholders will specifically be affected by the change—the impact on their skills, careers, positions, reporting relationships, etc. Active communications address the "what will this mean to me" questions, win buy-in, and are critical to successful change.

6. *Train key players in the change process.* Organizations undergoing major transformations should provide formal change process training to those responsible for implementing the change. Remember, change does not come easily to many

people; leaders need special skills to facilitate change. This type of change proficiency should be organic to the implementation project team and can also involve a network of designated change facilitators who represent different functional or geographic employee populations.

7. *Review progress against metrics.* Progress against the established metrics should be reviewed regularly and the results communicated to those affected. Assessments offer the opportunity to make adjustments and to realign implementation plans as necessary. This should continue through completion of the change project and beyond, so that the effectiveness of the change can be measured and the lessons learned can be applied to future change initiatives.

ACHIEVING EMPLOYEE ALIGNMENT

Some organizations have used a process that involves all employees (or all employees affected) in the change decision. Depending on the nature and scope of the change and the size of the target community, this approach can be very effective The process works especially well when the proposed change can be widely communicated (i.e., there is no legitimate reason for secrecy or confidentiality) and when large groups of employees are affected.

Let's assume, for example, that your organization is about to implement a new performance management system. There is general agreement that the old system is failing, but there is also considerable concern about whether the new system will be fair. Key steps to achieving employee alignment in this example would include:

• Top management announces the decision to develop a new system and, in a communication to all employees (in person if feasible), explains the rationale and timetable for the change and identifies the three to five person team that will be responsible for designing and recommending the new system.

- All employees are encouraged to direct any questions or pro-posals about the new system to any member of the develop-ment team.

- The development team is expected to take employee input seriously and to respond to each inquiry.

- At the conclusion of the design phase, the development team recommends a proposed new system to top management.

- Assuming that top management agrees with the proposal, *but before approving the new system*, top management presents the recommendation to all employees for their review and com-ment. Again, employees are asked to give the design team any feedback they have on the proposed system.

- Finally, with a good sense of how employees feel about the proposed system and with modifications made as necessary, management approves a new program.

This may seem like a simplistic approach, but it has proven to be very effective in creating lasting change. Employees are actively involved in creating and assessing a new system be-fore it is implemented, so they feel more aligned with the re-sult than they would otherwise. But they do not have a vote: Management retains full decision-making authority. If the pro-posal seems right but the employee reaction is widely negative, management has the option to defer the decision, modify the proposal, or go ahead with an understanding of the degree of employee resistance and therefore take steps to address that re-sistance during the implementation process.

Obviously, in situations that involve sensitive areas, such as possible layoffs, wide employee involvement is not advisable. For many organizational changes, however, this approach can speed the process and significantly improve the result.

CREATING A CHANGE-ORIENTED AGENCY

Here are some important principles for creating a change-oriented organization.

Become Change-Aware

Change awareness is the quality of understanding of the role that change has in supporting successful performance, the dynamics of the change process, the mechanics of creating the conditions for successful change, and the roles of political and career public servants in deploying these mechanisms. To begin with, it may be helpful for a leader to reflect upon the role of change in his or her own life, with particular consideration of professional experiences of change. For example:

- How has *individual willingness and ability* to change been a part of supporting or frustrating the success of changes I have been a part of? How has *organizational willingness and ability* to change affected those changes?

- What changes are underway currently in my own life, and how am I or others relating to these changes in terms of willingness to change?

These questions can assist a leader in making change tangible. The leader can begin to visualize the real impact that change has on success or failure at both an individual and organizational level, and thereby clarify the role of change in his or her ability to accomplish objectives.

Also important are the differing interests and "spheres of influence" of political and career leaders. Change capacity involves proficiency in executing two general types of change: project-based change and continuous-improvement change. Political appointee objectives that relate to particular policy goals generally rely much more heavily on project-based change, whereas career civil servants frequently view challenges with a more long-term outlook and therefore may find more significance in continuous-improvement change. Both are necessary for the agency to truly become more change-mature.

The following questions may help illuminate the relevant factors and dynamics involved in understanding how political appointees perceive change and how career civil servants view change. Recognize that there are no right answers here:

- How do short- and long-term policy objectives of an administration present essential requirements for the willingness and ability to change management direction, process, structure, and performance goals? What are the expectations for progress over the next year? Over the remainder of the administration's term?

- How do long-term management improvement objectives present unique requirements for the willingness and ability to change?

- What is the political leader's primary interest in and responsibility for supporting change?

- What is the career leader's interest in and responsibility for supporting change?

Finally, becoming change-aware requires that the leader have an understanding of the different levels of change maturity that organizations exhibit. These levels of change maturity include (from less to more change-mature): change-averse, change-knowledgeable, change-capable, and finally, change-aware. When a leader is able to have a sense of how change-mature the organization is, he or she is able to intervene strategically to enhance, improve, and sustain change.

Learn the Organization's Change Profile

The "change profile" is an organization's makeup for how it relates to change. Sometimes we meet individuals whose history and current circumstances predispose them to be very change-averse. At other times we encounter individuals who have a history and current life situation that have made them extremely well-adapted to change, and in some cases even good at it!

Organizations are not very different in this regard. Both the change history and current organizational conditions related to change have an impact on the organization's cumulative change profile. In government, past change efforts (such as restructurings and realignments) combined with current change conditions (such as the fear of competitive sourcing) could be keys to an organization's change profile. An indicator of a potentially government-wide change profile was noted in 2003 when the Office of Personnel Management released its "Federal Employee Survey" results, finding that "Only a third of survey respondents agreed that their organizations' leaders motivate and gain the commitment of the workforce. . ." while ". . .fewer than half of respondents gave their bosses positive scores on being receptive to change. . . ."[1]

Questions that can help political and career leaders understand their organization's change profile include:

- What has been the organization's historical experience with change events that were environmentally/externally generated (e.g., terrorism)? Internally generated (e.g., new agency leadership)? OMB or OPM rule-generated? Legislatively generated? Which experiences have been successes? Failures?

- How has the current agency culture come to regard these historical change events? In a negative context, positive context, or with indifference?

- Has the ability to change or innovate historically been a priority in the organization? Why or why not?

- How are different actors within the organization regarded with respect to their roles in creating, leading, or resisting change?

---

[1]*Government Executive*, March 2003.

- What internal and external conditions or developments currently frame the context of change in the agency?

- What is the level of dissatisfaction within the organization with regard to the current organizational state? Is some degree of change perceived as necessary?

- Is there clarity and widespread acceptance of a common vision of the agency's future? Do employees seem to have confidence and understanding of how to achieve that vision?

- What is the perception of how the current administration's "agenda" may or may not imply change? Is there openness to these implications of change?

- How do different groups within the organization relate to these different factors of change, such as labor unions, SES leadership, managers, front-line employees, functional groups such as human resources, financial managers, technology workers, and program managers?

- Who have been the historical and current proponents of change? Resisters to change? Of the proponents, who have been the critical change champions?

Build a Bridge to a More Change-Centered Organization

Particularly for political leaders, the first visible step toward creating a culture of change should be to "build a bridge" from the current organization to a more change-mature organization. For new appointees, it is extremely important to create a safe haven of openness and shared interest for both career and political leadership to discuss their concerns or fears and ensure that they become part of a shared vision. The critical ingredients of such a relationship are trust, mutual respect, and appreciation for each other's role and value to the agency as a whole, the current presidential administration, the larger function of government, and the public interest.

To establish this relationship, the new appointee uses his or her newly gained understanding of the agency's change profile to inform his or her actions, addressing change sensitivities and building on change strengths. Rather than presenting policy objectives as an ultimate and exclusive priority, the appointee should gain consensus on an integrated vision of the organization that includes both policy and management objectives and balances both short- and long-term agency interests. As part of this effort, the appointee should integrate the input and effort of the career change champions who were identified in the consideration of the agency's change profile and seek to include representation from all stakeholder groups within the organization.

Finally, in addition to gaining consensus on a policy and operational vision for the agency, the leader must ensure that change itself becomes a publicly recognized part of the management vision for the agency. This involves the recognition of change as crucial to performance. By officially sanctioning change as a core competency of the organization, the government leader can initiate a process of growing awareness that will evolve over time and improve the agency's performance.

Implement Change-Centered Practices

Change-centered practices involve shared responsibility between both political and career leaders. For political leaders, this process involves an external-facing role of gaining the support and recognition of executive and legislative stakeholders, and an internal-facing role of creating, communicating, and supporting the agency's vision while acting to remove any obstacles that impede the creation of change-centric processes and structures. Political leaders provide a conduit to external visibility and support while focusing internal effort on promoting an integrated vision and removing obstacles.

Removing obstacles is a key activity. You cannot "push" a plant to grow, but you can ensure that the conditions are optimal for it to do so. Career leaders can build the mechanics of change maturity within the organization, but they are only able to do so to the degree that the political leadership makes it possible.

Career leaders are the backbone of the agency's leadership, and they must play the role of the change champions who carry the commitment to change from one team of political leadership to the next. They are also the organizational memory; they can therefore also address how the organization views its change history and, in turn, its opportunities for change in the future. This involves maintaining emphasis on the importance of change to mission accomplishment while working to institutionalize change processes.

Leaders can progressively use general structural or process-oriented levers to build a more change-centered organization. For a less change-mature organization:

- *Change leadership skills.* These include problem-solving, project management, problem identification and diagnosis, business case creation, facilitation, change communications, process improvement, and conflict resolution.

- *Project-based change processes.* These include engaging stakeholders, creating the business case, developing a communications plan, assessing the impacts of change, and highlighting leadership commitment.

For a more change-mature organization, the more advanced levers include: maximizing change leadership skills and experiences; putting in place incentive and reward structures that support change; supporting the success of continuous change by encouraging employee input with good feedback; and communicating successes, failures, and changes in a timely fashion.

Optimize the Culture of Change

The final step in creating a change-oriented organization is to promote continual improvement. This involves continually assessing and seeking to understand the change enablers and change obstacles within the organization. Change leaders should emphasize change-oriented behavior and look for opportunities to enhance the organization's institutional memory through after-action program reviews and knowledge management systems.

FOR MEMBERS OF CONGRESS AND THEIR STAFFS

A lot of good things come from the separation of powers between Congress and the executive branch. Among these are strong oversight, thoughtful policy development, objective scrutiny of issues, and important checks and balances on spending.

From the perspective of managing change, however, the separation of powers can create problems. Organizations undergoing major change need strong and consistent leadership throughout the change process. To create change, they often have to choose one route from two equally reasonable but conflicting paths. In other words, they have to decide where they are going to go, gain employee commitment, accept some risk, and implement in a consistent and thorough manner.

This is difficult enough to do in the private sector, where you need the support of customers, employees, and the board of directors. To a change leader in the public sector, Congress sometimes feels like a 535-member board of directors, any one of whom can take you to task publicly at any time during the change process if any aspect of the change is encountering problems or has become unattractive politically.

Ideally, management in the public sector should be non-partisan, non-political, and (for the most part) not qualitatively affected by shifts in policy. Whether an administration wants to drill for oil in Alaska or not, the Interior Department and related agencies should be able to implement and monitor the policy effectively and efficiently. Whether education or foreign aid is a priority, the Education Department and the U.S. Agency for International Development should be able to meet the goals of Congress and the administration. Whether we attack terrorism overseas or on our shores, the Departments of Defense and Homeland Security should be organized and run to achieve our objectives.

Congress has a critical role in encouraging and directing change in the federal government. This role has been witnessed most recently by the creation of the Department of Homeland Security, Congress' intervention in the Defense Department's development of a new civilian personnel system, and the recent hearings on the recommendations of the 9/11 Commission, which may lead to a major restructuring of our intelligence operations.

This is a very appropriate role for Congress. Once legislation is passed, however, providing direction and setting the basis for change, the process of effecting change should be the responsibility of the executive branch. Congress should define the metrics by which successful change is measured and it should monitor progress. But members of Congress and their staffs should resist the temptation to dictate how change will be achieved or (barring major problems) to get involved while the change process is underway. Rather, Congress can support successful change most effectively by understanding the structural obstacles to agency change and ensuring that structural conditions are conducive to change leadership.

This approach to legislative leadership focuses congressional action on enabling and empowering agencies rather than directing them in detail. When Congress decides it is necessary to intervene, it should do so in ways that enhance change leadership, recognize what's working, and remove obstacles rather than create new ones.

Members of Congress and their staffs need a reasonable tolerance for risk and a realistic assessment of the requirements for transformation. Consider the Department of Homeland Security, which is now in the process of one of the most significant and complex reorganizations in history, public or private. The department's leadership of has done an excellent job of organizing for change, communicating with Congress and employees, evaluating options for new ways of managing, etc. So far, things appear to be going well.

But this change will take 10 to 20 years to complete—before DHS is truly a unified, high-performing organization—during which time mistakes will be made. If Congress can understand this and support a reasonable amount of risk-taking, the change process will be easier for everyone involved, and probably more successful. Throughout the process of implementing the change, Congress needs to understand the impediments and enable agencies to address them.

SUPPORTING CHANGE LEADERSHIP FROM THE OUTSIDE

External organizations can influence agencies' willingness and ability to change, including executive branch oversight organizations such as OMB, OPM, the Government Accountability Office (GAO), and non-governmental organizations such as labor unions, non-profit better-government organizations, policy advocacy groups, and the public.

For OMB and OPM, supporting agency change leadership means constantly striving to find the most effective ways to support agency success. Change requires support and involves risk; mistakes will be made along the way. OMB and OPM can best support change by focusing on enabling, empowering, and removing obstacles. By emphasizing their role as advisers to agencies, in much the same way GAO has begun to act, both have the opportunity to become "centers of excellence" that support agency change efforts and build agency capacity to change.

Non-government organizations can support government change in many ways, including the promotion and recognition of successful change efforts, the distribution of best practices, the establishment and support of centers of excellence that build change leadership capabilities, and the conduct of facilitated stakeholder forums that synthesize voices for change and clarify necessary actions. This has been demonstrated by many current better-government non-profits such as the Government Performance Coalition, the Coalition for Effective Change, the Council for Excellence in Government, the National Academy of Public Administration, the Partnership for Public Service, and the Private Sector Council. In each of these cases, non-profits offer unique vehicles for uniting diverse stakeholders in dialogue and proactive discussion.

Change is difficult to achieve in any organization, but managing change presents special challenges for federal agencies. Armed with an understanding of the basic conditions for successful change, political appointees, career federal executives, and members of Congress and their staffs will be better equipped to lead and manage change in the federal arena.

Unfortunately, change leadership is not currently a competency that is pervasive in public service. Leaders have the opportunity to recognize the role of change in public service and to make a place for change leadership in the government leader's toolkit.

CHAPTER 8

Achieving Results with State and Local Partners

Richard F. Keevey

"In return for federal support, the federal government should craft and enforce rigorous performance standards that measure state and local progress toward national goals—standards that replace bureaucratic micro-management of inputs and processes."

—William Galston and Geoffrey Tibbetts,
"Reinventing Federalism"

The federal government bears responsibility for ensuring that taxpayer-supported grant programs achieve their intended results. Congress and successive administrations have approved laws and policies that stress the need to determine more fully the goals and objectives for all federal programs, including those that are executed at the state and local levels. It has now become the norm for the federal government to ascertain if these goals are being achieved by developing, implementing, and tracking viable performance measures. It falls to appointed and career agency officials, as well as to Congress, to ensure that grant-funded programs achieve the intended results.

Richard F. Keevey *is Director of the Performance Consortium and Director of State Operations at the National Academy of Public Administration.*

Tips for Leaders and Managers

- Reach out to state and local governments to develop mutually agreeable performance measures for grant-funded programs.

- Emphasize to state and local government partners the mutual benefit of collecting good data on grant programs so that a central repository of measures will be seen as a valuable management tool.

- Consult with your staff, representatives of grantees, and respected researchers to find best practices to help grantees improve results.

- Devise a series of incentives or rewards to promote the achievement of better results.

- Develop performance partnerships with like agencies in the states to foster and encourage the development of better performance measures and streamlined grants administration.

- If your agency or program uses the same state or local agency for multiple programs, publish guidelines to standardize data requests for each program area within the states and localities.

- Ensure that the data being collected and reported by state and local grantees or third parties are accurate to the extent feasible.

- If you discover that the performance measures being used in your program do not accurately reflect program outcomes or results, make alterations to performance metric requirements to facilitate data collection that will support management better at all levels.

FEDERAL GRANTS TO STATE AND LOCAL GOVERNMENTS

Federal grant expenditures have risen dramatically over the past 34 years. Between 1970 and 2000, federal grant outlays to state and local governments rose from a little over $24 billion to almost $285 billion, an average increase of 98 percent every decade (see Table 8-1). Budgeted grant expenditures of $418.1 billion in 2004 are almost double the 2000 total.

Table 8-1: Trends in Federal Grant Outlays by Function
(in billions of dollars)

| | Actual | | | | Budget |
Function	1970	1980	1990	2000	2004
Natural Resources and Environment	0.4	5.4	3.7	4.6	6.5
Agriculture	0.6	0.6	1.3	0.7	0.9
Transportation	4.6	13.0	19.2	32.2	43.5
Community and Regional Development	1.8	6.5	5.0	8.7	14.8
Education, Training, Employment, and Social Services	6.4	21.9	21.8	36.7	56.9
Health	3.8	15.8	43.9	124.8	191.9
Income Security	5.8	18.5	36.8	68.7	88.3
Administration of Justice	0	0.5	0.6	5.3	4.3
General Government	0.5	8.6	2.3	2.1	9.9
Other (national defense, energy, social security, veterans benefits)	0.1	0.7	0.8	0.9	1.1
Total	**24.1**	**91.4**	**135.3**	**284.7**	**418.1**

Source: *Analytical Perspectives of the 2005 Budget,* Office of Management and Budget.

Most of the grant outlays (approximately 60 percent) currently go to education, social service programs, and Medicaid payments.

The Office of Management and Budget (OMB) also estimates that grant outlays to state and local governments for individuals, such as Medicaid payments, will represent 65 percent of total grants in 2005, with physical capital investment (15 percent) and outlays for training, education and social services (20 percent) making up the remainder.

TYPES OF GRANTS

Federal grants are payments to support public purposes or national interests. Grants fall into two major categories.

- *Discretionary*[1] (or competitive) grants are awarded to eligible grantees mostly on a competitive basis. They provide financial support for relatively clearly defined purposes and activities but leave considerable discretion to grantees to work out the details of how program goals will be accomplished. Discretionary grant program funding levels are usually determined annually through various appropriations acts. Examples include the Forest Legacy Program, the Department of Justice's Weed and Seed program, and the National Health Service Corps.

- *Formula* grant allocations to state and others (sometimes called block grants) are determined in authorizing legislation; their amounts can only be changed by altering eligibility criteria or benefit formulas by law. The total amount available each year is sometimes set in the authorization, sometimes in the annual appropriation. Annual appropriations acts can, but do not often, modify allocations for formula grants. Examples of formula grant programs are state grants for vocational rehabilitation, elementary and secondary education, the Workforce Investment Act, and the Community Development Block Grant. Federal administrative funds for these benefits are often appropriated separately as discretionary grants.

---

[1]The use of the term "discretionary" here is necessary but potentially confusing in light of another common use of the term: "Discretionary" appropriations are annually provided funds, and include both discretionary and formula grants.

SOURCES OF TENSION

Sources of tension between the federal government and state and local governments lie primarily in the nature of our intergovernmental system, which divides authority between the federal government and the 50 state governments. The Constitution reserves for the states any powers not specifically granted to the federal government (such as border control and national defense), but it also stipulates that the laws the federal government makes shall be the "supreme law of the land."[2] In the early history of the country, states and localities exercised sole responsibility for their own affairs without interference from the federal government. As the country matured and problems became more complex (particularly beginning during the Great Depression), however, the federal government assumed more power and responsibility for state functions, sometimes with state consent.

Notwithstanding this general shift in power, there were certain efforts, albeit brief, to provide significant grant autonomy and flexibility to state and local governments. The General Revenue Sharing Act, enacted in 1972, had as its goals more state and local discretion and less "interference." In effect, state and local governments were given a block of money that they could use for virtually any program; the only requirement was an end-of-year report on how the money was expended.

Ultimately, the tide swung back to those groups that argued for more accountability on what was being achieved with the federal taxpayers' dollars. The general revenue-sharing program was eliminated because many state and local governments simply used the dollars as an augmentation or substitute for state or local funds—just as the law intended—and did not necessarily connect the funds to specific and identifiable accomplishments that could be measured. The law was repealed in 1986.

In general, the close federal supervision and control that accompanies most discretionary grants breeds resentment on the part of state and local officials, who typically prefer greater leeway

---

[2]Anne Marie Cammisa, *Governments as Interest Groups* (CT: Praeger, 1995).

in deciding how to use grant resources. Three specific examples are noteworthy.

First, states and localities act in many respects as agents of the federal government by implementing a wide array of federal programs and policies. They distribute grant funds to subunits and enforce rules and regulations for programs that have been developed by the federal government. States and localities have complained over the years that some of these programs conflict with their priorities and are inadequately funded. Examples include the Americans with Disabilities Act, environmental protection laws, and homeland security requirements. While it is generally agreed that these laws embody goals that all levels of government should pursue, states and localities have looked to the federal government for most, if not all, of the resources to support them.

Currently, there is no consensus on the proportion of federal versus state responsibility for certain policies and programs, specifically, who should fund what. The federal manager must recognize that this conflict is inherent in our intergovernmental system and adopt approaches that work within this system.

Second, the federal government imposes matching requirements for many grants on states and localities; these can strain tight budgets. A 1997 Government Accountability Office (GAO) analysis found that every additional federal grant dollar results in less than a dollar of total additional spending on an aided program. Thus, one of the recommendations of the study was to require matching funds to obtain federal grant funding.[3] Matching requirements are imposed so that federal grant monies supplement rather than substitute for state and local spending on a particular program. For example, a matching grant may require states to spend anywhere from 10 to 50 cents from their own revenue sources for each dollar of federal funds provided.

Some have argued that matching requirements are usually relatively small, often take the form of "in-kind" contributions, give states a financial stake in the program as befits their role as pro-

---

[3]U.S. General Accounting Office, "Federal Grants: Design Improvements Could Help Federal Resources Go Further," AIMD-97-7, 1997.

vider of the service, and also strengthen the states' negotiating position with the federal government. Maintenance-of-effort requirements work similarly in that state and local governments must maintain a prescribed level of expenditures from their own sources on a particular program to qualify for funding.

Third, to qualify for most federal grants, states and localities must comply with certain conditions. These generally include quarterly reporting requirements, which are often viewed as unduly burdensome and time-consuming. Federal agencies have historically not done a good job of working with grantees to ease administrative burdens, obtain state and local feedback in developing common-sense program performance measures, and report results. While timely and accurate reporting is an essential part of good public administration, federal managers should do everything possible to (1) ensure that the reporting is a by-product of, rather than a new requirement on, state and local management systems, and (2) demonstrate the value of the reports to good management at all levels.

GOVERNMENT-WIDE FEDERAL REQUIREMENTS

Several government-wide federal requirements are changing the way performance measures and outcomes are incorporated into federal, state, and local grants programs.

Government Performance and Results Act

The Government Performance and Results Act (GPRA) of 1993 placed the issue of program performance squarely on the agenda of every federal department, including those federal agencies that depend on grantees (usually state and local governments) to accomplish their objectives. Some program statutes always included some form of performance requirements, and for decades, succeeding administrations sought to impose government-wide performance management and budgeting requirements. GPRA, however, elevated the issue to a government-wide statutory requirement. Among other requirements, GPRA requires policy makers and managers in each federal agency to develop strategic plans, provide annual data on the performance of each federal program, and provide information to show whether grant programs are being implemented effectively and efficiently.

During development of the GPRA legislation, much discussion focused on how to treat federal agencies that rely on state, local, and non-profit partners to implement grant programs. A significant area of debate related to how federal agencies could set goals, measures, and performance standards in policy areas where the federal government is a partner with a state or local government in program implementation.

Some, including state and local governments associations, and even federal program managers, argued that it was not possible to do so as the data were not readily available and the federal government would be creating yet another burden. Others argued that such data and information were critical in determining the effectiveness of these multi-million dollar programs and that surely mechanisms could be developed that would link the need for performance information with the concerns of state and local governments. Through a series of initiatives, including the establishment of performance partnerships, the skillful use of incentives, and mutually developed and negotiated performance measures, these concerns have largely been addressed, if not yet fully eliminated.

Federal Financial Assistance Management Improvement Act

The Federal Financial Assistance Management Improvement Act of 1999 established a requirement for agencies to "establish specific annual goals and objectives" in cooperation with "recipients of federal financial assistance" and to "measure annual performance in achieving those goals and objectives" as part of the agencies' responsibilities under GPRA. This law in effect applied the statutory requirements of GPRA to grant programs in the federal government. OMB, through the Office of Federal Financial Management and the budget examiners, works with the grant-making agencies to ensure that grants are managed properly and that federal dollars are spent in accordance with applicable laws and regulations.

Program Assessment Rating Tool

In 2002, OMB developed the Program Assessment Rating Tool (PART). This executive branch initiative is a management system that evaluates the performance of program activities across the federal government. By linking the GPRA and the PART processes, the federal government has moved a long way toward assessing the performance of program activities and focusing on their contribution to an agency's achievement of its strategic and program performance goals. There is now much greater emphasis on developing performance measures according to outcome-oriented standards.

The PART divides all federal government programs into seven categories—including two categories related to grant programs—and presents specific questions to be answered by the responsible agency personnel that are unique to that particular type of program. The PART questions are divided into four sections, each of which is given a score; the results/accountability section represents 50 percent of the overall score. Finally, each program can earn an overall rating of "effective," "moderately effective," "ineffective," "adequate," or "results not demonstrated."

On average, grant programs have received lower ratings than other types of federal programs. For example, in 2003, 46 percent of all grant programs received a rating of "results not demonstrated." It is perhaps understandable that grant programs would receive a lower rating because of their complexity and the lack of consensus among grantees and federal agencies on the performance measures to be used.

Although the appropriate legislative initiatives and management tools appear to be in place to manage grant performance for results, issues remain. These include: What is the best method for collecting the data? How can the integrity of the data be ensured? What should be measured? Some grantees, for example, object to the idea of the federal agency using their accomplishments as its own goals and metrics and suggest that the federal agency measure only what it controls—such as the time it takes to issue and process a grant. However, reporting only on process misses the key issue of results and would not justify the expenditure of taxpayer dollars.

While the statutes governing the majority of federal grant programs do not explicitly include performance data collection and reporting requirements, recent federal laws (e.g., Temporary Assistance for Needy Families, No Child Left Behind) have done so. Also, joint state and federal program agreements (e.g., the National Environmental Performance Partnership System) have begun to focus increasingly on the collection of data and performance measurements at the program and operational levels.

MONITORING GRANT PERFORMANCE IN AN INTERGOVERNMENTAL CONTEXT

Two examples demonstrate how grant performance can be monitored effectively in an intergovernmental context.

Department of Justice's Weed and Seed Program

Established in 1991, the Weed and Seed program is a Justice Department discretionary grant program. This joint federal, state, and local program provides funding to grantees to help prevent and control crime and improve the quality of life in targeted high-crime neighborhoods across the country. Weed and Seed grant funds support activities such as police bike patrols, community cleanups, youth and recreational activities, and computer training. A central goal of the program is for local Weed and Seed sites to develop partnerships with state and local governments as well as the private sector to leverage additional resources and eventually eliminate the need for federal support.

GAO conducted a study of the Weed and Seed program to examine its management practices, including whether the program has developed adequate performance measures to track program outcomes. The report found that while the program has started to develop measures to assess how well sites are meeting program objectives, it does not measure the extent to which grantees are weeding crime from neighborhoods and preventing it from recurring. In addition, no site's funding has been withdrawn as a result of becoming self-sustaining in the 11-year history of the program.[4]

As a result of its findings, GAO recommended that the program clearly define criteria for assessing when sites are self-sustaining and apply those criteria to sites when making further funding decisions. GAO also recommended that the program develop outcome performance measures that can be used to track progress toward program outcomes.

In a letter commenting on the GAO report, the program office essentially disagreed with GAO over the use of homicide rates as an effective indicator of program performance. It stated that external studies showed lower homicide rates in Weed and Seed sites when compared to host jurisdictions, and that program sites experienced a decline in homicides over a three-year period. GAO responded that the studies did not account for changes in population, used a faulty methodology in using host jurisdictions to compare performance in Weed and Seed sites, and evaluated program sites only on the basis of decreases in homicide when Weed and Seed was intended to reduce crime in general. This lack of federal/state agreement on performance measures and goals has persisted since the program began operation.

The Weed and Seed program also earned a PART rating of "results not demonstrated" in the 2005 budget. The PART report indicated that a large number of project sites had "inconsistent oversight and results" and that the program had failed to establish baseline data for performance objectives such as homicide rates. The PART report also stated that only a small number of sites have been independently evaluated, thus making it difficult to assess the effectiveness of the program.

Congress considered legislation in 2004 (H.R. 3036) that would impose more rigorous requirements on Weed and Seed program grantees, similar to other Justice programs like Commu-

---

[4]U.S. General Accounting Office, "Grants Management: Despite Efforts to Improve Weed and Seed Program Management, Challenges Remain," GAO-04-245, March 2004.

nity Oriented Policing Services and the Drug Free Communities Support Program. These include a matching grant requirement (currently none is required), a limit on the maximum number of years (proposed at 10) a grantee can receive funding, and a "timely and effective" plan to sustain the program independently when federal funding ends.

Congress' action, while useful to improve the management of the program, does not focus on results and thus falls short of what is necessary. Moreover, the disagreement between GAO and the Justice Department, as well as the program's mediocre rating on the PART, reflects the lack of collaboration among grantees and the federal officials responsible for managing grant-funded programs.

Temporary Assistance for Needy Families Block Grant

The Temporary Assistance for Needy Families Block Grant (TANF) program was the central feature of the welfare reforms contained in the Personal Responsibility and Work Opportunity Reconciliation Act of 1996, which replaced the federal entitlement program under Aid to Families with Dependent Children with block grants to the states. The TANF program had three broad goals:

- End the dependence of needy parents on welfare by requiring most recipients to work and prepare for self-sufficiency

- Promote the preservation of two-parent families

- Reduce the occurrence of babies born outside of marriage.

In addition, the law placed a five-year limit on welfare assistance to eligible parents and required recipients to participate in a job preparation program after two years.

TANF is one of the few programs that specifically provided for performance goals and measurement within the statute. For example, the law required states to have one-half of their welfare recipients in "work programs" for at least 30 hours per week by the year 2000. In addition, TANF required the Department of Health and Human Services to report yearly performance measures, including work participation rates, average annual earnings of participants, demographic characteristics of participating families, and employment trends of needy families with minor children living at home.

GAO conducted a review of TANF in 2001 and found that the program had gone a long way toward meeting its performance goals.[5] The report noted that "the states are transforming the nation's welfare system into a work-based, temporary assistance program for needy families." It found a 50 percent decline in the number of families receiving cash assistance, from 4.4 million in August 1996 to 2.2 million as of June 2000, and that most of the adults in families remaining off welfare rolls were employed at some time after leaving the program. Furthermore, states were training their "workfare" recipients to move off public assistance rapidly to paying jobs. The TANF program was not rated by the PART in the most recent reporting by OMB, but a number of independent studies have shown that this program has succeeded in moving individuals from welfare to work.[6]

TANF also includes provisions in the statute to improve performance. It rewards states that achieve the largest percentage reduction in the number of cash assistance cases, out-of-wedlock births, and abortions among program recipients. It also reduces grant funds to states that do not meet the requirements of the law by failing to provide data, failing to maintain specified levels of local funding, and failing to meet the work participation requirements of the statute.

As these two examples show, managing for grant performance presents a mixed picture. Successful programs like TANF reflect a willingness on the part of Congress and grant-making agencies to give guidance on what is required, and state and local grantees to cooperate and implement effective policies. On the other hand, programs like Weed and Seed reflect a lack of

---

[5]U.S. General Accounting Office, "Welfare Reform: Progress in Meeting Work-Focused TANF Goals," GAO-01-522T, March 2001.
[6]Jeffrey Grogger et al., "Consequences of Welfare Reform: A Research Synthesis" (Rand Corporation, 2002).

agreement between the federal agencies and grantees over how to measure results. Federal leaders must be willing to take on these issues and resolve them.

STATE AND LOCAL GOVERNMENTS ARE PART OF THE SOLUTION

Federal managers should not think that the federal government has a monopoly on the development of performance management tools like GPRA and PART. In fact, goal-setting, strategic planning, and the development and use of performance measures have long been in the tool kit of state and local governments. The National Association of Budget Officers and the National Conference of State Legislatures have for many years been reporting on the progress made by their member states in governing for results. Furthermore, both the Government Finance Officers Association and the Association of Government Accountants have programs to review the annual financial and accountability reports of state and local governments against an established set of criteria, including the degree to which the reports contain suitable performance metrics.

For the past several years, *Governing Magazine* has been reviewing and evaluating the progress that states, counties, and cities have been making in using the tools of performance management. State and local governments have taken many different routes toward governing for results, and needless to say some governments have shown better results than others. Nevertheless, there is no doubt that state and local governments have been in the business of strategic planning, performance budgeting, outcome and output measurement, and reporting for as long as, or longer than, the federal government.

Governing for results is now a universal paradigm in public administration. How do you manage programs that involve more than one level of government? This issue has been a major challenge at least since the New Deal, but it has become even more important as performance has become the signpost for better public management. Furthermore, GPRA and more recently the PART process have placed pressure on federal managers to ensure that they work collaboratively with state and local governments to develop and implement effective performance measures for grant-funded programs.

WORKING WITH STATE AND LOCAL GOVERNMENTS TO IMPROVE GRANT PERFORMANCE

The following observations are presented as a guide for current and prospective appointed and career federal agency officials, members of Congress, and their staffs to help state and local grantees focus more effectively on performance:

- *Whether or not your program statute explicitly calls for it, reach out to state and local governments to develop mutually agreeable performance measures for grant-funded programs.* Work cooperatively with state and local governments, as well as relevant interest groups such as national educational, environmental, and social service associations to gain a better understanding of what is needed to develop better program goals and performance measures. These groups all have a stake in good management of public dollars. Federal managers can foster an environment that promotes a better understanding of the need for performance measures and shows how cooperation can benefit all parties.

- *Emphasize to state and local government partners the mutual benefit of collecting good data on grant programs so that a central repository of measures will be seen as a valuable management tool.* It is in the interest of state and local officials to operate programs based on sound data, so that they know that these programs are working effectively for their populations.

- *Consult with your staff, representatives of grantees, and respected researchers to find best practices to help grantees improve results.*

- *Devise a series of incentives or rewards to promote the achievement of better results.*

- *Develop performance partnerships with like agencies in the states to foster and encourage the development of better performance measures and streamlined grants administration.* Performance partnerships give states and localities more flexibility to solve problems the way they want to in return for being held accountable for results. They also eliminate federal micromanagement, share decision-making, and focus on public outcomes rather than outputs. A good example of such a strategy was developed by the Environmental Protection Agency (EPA) when it formed its National Environmental Performance Partnership System (NEPPS). Discussions with EPA program managers and state departments of environmental protection suggest that this is an excellent model.

David Ziegele, the Director of Planning, Analysis and Accountability at EPA indicates that "NEPPS has proven to be an important mechanism for promoting joint planning and priority setting and strengthening the collaborative relationship between states and the EPA." Call on EPA officials to discuss in more depth the details of this kind of partnership.

• *If your agency or program uses the same state or local agency for multiple programs, publish guidelines to standardize data requests for each program area within the states and localities.* This will ensure that all states and local governments are reporting the same information, making comparisons more valid, enhancing data integrity, and reducing the paperwork burden.

To this end, the Department of Education has recently visited each state department of education to establish common measures and collect common data elements. This kind of up-front work will pay big dividends in the future. According to Hugh Walkup, Director of the Strategic Accountability Service at the Department of Education, when the system is implemented the reporting burden on the states should be reduced by half (see Chapter 6).

• *Ensure that the data being collected and reported by state and local grantees or third parties are accurate to the extent feasible.* Even though agency Inspectors General conduct internal audits of program and financial information, proactive leaders take the initiative to ensure that there are no surprises. The process of data verification is difficult for almost all grant program areas, whether it be education, social services, or the environment. But, if the data are flawed, all the benefits of benchmarking, best practices, and program performance will be negated and the conclusions will be invalid.

- *Make alterations to performance metric requirements to facilitate data collection* if you discover that the performance measures being used in your program do not accurately reflect program outcomes or results. State and local government program managers are often in a better position to know what kinds of data are available and what information is better suited to measure effectiveness. Your staff, GAO reports, and OMB are good sources. In such cases, federal and state and local governments and associations should promptly negotiate a better set of performance measures. This will lead to better intergovernmental relationships, improved performance measures, and better program outcomes.

Congress should also play a key role by taking the following steps:

- *Step up to its oversight responsibilities by holding frequent hearings focused on federal grants to states and localities.* (Public Law 97-258 makes provision for congressional review of grant programs to determine "the extent to which the purposes of the grants have been met.") To date, Congress has not fully used the data from GPRA and the PART in its budget deliberations. Recently, the House Government Reform Committee passed the Program Assessment and Results Act, which would mandate that OMB review every federal program every five years. For this initiative to be truly effective, Congress should become more involved in the performance review process as part of its oversight responsibilities.

- *Ensure that taxpayer dollars are well spent by providing enough funding for high-quality data collection and program evaluations.* Make certain that the grant-making federal agencies have the capacity to maintain and enhance existing performance data standards and analytical tools.

- *Give federal grant-making agencies the explicit statutory authority, if they don't already have it, to reward states and localities for achieving intended performance outcomes.* TANF is a good model for how agencies can be given the power to sanction states and localities for failing to attain their performance objectives.

These suggestions should not be viewed as a panacea for what ails the U.S. grants administration and implementation process, but as a guide to help decision-makers put in place a system based on accountability, cooperative partnership, and results.

Effectively managing federal grant-supported programs for results is extremely difficult but exceedingly important. The size and complexity of federal grant programs mean that federal managers and Congress both bear responsibility for ensuring that taxpayer dollars support programs that produce results. Recent federal initiatives such as GPRA and the PART move the government in the right direction, but there is still a long way to go. The challenge for federal managers is to work cooperatively with state and local government managers who best understand local conditions and have been part of the effort to institute performance management in their communities.

CHAPTER 9

Achieving Results with Contractors

Carl DeMaio

"Where performance-based contracting is working well, it is
a partnership—both the government and the contractor are
working together for mutually beneficial results. When done
correctly, performance-based contracting is actually less difficult
to manage than traditional contracts. And last, just as we hold
the contractor accountable, government employees must also be
held accountable—and both should be rewarded for achieving
the desired results."

—Ronne Rogin, former procurement analyst,
Treasury Department

"Federal procurement is undergoing a major transformation. It
has ceased to function simply as a support activity. Instead, federal procurement has evolved into a primary management and
administrative function that is playing an increasingly critical
role in enabling federal departments and agencies to discharge
their primary missions."

—Lawrence L. Martin, Associate Professor,
School of Social Work, Columbia University

"Ineffective contracting does long-term damage to the government's credibility with the governed and thus, to our collective
ability to lead."

—David Safavian, Counselor to the Deputy Director,
Office of Management and Budget

Carl DeMaio is President of The Performance Institute.

Competition and performance-based contracting enable government managers to elicit the best performance from those who provide services for the government. They also provide taxpayers assurance that the government is acting responsibly with their tax dollars by achieving the highest level of performance at the lowest cost.

Tips for Leaders and Managers

- Prioritize contracting opportunities to target high-impact functions.

- Get the vocabulary straight to avoid miscommunication.

- Invest in employee training and support.

- Set clear cost and performance measures to guide competitions.

- Enrich contracts with efficient performance measures.

- Hold winners accountable for delivering results.

THE CHALLENGE OF CONTRACT MANAGEMENT

The federal government carries out its various missions on behalf of taxpayers with the help of thousands of contractors each year. Indeed, by making over $200 billion in purchases annually, the federal government is the largest single purchaser of goods and services on the planet. By some estimates, over 10 million contract staff support the federal government—with some dubbing these masses of contractors government's "shadow" workforce.

Substantial reforms have been enacted over the past decade to streamline contracting functions in the federal government. Implementing those reforms has been a key initiative for every federal agency. Contracting has also become a political issue.

In some cases, the use of contracted services has been criticized for "outsourcing" key functions of the federal government. In other cases, contractors have brought embarrassment to the agencies they serve.

Despite the controversy surrounding contracting in government, it remains a critical management tool. Effective management of contractors is not only important to keep your agency off the front page of the *Washington Post*, but it is vital to ensuring the effective delivery of services to the American taxpayer.

The challenge of contractor management can be broken down into two key phases: (1) deciding when contract, and (2) managing contracts for results.

Deciding When to Contract

Over the years, a number of agency functions have been contracted out as management came to the conclusion that having outside providers do the work was more advantageous (either from a cost or performance perspective) than having federal workers do the work. How agency managers arrived at that conclusion for each function—and whether that conclusion still holds true—has been the subject of great controversy. Understanding the various processes available to help agency mangers decide when to contract is the first key step in managing contracts for performance.

The three principal methods for engaging outside entities in service delivery are privatization, outsourcing, and competitive sourcing. It is extremely important to understand that these three terms are *not* synonymous.

Privatization is the decision by government to discontinue a responsibility (i.e., funding and management) in favor of non-governmental entities providing the service on the open market. Privatization is a specialized approach that occurs infrequently and does not involve government contracting.

Outsourcing is the contracting out of a government activity to a non-governmental entity (either private or non-profit). Government retains the responsibility for the service and continues to provide funding for it, but allows the actual work to be done outside the agency by vendors. Outsourcing involves the use of the Federal Acquisition Regulation (FAR) process and typically involves soliciting bids from vendors—sometimes including even governmental vendors such as other federal agencies. In special cases, non-competitive approaches may be used.

In some cases, agencies have opted to proceed directly to "outsourcing" a function when management has little to no doubt that the service could best be provided by a vendor outside the agency. In these instances, the agency solicits bids for work under the FAR and evaluates the cost and performance offered by each bidder. Not all outsourcing goes to the private sector; agencies sometimes contract with other federal agencies for services. Many non-profits receive federal contracts as well.

Competitive sourcing is a process used in situations where the "management call" is not so clear. Competitive sourcing offers a standardized and managed process for comparing the costs and performance of work currently done by government employees against alternatives available from private and non-profit groups.

Although competitive sourcing has been a federal policy for over 50 years, aggressive marketing of competitive sourcing during the Bush administration provoked an unusually severe backlash, primarily from federal employees and employee unions and their congressional supporters. The backlash generated rhetoric from both antagonists and advocates that has muddied the concepts and obscured the facts of the situation.

At its most basic level, competitive sourcing involves the examination of an agency activity to determine whether the activity should continue to be carried out within the agency or should be performed by an outside entity. Put simply, should the agency "make" or "buy" this activity?

In a larger sense, the purpose of competitive sourcing is to analyze an agency's various options for achieving the performance results of a given activity. Indeed, competitive sourcing goes beyond the decision to "make" or "buy" to examine such considerations as:

- Whether an activity is needed in the first place

- Whether an activity should be "reengineered" to be more efficient

- Whether an activity should be "sourced" differently, possibly through another staff unit, another agency, a non-profit organization, a program partner, or a private-sector vendor.

If competitive sourcing is implemented effectively for an activity, the issue of improving performance should dominate these three considerations—with the concept of "competition" driving the process to ensure that the agency adopts the best sourcing solution. However, true competition can be achieved only when multiple players are competing under a fair and transparent process where performance results expected from the activity in question are clear.

When it results in constructively redeploying part of the workforce to citizen-centered, mission-critical activities, competitive sourcing offers a vehicle to help respond to the government human capital crisis. It can strengthen recruitment and retention by ensuring that government employees are valued, trained, and utilized to their fullest potential. Employees rose to the challenge in the phase of competitive sourcing that began in FY 2003 by winning around 89 percent of job competitions using innovative strategies to serve the taxpayer.[1]

Competitive sourcing is designed to help federal agencies operate in the most efficient manner possible. With the 662 compe-

---

[1]Office of Management and Budget, "Competitive Sourcing," May 24, 2004.

titions completed in 2003, the government expects to realize a 15 percent cost efficiency estimated to produce $1.1 billion in taxpayer savings over the next five years.[2] These savings could be just the beginning. With more experienced managers leading more competitions, the taxpayer could see even greater savings from competitive sourcing. If successfully targeted at commercial functions, competitions can free up resources that can be shifted to activities that directly serve the citizen.

Through the combined impact of these benefits, competitive sourcing has the potential to deliver more staff and money for habitat restoration and park services at the Department of Interior; more staff and money for teacher training at the Department of Education; more staff and money for quality healthcare at the Department of Veterans Affairs; and more staff and money for the soldiers in the field at the Department of Defense. When viewed in these terms, properly implemented competitive sourcing is well worth the effort.

To that end, OMB updated its Circular A-11 in the spring of 2004 to require that agency budget requests contain detailed information about competitions performed—including the projected savings and how those savings will be spent. The intent is to bring an added element of transparency to the process and to demonstrate the direct impact that competition can have on the delivery of services to taxpayers.

Once completed, a competitive sourcing process must then involve holding the winner of competitions—government or non-government—accountable for delivering on cost and performance. This is best done through the implementation of performance-based contracts for the services.

Finally, competitive sourcing is not driven by any one administration's view of the role of government, nor is it either a conservative or a liberal philosophy. Conservatives may value highly the effects of competitions that can save taxpayers money and create a lean government. Liberals may value highly the effects of competitions that can allow government to free up and save money that can be used to provide more services to taxpayers.

[2]Office of Management and Budget, "Competitive Sourcing," May 24, 2004.

It is a management practice that dates all the way back to the Eisenhower administration, with each administration since endorsing and using the tool.

Helpful Practices for Successfully Implementing Competitive Sourcing Initiatives

1. Demonstrate senior agency leadership's commitment to the competitive sourcing initiative.

2. Develop an internal communication plan to address employee concerns.

3. Prioritize competitive sourcing opportunities to target high-impact functions.

4. Link human resources planning to competitive sourcing.

5. Invest in employee training and support before, during, and after competitions.

6. Set clear cost and performance measures to guide competitions.

7. Communicate a clear business case to employees, Congress, and OMB.

8. Hold winners accountable for delivering results.

Managing Contracts For Results: Performance-Based Contracting[3]

Once the decision to contract has been made, managing contractor performance is the second step in government becoming a "smarter shopper." The last 10 years of acquisition and procure-

---

[3]For additional information on performance-based contracting, see "The 7 Steps Guide to Performance-Based Services Acquisition," *Federal Times*, August 4, 2003; and "Making Performance-Based Contracting Perform: What the Federal Government Can Learn from State and Local Governments," IBM Center for The Business of Government, November 2002.

ment reform have changed the landscape of how our government contracts for services. The intent has been to equip government contracting officials with the same tools and techniques for procuring services that the private sector has used successfully: streamline the process, open contracts up to more bidders, and enhance accountability for results at a competitive price.

The latest round of procurement reforms has occurred with the recently passed Service Acquisition Reform Act (SARA), which places a premium on managing contracts for results through the expansion of performance-based contracting (PBC) techniques. Performance-based contracting is defined as:

- *Soliciting bids and awarding contracts based on results rather than activities.* PBCs describe the work that needs to be done by the service provider in terms of impact or performance, but leave the details on how to achieve those results up to the contractor. This allows the government to develop contracts without describing every detail, which takes time, staff resources, and, obviously, money.

- *Providing flexibility in exchange for accountability.* Old methods of government contracting permitted little flexibility and provided few incentives to perform the work more efficiently and at higher levels of performance. PBCs focus on results, granting operating flexibility and often providing incentives for greater results and lower cost.

- *Using performance measures to evaluate results.* PBCs use a limited number of results-oriented performance measures to establish quality standards for a contract.

- *Basing payment on performance rather than contractor costs.* Old contracting methods often relied on a "cost reimbursement" approach that paid contractors for time and materials—effort alone! Often, the more time it took a contractor to perform the function, the more money the contractor was paid. In contrast, PBCs pay for results.

Think for a minute about the process you would use to buy a new roof for your house. First, you would determine that you need a new roof, based on either visible damage or an assessment by an outside expert. Essentially, you are establishing a basis for a contract: Your current roof is not meeting the level of performance you would like and you determine whether it is time to contract with a service provider to install a new roof.

In this example, the results you seek are fairly simple. First, you would like a secure roof that keeps out the weather. Second, you want this roof in a particular color and style that match the exterior of your house. Third, you would like the roof installed by a certain date and within a certain price range. Finally, you may want to make sure the roof lasts a certain of length of time before any deterioration occurs, barring any natural disasters. Further, if the vendor who is installing your roof does not finish the project in the time and within the cost you and he agreed to, you both expect—by the terms of the contract—that he will finish the job anyway, without additional compensation.

Using this approach, you have essentially set up the conditions for a performance-based contract. This is the type of purchase you make all the time in daily life—and it shouldn't be any different when using government money instead of our own.

Now, let's take this example and make it an activity-based contract. Even though you are not the roof expert, you contract with the vendor telling him what type of shingles and nails to use, how many workers to employ, how many shingles and nails to use, what type of ladder to use, when the lunch breaks are, what the starting and quitting times are, etc., etc., etc. This approach does not allow the vendor the flexibility to do what he does best: Install your roof within the agreed-to time and cost. Yet these are the kinds of details that are often included in government contracts with service providers.

CREATING PERFORMANCE MEASURES TO GUIDE COMPETITIONS AND CONTRACTING

Performance measures are an essential tool for improving results in government contracting. However, effective performance-based contracting requires something better than just having things labeled "performance measures" in the contracts. Contracts with multiple measures of non-critical information, and without measures that bear on results, are not effective performance-based contracts. They just create more work for the government and the vendor to ensure compliance without advancing results. PBC performance measures should address the things that actually count toward achieving results instead of measuring what is easily counted, like processes and activities.

One way to look at measures is to view them as "indicators of success." Performance measures should indicate whether success or failure is occurring, whether something of quality and importance to achieving the desired outcomes of the contract is happening. By focusing on a few of these important measures, the government can gauge the likelihood of success of the contract while still allowing the vendor flexibility for innovation, efficiency, and higher performing services.

In the end, performance measures should be "SMART":

- *Specific*: Clearly identify what will be "counted" or tracked by the measure and why that is significant for the ultimate results goals of the contract.

- *Measurable*: Provide (i.e., negotiate) a target and a definitive way to determine whether the target has been met.

- *Accountable*: Demonstrate that the use of the performance measure imposes an appropriate level of accountability that directly relates to the span of influence exercised by the contract.

- *Results-oriented*: Demonstrate how the performance measure evaluates real results rather than processes or level of effort.

- *Time-bound*: Establish a clear due date for each major performance achievement under the contract—allowing performance to be evaluated on an ongoing basis rather than just at the end of the contract term.

It is important to develop measures that not only indicate success or failure in terms of the results achieved, but that also motivate greater success, with incentives and rewards for vendors to deliver higher levels of service and success. Quality performance measures are vital to achieving long-term success in contracting and will help ensure that the government provides the cost-efficient, effective, and high-performing services that taxpayers expect from government leaders.

SEVEN STEPS FOR IMPLEMENTING PERFORMANCE-BASED CONTRACTS

Performance-based contracts are dependent on the development of the right performance measures, but they are also dependent on a step-by-step process for designing and managing contracts. Seven steps have emerged from the PBC lessons-learned in government—steps that each federal agency should institutionalize to manage contracts for results successfully:

Step 1: Establish the contracting team. Involve a diverse group of agency officials (e.g., procurement, finance, human resources, program managers, users) in the development of the statement of work for the contract and the review of bids.

Step 2: Identify scope and anticipated end outcomes. Clearly state how the contract aligns to agency mission and goals—complete with a way to measure the specific contribution of the contract to those goals.

Step 3: Examine private sector and public sector solutions. Canvass industry groups and other federal agencies to study various business solutions to your agency's service requirement, providing for an innovative look at your options.

Step 4: Select performance measures for the service being contracted. Identify a limited set of performance measures (3–5) that will allow the contract to be managed for results, emphasizing measures that track results and quality rather than process and effort.

Step 5: Develop the performance work statement or statement of objectives for the contract. Create solicitation and selection criteria that focus on results to be achieved from the contractor, while allowing ample flexibility for the kinds of technical proposals that vendors could make to deliver those results.

Step 6: Select a contractor. Based on the selection criteria and bidder performance record, determine which bid provides the best solution for achieving results most cost-effectively.

Step 7: Monitor and manage performance. Often the least well-implemented step in contracting is the vital role of effectively monitoring and managing contractor performance on an ongoing basis. The agency should track performance on a timely basis and ensure correction of problems throughout the contract term.

In the end, competition—whether through the traditional bidding process or the competitive sourcing approach—combined with performance-based contracts, can work to maximize the performance of service providers to government. Taxpayers must be assured that the government is acting responsibly with their tax dollars and achieving the highest level of performance at the lowest cost. Increased knowledge and understanding of competitive sourcing should be valued by federal managers (as well as by Congress and the public) because competitive sourcing has proven to be an important way to achieve program success and taxpayer savings.

Once a decision is made to contract out a function, government needs to continue to move away from "activity-based" contracts and toward performance-based contracts that use effective, efficient performance measures and provide performance incentives for improved results. Properly implemented competition, along with performance-based contracting, has the potential to enhance substantially the values of transparency, accountability, performance, and competition in the federal government.

PART THREE

Communicating Results

Your responsibility as leader includes not only achieving results but communicating your results. When results are positive, the public, Congress, and the administration need to know that to justify the investment they are making. When results are negative, the public, Congress, and the administration need to know that you are correcting problems or are stopping unproductive spending when you can. Both kinds of communication are essential responsibilities of successful leaders and managers.

Chapter 10 once again shares *Maurice McTigue's* perspective from his direct experiences with results-based management in New Zealand and his studies of comparable American and international approaches. Here he helps you get the results message framed right, even when not everyone wants to hear it.

Chapter 11 explains your agency's most important formal report to the public and Congress on results: the statutorily required annual Performance and Accountability Report (PAR). The heads of the two outside organizations that publicly critique PARs present their organizations' perspectives: *Harold Steinberg,* Technical Director of the Certificate of Excellence in Accountability Reporting of the Association of Government Accountants, and *Maurice McTigue,* Director of the Mercatus Center's Government Accountability Project.

In Chapter 12, *Dr. Philip Joyce* of The George Washington University (and former state and congressional budget official) shows you how results data can be communicated in the executive branch and congressional budget processes to support your resource requests as well as to improve your internal program management.

Chapter 13 provides a concise discussion of the most successful ways for you to communicate results to Congress and the public. *Carl DeMaio,* President of The Performance Institute, offers the lessons he learned while serving in several staff capacities in Congress; he is joined by his Communications Director, *Ian Koski,* who helps agencies use these lessons every day.

CHAPTER 10

Getting the Results Message Right

Maurice McTigue

Accountability in government means that organizations are responsible for disclosing performance fully and honestly to those who are entitled to know. The government exists to benefit the public, so being "accountable" means demonstrating clearly how society is better off because of your work. No longer is it good enough to demonstrate that you spent your resources carefully, without waste, fraud, or abuse. There is increasing pressure on public sector organizations at the federal, state, and local levels, as well as around the world, to demonstrate exactly what public benefit—that is, what outcome—flowed from the expenditure of public dollars.

These public benefits are certainly being presented through required reports (for example, see Chapter 11 on Performance and Accountability reports, or PARs). Regardless of externally imposed reporting requirements, however, an accountable organization should conduct ongoing assessments of performance and be able to identify achievements and failures to stakeholders at any time throughout the year. Reporting should be viewed as an opportunity to communicate your organization's successes and seek feedback on failures or new ventures from your stakeholders. Organizations must shift the focus of their communications away from simply recounting their activities to describing their achievements and the benefits they provide to the public.

It is important to use reporting as an opportunity to tie activities to broader public benefits. For example, the Department of

Maurice McTigue is Director of the Government Accountability Project at the Mercatus Center, George Mason University.

Veterans Affairs was particularly good at explaining how its work contributes to the well-being of veterans in its PAR for fiscal year 2003. The department then went further to explain how its medical research at VA facilities benefits the broader public.

In the private sector, organizations spend a significant amount of time communicating their successes, which typically represent 95–97 percent of their total activities. In the public sector, organizations spend most of their time explaining their failures, which arguably account for only 3–5 percent of their total activities. As a result, most public sector organizations spend countless hours finding solutions for failures when they could be putting time and resources into improving successful activities. It is impossible to create a "culture of success" when so much emphasis is placed on failing activities.

Tips for Leaders and Managers

- Recognize that accountability means full disclosure of benefits and failures—not financial compliance.

- View reporting requirements as an opportunity to communicate with stakeholders and the public.

- Learn from private sector organizations to focus on success and spend less time explaining failure.

- Communicate with various audiences as appropriate, but with the same message: Focus on success and demonstrate specific benefits.

CREATING A CULTURE OF SUCCESS

Success-oriented cultures employ a communications strategy whereby everyone in the organization understands and accepts that failing activities should be terminated or repaired rather than being allowed to persevere as they currently exist. Management should seek opportunities to foster this behavior at every level. The head of the organization should praise publicly those who use sound judgment to terminate failures as well as those who succeed in their ventures. When an organization has valiantly tried to repair a failing activity but is unable to make it succeed, it is essential that the failure be made transparent—both internally to its own workforce and externally to the public and stakeholders.

Sometimes a leader has the evidence that a program has failed and has made reasonable efforts to turn it around without success, but is required by the policy of the current administration or pressure from Congress to maintain that program anyway. In these not-uncommon cases, leaders need to make the evidence of performance very transparent to avoid misleading the public into thinking the program is a success. Failure to do so allows public funds to be deployed poorly without appropriate scrutiny; it also has the potential to reflect badly on the performance and integrity of the leader.

Many public sector organizations have become focused on explaining their failures rather than highlighting their successes because of legislative inquiries. If they can begin to report their performance in clear, outcome-oriented terms, it will become apparent whether the failure is a result of poor design, poor execution, or legislative requirements that mandate processes that are doomed to failure. Applying these principles to communication strategies will allow greater transparency and more perceptive judgments about the cause of the failure.

Legislators and the White House want to be associated with successes, not failures, as do most interest groups. Use every opportunity to lay out the evidence of failure and build support. It may take more than one year to achieve your goal, but stopping failure and redirecting resources toward success is worth the effort. When a fatally flawed activity cannot be stopped or fixed, the government should get out of the activity.

Keep in mind that there is nothing sacrosanct about a particular program; it is a tool used by managers to achieve a certain outcome. If that tool has been superseded by new and better tools, the responsible manager has only one acceptable choice: to use the superior tool.

Not only is it good management, but it is a more responsible approach to the public when the legislature and administration agree on a clearly articulated description of the public benefit to be achieved by government programs. Often arguments will erupt over whether to cut or give more money to a failing program. The argument to stop a failing activity is more sustainable when it is evident that the program does not achieve the public benefits intended. It is much harder to kill or suggest increased funding for an activity when no one is sure how it measures up to what it is intended to achieve. The basis for making the judgment about whether a program is failing should be founded in an evaluation process that produces credible evidence about the effectiveness of an activity. (See Chapter 14 on program evaluation.)

The most successful organizations have developed clever communications strategies where they identify and admit failures first—before someone else does. An early admission of failure often prevents a scandal. When a hidden failure is uncovered by an external source, the organization finds itself in the unfortunate position of having to explain and defend, while being presumed guilty of a cover-up.

The National Aeronautics and Space Administration (NASA) is particularly adept at managing public relations around high-profile projects. NASA adopts a strategy of managing public expectations downwards. Then the agency keep the public well-informed as a project proceeds. NASA has generally been able to get in front of issues to manage expectations and explain failures. As a result, NASA retains a high degree of public support despite catastrophic incidents and mishaps.

Warren Buffet brilliantly and humbly discloses Berkshire Hathaway's failures in his chairman's letters (see www.berkshireha-thaway.com/letters/letters.html). He is even reported to have admitted to his shareholders that they would have been better off if he had been on the beach instead of managing their portfolio!

Proactively admitting failures immediately focuses the debate on the solution, rather than trying to assign blame. This allows the organization to recover more rapidly and avoids the extraordinary consumption of senior managers' time and morale on the pointless exercise of mitigating blame.

ADAPTING YOUR MESSAGE FOR DIFFERENT AUDIENCES

While the premise surrounding the "culture of success" remains the same regardless of the communication, the message will vary slightly to address the needs of your core audiences: the White House, the Office of Management and Budget (OMB), Congress, and the media/public.

In communicating with the White House, in addition to explaining what you do to make the United States better, you need to answer the question, "How successfully is this organization addressing the administration's agenda?" Answering this question requires a clear articulation of outcome-oriented goals, measures of public benefits, and delineation of actual outcomes.

A good example of the right types of goals, measures, and public benefits can be found in the State Department's fiscal year 2003 PAR. The mission of the State Department is to "Create a more secure, democratic, and prosperous world for the benefit of the American people and the international community." From that the department has tiered down to strategic objectives, one of which is "achieve peace and security." One of the strategic goals under that objective is "regional stability." To measure performance, the State Department has chosen to measure "Existent and emergent regional conflicts are contained or resolved." The department has developed a very clear goal structure and has articulated its goals in outcome terms. The State Department then has to place program results alongside the measures and objectives so that a judgment can be made regarding a program's level of success.

OMB will want to know that your performance is consistent with the priorities and direction of the administration and that your activity creates considerable value for the resources it expends. For cost information to be useful and interesting, it should be linked to what it costs to produce a unit of success. The Small Business Administration and the Department of the Interior have successfully engaged in activity-based costing for some time. This is the first step in developing the capability to link costs to outcomes.

Communicating with Congress could be the trickiest of all, as you are not interacting with a unified body but with many "fiefdoms" and competing interests. Here your job is to focus on the big picture and minimize the minutiae. The questions you answer for Congress can be the same as for the White House and OMB, as long as you remain in the larger picture instead of in the details. Members of Congress will ask for details when they aren't satisfied with how well you know what is happening. If you can succinctly and confidently produce evidence of how your organization is making the United States a better place, you are less likely to get micromanaged.

The media and the public need to know how you are making things better for them, personally. They need anecdotes of how you are expanding the good that you do or diminishing an existing harm. They also need to know whether the individual stories are examples of what is typically true or just hand-picked accounts intended to show the agency in the best possible light. For this reason, it is critical that anecdotes be backed up by solid data that accurately reflect the results of programs.

The media won't report anything that is not interesting—and controversy is always more interesting than smooth sailing. Failure and blame are more likely to be reported than success and reward. You must be conscious of journalists who are looking behind the story in search of controversy. These negatives can often be offset by a good depiction of the public benefit achieved, especially if it is presented in terms of the benefits accrued to individuals. (See Chapter 13 for more detailed guidance on taking the results message to Congress, the media, and the public.)

> Accountability in government requires that public managers employ strategic management of resources to maximize public benefit, while reporting successes and failures transparently to the public and interested parties. The opportunity to report to stakeholders should always be maximized—both as good practice and as an insurance policy for your future.

CHAPTER 11

Communicating Results through the Performance and Accountability Report

Harold I. Steinberg
Maurice McTigue

"The American taxpayer deserves and wants to see his or her government's results. To have results, there must be accountability. And accountability requires reporting. The government needs to "open the kimono" and show the public its results."
— Clay Johnson, OMB Deputy Director for Management,
Bush administration

"The required Performance and Accountability Reports perform the important role of advising the Congress and the public about an agency's results for the year. But positive results presented poorly are not far ahead of disappointing results discussed clearly and thoughtfully. Leaders and managers need to present their successes and failures effectively for both internal and external audiences.
— John Koskinen, OMB Deputy Director for Management,
Clinton administration

Each executive branch agency must publish an annual Performance and Accountability Report (PAR) on the agency's achievement of results and its financial management. These re-

Harold I. Steinberg is Technical Director, Certificate of Excellence in Accountability Reporting, at the Association of Government Accountants.
Maurice McTigue is Director of the Government Accountability Project at the Mercatus Center, George Mason University.

quirements are exerting growing pressure on agency managers to make the PAR as candid and objective as possible.

Two independent, non-profit, non-partisan organizations operate programs that annually assess and publicly evaluate PARs: the Association of Government Accountants (AGA) conducts the Certificate of Excellence in Accountability Reporting (CEAR) program, and the Mercatus Center at George Mason University conducts the Government Accountability Project. While these organizations take different approaches to assessing PARs and do not always agree, between them they provide Congress, the media, and the public the only independent assessments of the quality of agency reports on results. Each organization willingly meets with agencies to discuss its findings and recommendations for improvement.

In the fall of 2004, the two top government officials from the legislative and executive branches who focus most on agency results participated in the events marking release of the assessments of FY 2003 reports: Office of Management and Budget (OMB) Deputy Director for Management Clay Johnson for CEAR and Comptroller General David Walker for Mercatus.

Attention to the preparation of these reports in agencies is inconsistent, with some program managers still scarcely aware of them. Attention to the reports in Congress and OMB also varies. However, the participation of the two top results officials signals that these reports are gaining currency and notice. Program managers will ignore them at their peril.

Tips for Leaders and Managers

- Understand that the annual PAR presents information on how you managed your programs and resources, what your programs have accomplished compared to plans, and your agency's related financial position, results, and management systems.

- Treat the PAR as an annual shareholder report.

- Consider that writing the report—and the accompanying self-reflection—is as valuable to your organization, if not more so, than the publication and release of the report.

- Understand that with steadily increasing scrutiny of agency results by Congress, the executive branch, and the public, the importance and impact of reporting results cannot be overstated.

- Recognize that without quality results and cost information, high-quality performance management is not possible.

- Do your own results analysis and find the failures or successes—or someone else will.

WHAT IS THE PAR?

PARs are a relatively new phenomenon. Until recently, the primary way agencies reported their results to Congress or the public was with an "annual budget justification" that was intended to support the administration's budget proposal. Starting in the late 1980s and 1990s, Congress enacted a series of management reform statutes that called for two separate streams of annual reporting. One stream, which flowed from such statutes as the Federal Managers Financial Integrity Act, the Chief Financial Officers (CFO) Act, and the Government Management Reform Act, focused on financial management and integrity. The second stream, which flowed from the Government Performance and Results Act, focused on program performance. Each agency is required to issue a strategic plan every three years, an annual performance plan, and an annual performance report disclosing the extent to which the performance goals presented in the annual performance plan were achieved.

Unfortunately, there was little connection between the two streams of reports. Nor was there a focus in either stream on the cost-effectiveness of spending to achieve results. In the political world, there is often a presumption that incremental increases in spending result in equally beneficial increases in public benefit. Cost/benefit data make the proper relationships between spending and performance transparent.

Virtually all agencies are now required to issue an annual "integrated" Performance and Accountability Report. In 2000 Congress enacted the Reports Consolidation Act (RCA), which authorized the integrated reports for CFO Act agencies. Eight agencies began to follow the integrated approach for FY 2000 and 10 more followed for FY 2001. On October 18, 2002, OMB issued a memorandum directing that for the FY 2002 reporting cycle, all CFO Act agencies issue an integrated report. On August 13, 2003, OMB extended this requirement to agencies covered by the Accountability of Tax Dollars Act of 2002, which included virtually all the executive branch agencies.

All executive branch agencies must now issue, 45 days after the fiscal year ends, a PAR describing what the agency has accomplished, how it has managed its programs and resources, and what challenges must be addressed. New managers taking office in 2005 should find the reports issued in November 2004 a useful information source on their agency's results and plans for improvement.

The complete requirements for a PAR are not listed in any one official document. Instead, they are an amalgam of requirements contained in the Reports Consolidation Act, OMB's Circular A-11 (updated annually), OMB's memoranda of October 18, 2002, and August 13, 2003, and other directives. The PAR typically presents required information in three sections:

- *Management's discussion and analysis,* the "MD&A," provides an opportunity for the agency head to summarize what has been accomplished during the year. It typically includes the agency's mission and organizational structure, highlights of the agency's "most important" performance goals and results (both positive and negative, with trends identified), and descriptions of actions taken or planned for achieving unmet goals.

The MD&A also covers the significant demands, risks, uncertainties, events, conditions, or trends facing the agency, including: financial implications; highlights of the financial statements; a description of the agency's systems, controls, and compliance with financial management statutes and regulations; and other important information. In the Bush administration, MD&As also reported the agency's progress in implementing the President's Management Agenda.

Essentially the executive summary of the PAR, the MD&A highlights agency results.

- The *performance* section presents the agency's program performance in greater detail, linked to the goals and objectives published in the agency's strategic plan and annual performance report. (In recent years, agencies have begun making efforts to make this section more readable and accessible by reducing excessive detail.) This section includes the agency performance measurement and management structure; the strategies and resources used to undertake the agency's programs and meet its published goals; a comparison of the current and prior years' results for each performance measure, related to targets established for the year; explanations of trends; reasons why targets were not met and plans for achieving those targets in the future; information with which readers can assess the reliability and completeness of the performance data; and a summary of the findings and recommendations of program evaluations completed during the year, including, in the Bush administration, the results of the Program Assessment Rating Tool (PART) program reviews.

- The *financial* section is comprised mainly of the agency's audited financial statements and the auditors' reports thereon. It also presents the chief financial officer's plans for correcting weaknesses in financial management controls and a summary of what the agency's Inspector General considers to be the agency's most serious management and performance challenges and the agency's progress in addressing these challenges.

THE CEAR REVIEW[1]

Imagine a situation in which there are plenty of plans, estimates, and promises of what will be accomplished, but never any reports of what actually happened. That is precisely the way the government operated until recently—but no more. Fortunately, agencies are now required to issue an annual Performance and Accountability Report that describes what the agency has accomplished, how it has managed its programs and resources, and what challenges must be addressed. The PAR is a key way that appointed and career leaders can publicly describe the results they have achieved, what they did to achieve them, and how they plan to improve them.

In 1997, the Association of Government Accountants (AGA), the professional association for persons working in governmental financial management, initiated a program to help agencies report effectively on their financial management: the Certificate of Excellence in Accountability Reporting program. The CEAR program reviews an agency's report, recommends how the report can be improved, and identifies those reports that are most complete and inviting to read. While others can submit their reports to CEAR for the benefit of the recommendations for improvement, only agencies that have received a clean audit opinion for the reporting period can qualify for a certificate.

Since the statutory and administrative changes that began in FY 2000, the CEAR review has expanded to embrace the concept of the integrated performance and financial report. The CEAR program has prepared a 50-page guidelines document (see www.agacgfm.org/performance/cear/) that lists in one place all the legislative and administrative reporting requirements and commendable reporting practices for a PAR. Agencies use this document to guide the preparation of their PARs.[2]

---

[1]This section was written by Harold I. Steinberg, Technical Director of the CEAR Program at the Association of Government Accountants.

[2]Another document that can be referred to for preparation of a PAR is *Accountability Reports Trends and Techniques,* published by KPMG LLP. The publication summarizes the manner in and the extent to which the agencies that prepare PARs each year address the various requirements. It also provides examples of how individual requirements were met. It is available at www.us.kpmg.com/federal.

The CEAR review of each PAR is conducted by a team of five persons who represent the perspectives of chief financial officers, Inspectors General, certified public accounting firms, and the program management community. Joined by the CEAR technical director, a different team reviews each report and drafts recommendations for improvement and citations of good practice. The recommendations are organized into four categories:

- Improving the presentation of the information

- Eliminating reporting or disclosure deficiencies

- Making the report more informative

- Addressing editorial matters.

The team members for each PAR meet to discuss and decide which recommendations should go forward to the agency and whether the report should be awarded the certificate. Criteria for awarding the certificate are:

- The report complies with the technical, statutory, and regulatory requirements accurately and candidly.

- The report is integrated and flows well.

- The report is readable and inviting to the intended audience.

- The report reflects the agency's effort and intention to continuously improve its performance and accountability reporting.

AGA sends the recommendations and notification of award of the certificate, if applicable, to the agency. An awards ceremony is then held in the fall to honor the agencies awarded the certificate and the individuals who prepared the reports.

AGA charges a small fee for the review. The agencies feel the fee is small in relation to the extent and quality of the recommendations for improvement they receive.

Eighteen agencies submitted their FY 2003 reports for review. Two of these agencies knew in advance that they would not receive the certificate since they were unable to obtain an unqualified opinion on their financial statements. They nonetheless participated, believing that the reviewers' recommendations would be extremely useful for improving their reports.

Ten agencies were awarded the Certificate of Excellence in Accountability Reporting for their reports on FY 2003: the Departments of Education, Interior, Labor, and State; the General Services Administration; the Nuclear Regulatory Commission; the Social Security Administration; the Federal Aviation Administration; the United States Patent and Trademark Office; and the Government Accountability Office. The Social Security Administration has received the certificate for six consecutive years, ever since the program's inception. Labor and Interior received the certificate for the fourth consecutive year, and State and GAO for the third consecutive year.

The PARs, along with the wealth of information they are required to present, should be used to report the agency's efforts to achieve results, and more important, the results for which the agency is being held accountable.

Specifically, a PAR should answer the reader's fundamental concern: "How well is your agency managing the resources with which you are entrusted?" One way to begin to answer this question is to present a letter from the agency head that: summarizes major results accomplishments as well as major problems, and how those problems are being addressed; provides assurance that the agency either has no material financial control weaknesses or identifies the plans to address them; and assures readers of the reliability of the information the agency uses to manage activities and make day-to-day decisions or indicates strategies to fix any reliability issues. A reference to the agency's independent auditors' opinion on the financial statements will reinforce such assurances.

The management of agency programs, however, should be the major focus of the PAR. People want to know not only whether and how the agency is fulfilling its responsibility to provide specific services to the public and meet statutory goals, but whether it is doing so effectively. The PAR can be used to present an understanding of agency programs, the results achieved, and whether the agency is demonstrating forward-looking leadership. For example, the PAR should enable readers to determine whether an agency is establishing ambitious goals; whether it is meeting these goals and if not, why not, and what it plans to do about that; and whether the agency's year-to-year performance is improving or deteriorating.

Appointed and career leaders in every agency should, as does their Inspector General, use the Performance and Accountability Report to identify the challenges their programs and the agency as a whole face and must surmount. The PAR is an important tool for managers to use to gain the confidence of the public, Congress, and the media by candidly explaining what they will do to improve results. The PAR enables leaders and managers to gather and publish in one place the breadth and depth of information that fully explains what the agency has accomplished and how its resources have been managed. It should not be overlooked by anyone accepting a position to make government more effective.

THE MERCATUS REVIEW[3]

Much as any publicly held corporation must present an annual report to its shareholders, a public sector organization must present an annual statement to its stakeholders: the President, Congress, and the American people. That statement is the PAR.

While the particular requirements vary across the private and public sectors, the purpose of annual reporting is the same: to share your progress on goals, tie that progress to broader benefits, explain failures, and set a vision for the future.

Preparing the report is half the battle. Although it may seem like a paper exercise, the actual process of preparing a performance report is just as important and valuable as the final product. Reflecting on the activities, results, accomplishments, and

---

[3]This section was written by Maurice McTigue, Director of the Government Accountability Project at the Mercatus Center.

failures of the previous year is essential to optimizing strategic management for the future of the organization.

When preparing the report, an organization conducts a self-reflection, identifying and homing in on its strengths and weaknesses. Based on that information, the leadership outlines solutions for the future. This process of internal communication and collaboration can reinvigorate employees and remind everyone why they come to work each day.

Each year, the Mercatus Center at George Mason University evaluates the annual performance reports produced by 24 major federal agencies. ("Major" agencies include all Cabinet departments plus the non-Cabinet agencies covered under the Chief Financial Officers Act.) The Mercatus Center researchers have employed the same criteria each year since integrated performance and financial management reports were first issued in 2000. The Mercatus scoring process evaluates: (1) how transparently an agency reports its successes and failures; (2) how well an agency documents the tangible public benefits it claims to have produced; and (3) whether an agency demonstrates leadership that uses annual performance information to devise strategies for improvement.

Transparency

1. Is the report easily accessible via the Internet and easily identified as the agency's annual PAR?

2. Is the report easy for a layperson to read and understand?

3. Are the performance data valid, verifiable, and timely?

4. Did the agency provide baseline and trend data to put its performance measures in context?

Public Benefits

5. Are the goals and objectives stated as outcomes?

6. Are the performance measures valid indicators of the agency's impact on its outcome goals?

7. Does the agency demonstrate that its actions have actually made a significant contribution toward its stated goals?

8. Did the agency link its goals and results to costs?

Leadership

9. Does the report show how the agency's results will make this country a better place to live?

10. Does the agency explain failures to achieve its goals?

11. Does the report adequately address major management challenges?

12. Does it describe changes in policies or procedures to do better next year?

By assessing the quality of agencies' reports (but not the quality of the results achieved), the Mercatus Center seeks to show which agencies are supplying the information that citizens and their elected leaders need to make informed funding and policy decisions. The goal of this annual assessment is to inform not just decision-makers, but also the American people more generally. By injecting the American spirit of competition for scarce resources and accountability for using those resources into performance reporting, we hope to assist and encourage agencies in improving the quality and cost-effectiveness of the services they deliver. The Mercatus report ranks the 24 CFO Act agencies from best to worst, giving each agency a cumulative score and ranking them 1 to 24 (see www.mercatus.org/governmentaccountability/subcategory.php/131.html).

With society's increased emphasis on accountability, transparency, and disclosure, it is incumbent on the federal government and its agencies to meet the highest standards in their external reporting efforts. Effective accountability in public service requires that agencies present a comprehensive, concise, accurate, and reliable assessment of the benefits created for the public, as well as the costs of producing those benefits. Equipped with such information, the administration and Congress can allocate federal resources in ways that continually advance government's contribution to citizens' quality of life.

The move toward managing for results forms the foundation upon which the Government Performance and Results Act, the Clinton administration's National Performance Review, and the Bush administration's President's Management Agenda are built. While the President's Management Agenda is ostensibly focused on five key elements of good management, every initiative relies on quality results information as gathered and reported by the agency. Without quality results information, all performance and management initiatives will founder.

Only when agencies are able to fully account for results and costs will comparisons between programs by policymakers be possible. In a time of limited resources, the ability to discern performance quickly—and reallocate funds accordingly—will be critical. Why not have the data analysis complete and be in a position to truly understand the value your organization brings to the citizen? The alternative is to have someone speculate about your effectiveness for you, making decisions about funding that are ill-informed at best or that bring about erroneous spending at worst. Rather than being bound by paperwork requirements, use reporting as an opportunity to bring shareholders into your business in an appropriate and informative way.

CHAPTER 12

Linking Performance and Budgeting[1]

Philip G. Joyce, Ph.D.

Government reformers have been trying to increase the use of performance information in budget processes for more than 50 years (see Chapters 3 and 4). Why does this recurring reform have such current relevance? In short, because budget processes allocate scarce resources among competing purposes. Taxpayer dollars are limited, so understanding the effects of resources on the objectives of government action is critical to using them well. In fact, the more scarce the resources, the more important it is that they be allocated wisely. In such an environment, it is vital that resource allocation decisions be focused primarily on the effectiveness of spending and tax policies.

Governments have consistently reported some kind of performance information in budget documents for many years. Unquestionably, performance information has increased at all levels of government over the past 20 years. For example, research on U.S. state government reporting of performance information in budget documents demonstrates a steady increase in the

[1]This chapter is a revision of a much longer report on the same topic prepared for the IBM Center for The Business of Government. The author wishes to thank the IBM Center, and particularly Mark Abramson, Jonathan Bruel, and John Kamensky, for support and previous comments. That paper, and therefore this chapter, also benefited from comments from Paul Posner, Barry White, and Rita Hilton. The full report, entitled "Linking Performance and Budgeting: Opportunities in the Federal Budget Process," is available on the IBM Center's website, www.businessofgovernment.org/pdfs/Joyce_Report. pdf.

Philip G. Joyce, Ph.D., is Professor of Public Administration at The George Washington University.

number that present information on performance.[2] There is less evidence, however, of the *use* of performance information by these governments—that is, of performance information having widespread influence on government funding decisions. Increasing the influence of information on the results of government is a key duty of appointed, career, and elected officials.

In part, the apparent lack of evidence of the use of performance information for budgeting arises because observers have not looked in the right places. That is, the implicit assumption is that resource allocation is something that occurs only (or at least mostly) in the central budget office or in the legislature. Acting in accord with a more comprehensive definition of performance-informed budgeting, leaders and managers can use performance information in decision-making and thus have an impact on the achievement of results at all stages of the process—in the agency, in the Office of Management and Budget (OMB), and in Congress.

Public sector leaders and managers have many factors within their control as they pursue better results at the program and agency levels as well as better stewardship of taxpayer dollars.

Tips for Leaders and Managers

- Be sure you have systems that produce timely, accurate information on program costs and performance so that you can use performance and cost information effectively to manage toward results.

- Keep the preparation of budget requests and the management of budgetary resources under your direct control.

- Focus the conversations with higher levels in your agency and with OMB, the White House, and Congress on results. With Congress, work to get clear results expectations into the authorization and appropriations actions.

---

[2]Robert D. Lee, Jr., "A Quarter Century of State Budgeting Practices," *Public Administration Review* 57 (1997): 133–140.

- Use the discretion available in many venues to manage resources to get better performance.

- Use "feedback loops" of evaluation and assessment to enable you to determine whether programs have worked and what needs to happen to make them work.

A COMPREHENSIVE FRAMEWORK FOR LINKING PERFORMANCE AND BUDGETING

Past and current reforms have in common their attempt to bring together more explicitly performance information, the budget processes, and program management. Understanding what that really means, however, has been less than straightforward. Scholars, practitioners, and successive administrations have used many different terms to describe this linkage, including performance budgeting, performance-based budgeting, results-based budgeting, performance funding, and budgeting for results.[3] These terms have in common some linkage between the budget and performance as well as the rejection of a budget process that focuses primarily on the use of inputs, on the marginal change in inputs purchased (so-called "incremental budgeting"), or exclusively on the purchase of outputs.

If the budget process is to become centered more effectively on the achievement of results, the transformation from traditional budgeting will involve the simultaneous consideration of two factors: (1) the availability of appropriate information on strategic direction, results, and costs; and (2) the actual use of that information to make decisions at each stage of the budgeting cycle.

How does a leader of an agency or program clearly articulate a strategy to incorporate better performance information into

---

[3]Philip G. Joyce and Susan Tompkins, "Using Performance Information for Budgeting: Clarifying the Framework and Investigating Recent State Experience, in K. Newcomer, E. Jennings, C. Broom, and A. Lomax, eds., *Meeting the Challenges of Performance-Oriented Government* (Washington, D.C.: American Society for Public Administration, 2002).

the budget process? First, the leader should recognize that the budget process has clear (if not always smoothly functioning) stages:

- *Budget preparation,* when agencies develop internal budget allocations and requests that are eventually (after some give and mostly take) integrated into the President's budget

- *Budget approval,* when Congress and the President ultimately enact the laws that will permit taxing and spending to occur

- *Budget execution,* when agencies implement the budget, within the constraints established by Congress and the administration

- *Audit and evaluation,* when agencies and auditors/evaluators decide (after the fact) what the effects (i.e., financial and performance) of budgetary activities have been.

If we recognize that traditional discussions of "performance-based budgeting" involve discussions of a portion of the first stage (decisions by OMB and the President) and the second stage (decisions by Congress), a further articulation of the process permits us to recognize that there is ample opportunity for asking questions about the availability and use of performance information at each of these stages (see Table 12-1).

To What Extent Is Performance and Cost Information Available for Budget Preparation and Negotiations?

Three separate activities affect the extent to which performance and cost information is available for budget preparations and negotiations:

1. *Public entities need to know what they are supposed to accomplish.* Figuring that out is not an academic exercise. It implies the necessary strategic planning that establishes the context in which program leaders and managers can best use performance and cost information.

Table 12-1: Stages of the Federal Budget Process

Stage of Budget Process	Key Actors Involved	Description of Activities	End Product
Budget Preparation— Agency	Agency budget offices, agency subunits, program managers	Agency prepares budget for submission to OMB	Budget request
Budget Preparation— OMB	Agency heads, agency budget offices, OMB, White House, President	Analysis of agency budget request on behalf of President; negotiation with agencies and White House staff on budget allocation levels	President's budget
Budget Approval— Congress	Agencies, congressional committees, congressional leadership	Congress makes overall fiscal policy, authorizes programs, and appropriates funds	Budget resolution, authorization bills, appropriation bills
Budget Approval— President	President, agencies, OMB	Action on congressional legislation affecting budget	Negotiation, signature, or veto
Budget Execution	Agencies, OMB	Implementation of programs by federal agencies; allocation of dollars by agency subunit	Administration of programs
Audit and Evaluation	Agency managers and evaluators (internal and external), OMB, GAO, and auditors (internal and external)	Review of tax and budget actions after the fact, recommendations for changes	Audits and evaluations, guidance for program redesign and improvement

2. *Valid measures of performance are needed.* It is often hard to convince agency staff to be held accountable for outcomes; many find it much more comfortable to focus on outputs that are largely within their control. The challenge facing a new leader is to get past that kind of thinking by defining outcomes in the context of all the factors that influence them, since the goal is to achieve important results with scarce resources.

3. *Accurate measures of cost need to be developed.* Connecting resources with results implies knowing how much it costs to deliver a given level of outcome. When a leader or manager discovers that his or her organization cannot accurately measure the cost of results, it is crucial to develop better cost measurement systems or it will not be possible to know whether programs are successful or cost-effective.

To What Extent Are Performance and Cost Information Actually Used to Make Decisions about the Allocation, Management, or Monitoring of Resources?

The message here is simple: *Every agency leader and every agency manager can use timely and accurate performance and cost information to manage their programs,* even if they do not receive those resources through a performance-informed process. They can use that information to direct and redirect resources and hold responsible staff accountable for achieving results.

There is no simple decision rule for relating cost and performance in the public sector, at least at a macro level. A simple, but incorrect, approach (allegedly embraced by some members of Congress) would be to take money from programs that fail to meet performance targets and give more money to programs that meet targets.[4] In fact, there are a great many reasons why programs may not meet their goals, including poor management, poor program design, or insufficient funds.

When performance expectations are not met, it is important to ask why. If the program design is flawed and program manage-

---

[4]Paul Posner, presentation before a conference on performance-based budgeting, Queenstown, Maryland, March 31, 2003.

ment is bad, no amount of money will solve these problems. If the program is conceptually strong with good management, then a mismatch between resources and expectations may be the issue. Moreover, budget decisions are appropriately influenced by other (non-performance) concerns, such as relative priorities, unmet needs, and equity concerns.

Beyond the conceptual underpinnings of the relationship, however, participants in the budget process must have incentives to use performance information. Good managers and leaders work to create these incentives, again by asking why agency employees are not using performance information to manage and why policymakers are not using the information to allocate resources. In fact, the incentive question is probably the most important one to focus on in determining the possibility that performance information will actually be used as an input in the various stages of budget decision-making.

The crucial leap in a more robust understanding of the role of performance information in the budget process involves looking at the whole process, from start to finish. The usual preoccupation with OMB and Congress fails to acknowledge the formal and informal use of discretion by program managers—which is also policymaking—that occurs in federal agencies. Agency leaders and managers can incorporate performance information into the budget process at many decision points.

For example, agencies might make substantial use of performance information in building the budget (an effort that can pay dividends for resource management in budget execution), even if other actors (OMB and Congress) make little or no use of that information at subsequent stages. Conversely, the absence of performance concerns in preparation and approval would not prevent an agency from using its discretion to execute its budget by considering the effects of different execution strategies on its goals and objectives (i.e., applying outcome measures).

POTENTIAL USES OF PERFORMANCE INFORMATION IN THE FEDERAL BUDGET PROCESS

Performance information can be use during the various stages of the federal budget process.

Budget Preparation

The budget preparation stage of the budget process is itself divided into two phases: (1) the development of the request from the agency to OMB and then analysis of the request by OMB, and (2) the related decision processes involved prior to transmittal of the budget by the President to Congress. Performance information can be used during both of these portions of the process, either to maximize the effects of funding on performance or to justify the budget request as it goes forward to OMB or from the President to Congress.

Development of the Agency Budget Request

Budget preparation begins with initial planning by the agency. This can start a year or more prior to the submission of the budget request to OMB. For large agencies, this process can be quite time-consuming. Many Cabinet departments, for example, contain a great many subunits or bureaus, each of whose requests needs to be developed and then reconciled into a departmental budget proposal.

Budget preparation is constrained by many factors, including political constraints imposed by interest groups and Congress. Within those limitations, the budget request itself—and the information required to be included in the request—is dictated by OMB Circular A-11, in particular Part 2, entitled Preparation and Submission of Budget Estimates. Circular A-11 is a crucial agenda-setting tool for focusing the agency budget request on performance. Managers and leaders must tap the knowledge of A-11 in their budget experts at the department, bureau, or other level.

Making budget development more focused on performance normally requires that the agency budget office, through frequent interaction with agency leaders and program managers, develop a framework for budget requests that clarifies the relationship between resources and performance. Such a budget request made to the agency budget office would include:

- *Performance information*. Agencies should have output and outcome measures related to programs that are in turn related to the agency's larger strategic vision. They should also have indicators of program success in meeting objectives. These measures may be at several levels (e.g., output, intermediate outcome, final outcome) but if done right, the agency can show a logical relationship between its various types of measures and its strategic objectives at all levels.

- *Cost information.* The budget request should identify the true cost of providing services, with costs charged to the appropriate bureau or program. This will not be possible without relatively sophisticated means of allocating overhead or indirect costs, still far from fully developed in most agencies. Administrative costs are now often accounted for separately and are not allocated to individual programs.

How can this information be used? First and foremost, it can be used to justify budget requests. Managers could ask a number of specific questions at this level:

- How well are my programs working to achieve their goals and objectives?

- How productive is my staff (usually defined as the relationship of inputs to outputs) compared to past productivity or perhaps benchmarked against staff in some other agency or organization?

- What opportunities exist to contract out or competitively source particular services to save money while maintaining or improving performance, understanding that contracting does not relieve the manager of ultimate responsibility for results?

- Does my organization have the right mix of skills (from staff or contractors) at the right place at the right time to maximize the achievement of performance goals?

- What are the effects of different levels of funding on the performance of the bureau, given key performance measures?

It is hard to overstate the importance of agency budget preparation to the overall effort to make the budget process more informed by performance. If the agency budget request at all levels has not laid the groundwork for relating funding to performance, it is highly unlikely that, as changes are made at higher levels of the agency, in OMB, and in Congress, managers will be able to understand the performance implications of those changes. If these relationships are not well understood, agency managers and line employees may later find themselves managing "pots of money" without any clear understanding of how their actions can contribute to—or detract from—the overall performance of the agency.

In the end, having appropriate performance and cost information can enable the agency head (and the agency budget office on behalf of the agency head) to analyze budget requests in the context of their performance implications, make tradeoffs in a way that maximizes performance, and build a better-justified budget request to OMB and Congress.

OMB Analysis of the Agency Budget Request
Once the agency submits the budget request to OMB, the President's budget office begins the difficult job of attempting to fit too many expenditure requests into too few revenues. That is, invariably the sum of agency requests far exceeds the total amount that can (or at least will) be included in the President's budget. This means that the process of arriving at a recommendation for each agency will involve, in most cases, attempts by OMB to reduce the agency's budget request to a number that will fit within the overall budget constraint.

The same performance, cost, and strategic planning information that is necessary at the agency level is also necessary for OMB's evaluation of the budget request, with one addition. Frequently only a limited number of resources are actually "in play" in a given budget. Expenditures that are relatively "uncontrollable" (e.g., interest on the debt, most entitlement expenses for current recipients) account for approximately 65 percent of the current federal budget. Presidents routinely propose, and Congress routinely enacts, changes that affect entitlement programs for future recipients. (Also in play in each budget are resources for the many benefits provided through the tax code via tax credits and other preferential treatment to encourage particular activities, such as homeownership, child care, and research and development.)

Even for the remaining 35 percent of the budget, representing discretionary (appropriated) accounts, the process is not "zero-based." Decisions are almost always being made "at the margin": How much more or how much less will the agency receive compared to last year? The decisions concerning how these marginal dollars are to be allocated are the decisions most likely to be informed by performance considerations. That is, the performance of the current or base program should be a major influence on resource decisions at the margin.

This is what distinguishes this aspect of budgeting from "incremental budgeting," which only examines the potential benefits of the increment without reference to the base. Responsible budgeting never simply assumes the continuation of the base; that would run the risk of freezing current priorities and policies in place rather than continually evaluating expenditures to determine which mixture of policies will best achieve the legislative purposes and the President's aims.

Perhaps the greatest payoff to the use of better performance and cost information during this stage will come in the "conversation" between the agency and the OMB budget examiners. To the extent that cost information and performance information are available and are brought together, the debate between the parties can truly focus on whether the level of funding requested is justified by the results that will be achieved, as opposed to being driven solely by anecdotal evidence on one side or the other. This may prove advantageous to agencies that can build a strong case for the performance effects of their programs. It may prove advantageous to OMB in cases where programs or agencies have continually received funding despite a general lack of evidence of the success of their programs.

Of course, the introduction of more performance information into the budget process is not neutral. Clearly, there are also cases where agencies and OMB would prefer that the performance effects of funding not be known. In fact, there are probably relatively few places where both OMB and the agency would be equally enthusiastic about having more performance information brought into the budget process. To the extent that performance information is available and is used uniformly, however, it is less likely to become simply a political tool.

At higher levels, the President or White House staff may make decisions concerning funding based on performance considerations, based on other factors, or more usually, based on a mix. Obviously, Presidents have priorities, and presidential decisions take into account the policies and preferences of the administration. A program with excellent data on results and unmet needs may not receive more resources and may even have its budget reduced if its purpose is not a high priority for the administration, if senior officers prefer a different approach, or if those resources are needed for another purpose. Conversely, a program with data showing poor results may nonetheless be important to the administration and therefore be funded, perhaps with actions aimed at improving the program.

The Bush administration, building on the progress made in the Clinton administration, has stressed the use of performance information for decision-making. This approach has manifested itself in the Program Assessment Rating Tool (PART) and in the efforts of federal agencies to negotiate performance budgets with Congress. This represents the logical next step in performance-informed budgeting and should continue with future administrations.

Budget Approval

Once the President's budget is transmitted to Congress, the budget approval stage begins. Budget approval is largely the province of Congress as it approves legislation that affects both taxes and spending. The approval stage involves the President in the sense that he must approve the bills that are passed by Congress prior to their becoming law, and the administration is heavily involved in negotiations with Congress on legislation as it is being considered. How might Congress make better use of performance information? The answer lies in the various parts of the congressional process: the development of the budget resolution, the authorization process, and the appropriations process.

Development of the Budget Resolution
The budget resolution lays out the "big picture" of fiscal and budget policy, creating the overall framework for specific deci-

sions on taxes and spending that must be made by congressional committees as the process goes forward. The budget resolution does not deal with the details of the budget, but rather creates a framework within which decisions on those details can be made by congressional committees. Budget resolutions nonetheless set the context for decisions at the agency or program level that are made in the authorization or appropriation process.

Authorization Process

The authorization process creates and extends programs, creates the terms and conditions under which they operate, and may create performance expectations for programs and agencies. This can include creating or making changes in mandatory spending programs—such as Social Security and Medicare (where funding of benefits is provided in authorizing law; funding of most administrative costs is provided in appropriations law)—or making changes to laws governing the collection of revenues. Authorization bills often include direction concerning performance expectations, but frequently do not include any specific performance targets.

In this context it would be very useful for federal agencies and programs if performance expectations were made clearer in authorizing legislation. This would assist agencies in developing priorities, since authorizing legislation involves reaching consensus between Congress and the President. Including performance expectations would necessitate more frequent authorizations for some programs than has historically been the case, since meaningful performance expectations must be consistent with the views of the current Congress and the current President.

The authorization process is crucial to developing expectations about the performance of programs and it is therefore the most logical place for performance information to gain a foothold in the congressional budget process. Program managers can influence congressional authorization action by working to incorporate performance goals in administration bills, making performance expectations part of the normal negotiations with Congress, and focusing on performance expectations in hearings and meetings with congressional staff.

Appropriations Process

Agencies and programs funded from discretionary appropriations have no legal authority to spend money without the appropriation of those funds. Thus, the appropriations process is an important (in many years, *the* important) annual budgeting ritual. Critics of the appropriations process usually cite the following as among the limitations of this process, each of which is a criticism that some also make of the executive branch process:

- The process is usually focused only on marginal decisions rather than on the comprehensive effects of spending.

- There is little evidence that appropriations committees consider performance information in any systematic way when making decisions on allocations, relying instead on anecdotal information on program and agency performance.

- Members of Congress use the appropriations process, in part, as a vehicle to dole out money for "member priorities" (frequently referred to as "pork barrel projects"), sometimes at the expense of program or agency performance.

In addition, many appropriation accounts are not connected to programs or specific activities of the agency. Frequently the accounts are aggregate "salary and expense" items, which commingle several programs or activities into one relatively large account. This can make it difficult to tie the costs to specific programs, let alone to the performance of particular programs.[5]

How could performance and cost information be used in the appropriations process? First, accounts could be reorganized so that they tie more specifically to agency missions or programs. A reform of account structures might allow for a more transparent illumination of costs that are associated with programs and could lay the groundwork for relating program costs to program performance.

---

[5]Jonathan Breul, "Performance Budgeting in the United States," paper prepared for the Strategic Planning and Enviornmental Governance Conference, Ministry of Environment and Territorial Protection, Formez, November 28–30, 2002, Rome, Italy, pp. 13–14.

Changes in account structures are already being advocated by executive branch agencies, some of which have had some success in convincing Congress to allow them to restructure accounts. For example, the U.S. Marshals Service completely restructured its accounts in the context of its fiscal year 2004 budget request.[6] Restructuring accounts, however, requires managers and agency budget offices to engage in often difficult negotiations with Congress.

Second, the appropriations committees could demand, and make better use of, performance information as a part of the appropriations process. To the extent that many members of Congress attempt to focus on pork barrel spending or on anecdotal information when making budget decisions, they may be less likely to demand information on the effects of overall spending. If such information became a normal part of the congressional debate, however, the effects of appropriations decisions on performance would likely become more transparent.

Third, the appropriations committees could consider agency budgets more comprehensively, reducing the number of cases where they are focused on changes at the margin. That is, they could relate program performance to cost at different funding levels, including the baseline level as well as levels that deviate from the baseline level (either positively or negatively). This would give members of Congress a better idea of the performance tradeoffs inherent in providing different levels of funding to different agencies and programs.

What can federal executives do to make the congressional process more focused on performance? First, when authorization bills are considered, they can propose legislative language that makes clear the performance expectations associated with various programs. Further, they can get agreement on performance measures that will be used to gauge progress toward authorization goals. In the appropriations process, they can ensure that

---

[6]Office of Management and Budget, "Budget and Performance Integration," chapter 1 of *Budget of the United States Government, Analytical Perspectives, Fiscal Year 2004* (Washington, D.C.: U.S. Government Printing Office, 2003). The Government Accountability Office has also done a significant amount of work on account structures in federal agencies.

budget justifications focus not just on dollars, but on the performance that is being purchased for those dollars. By helping put performance on the congressional agenda, executive branch leaders can enable clearer performance signals to be sent and can assist Congress in making performance-informed choices.

Budget Execution

Without question, there are important potential applications of performance information in each of the preceding stages of the budget process. But even if none of these preceding applications has occurred, there is a myriad of ways in which federal agencies can use performance information for budget execution—that is, for implementing the budget after it has become law.

Put simply, agencies have discretion. Agencies and their management need to "fill in the details" during the implementation (or budget execution) stage of the process. There are many specific ways in which performance information can be brought to bear on managing resources (see Table 12-2).

UNDERSTANDING THE SPECIFIC IMPLICATIONS OF THE APPROVED BUDGET FOR PERFORMANCE

Once the budget is approved, agency leaders and program managers can evaluate how all the factors that affect results—such as funding, legislative factors, environmental or economic conditions, and regulations—can be expected to affect performance. Then leaders can communicate the expected performance from the approved budget to agency staff and other interested parties. If the approved budget is different from the proposed budget, these expectations might be revised based on the budget as approved. As noted, it is most likely that the performance expectations associated with the approved budget will be transparent if the performance implications of the budget were made clear at earlier stages, beginning with the development of the budget request from the lowest levels of the agency.

Table 12-2. Performance-Informed Budgeting in Budget Execution

Potential Information Sources	Potential Uses	Could be Used by
• Agency and governmentwide strategic plans • Levels of funding (through apportionments and allotments) • Performance (outcome) measures • Output (activity) measures • Cost information	• Understanding legislative and other constraints and their effects on the achievement of agency performance goals • Allocating funds to agency missions, subunits, or regions/ local offices • Allocating funds to third parties • Monitoring cost and performance during budget execution	*Agency Head:* Allocating funds to agency subunits; communicating performance expectations *Program Managers:* Using flexibility to spend money in line with strategic priorities; communicating performance expectations *Individual Employees:* Managing funds/spending money consistent with their contributions to strategic objectives *Grant Recipients:* Purchasing goods and services with an eye toward overarching program goals

Using the Agency's Discretion to Allocate Funds within the Agency

The approved budget from Congress normally leaves the agency significant discretion to allocate resources. For many agencies, this means allocating dollars toward different agency programs, regional subunits, or both. In either of these cases, the agency can use information on the relationship between dollars and performance to maximize the level of performance that can be leveraged from a given budget. For example:

• The Food and Drug Administration restructured staff assignments to enable it to complete reviews of generic drugs in a more timely fashion.[7]

---

[7]Harry Hatry, Elaine Morley, Shelli Rossman, and Joseph Wholey, *How Federal Programs Use Outcome Information: Opportunities for Federal Managers* (Washington, D.C.: IBM Endowment for The Business of Government, May 2003), p. 35.

- The Internal Revenue Service allocated training resources among its toll-free customer service centers based on needs as indicated by the error rates across the different centers.[8]

- The Administration for Children and Families often allocates Training and Technical Assistance funds and salaries and expense dollars to its different programs "based on program performance and needs."[9]

- The Department of Agriculture's Animal and Plant Health Inspection Service's Fruit Fly Exclusion and Detection program uses outcome data to "allocate field personnel, vehicles, supplies, and other resources to. . .problem area(s)."[10]

- The Department of Housing and Urban Development uses outcome information, in part, to prioritize its use of resources for its Public and Indian Housing program and uses information on physical conditions of buildings to prioritize capital spending.[11]

- The Veterans Health Administration allocates funds to its 22 health care networks (or VISNs) based on the number of veterans being served, but performance information plays an important role in the allocation of resources to different hospitals, clinics, and offices within each VISN. VISN directors are held accountable for the achievement of outcome goals within their network, giving them incentives for maximizing performance partially by using their discretion to allocate dollars where they are most needed.[12] In 2002 the recently renamed Government Accountability Office (GAO) reviewed budget execution practices at two VISNs and found that "(i)ntegrating performance information into resource allocation decisions is apparent" in these networks.[13]

---

[8]Hatry, Morley, Rossman, and Wholey, pp. 58–59.
[9]U.S. General Accounting Office, "Managing for Results: Efforts to Strengthen the Link Between Resources and Results at the Administration for Children and Families," GAO-03-9, December 2002.
[10]Hatry, Morley, Rossman, and Wholey, pp. 19–20.
[11]Hatry, Morley, Rossman, and Wholey, pp. 41–42.
[12]Hatry, Morley, Rossman, and Wholey, pp. 61–62.
[13]U.S. General Accounting Office, "Managing for Results: Efforts to Strengthen the Link Between Resources and Results at the Veterans Health Administration," GAO-03-10, December 2002.

This is by no means a comprehensive listing of performance-informed budget execution strategies by federal agencies. Clearly, performance-informed budgeting also has a payoff in the detailed budget allocation practices that are followed at the lowest managerial levels of the organization—in an individual veterans hospital, in a national park, or in a local immigration office. For example, a hospital administrator can allocate staff between missions or between shifts based on the implications for veterans' health; a national park superintendent can use resources in a way that best assists the National Park Service in achieving its customer service, conservation, and maintenance objectives.

Allocating Funds to Third Parties

Many third parties, including state and local governments (for example, for Medicaid) and private contractors (for example, defense contractors) play important and necessary roles in managing federal programs. Clearly, agencies may use performance information to allocate resources to these external parties in a way that best leverages performance. Two specific uses are: (1) allocating and reducing funds to grant recipients; and (2) deciding whether to contract or provide a service in-house and monitoring the performance of contractors.

Allocating Funds to Grant Recipients

An inherent challenge of managing grant programs (as discussed in Chapter 8) is that the agencies with the grant funds do not directly control the behavior of the grant recipients. In the case of formula grants, performance considerations do not influence the bulk of budget allocations during budget execution, but they can influence the design of the program and the formula itself and, when the laws permit, the withholding of funds or the imposition of new conditions on fund use if performance is not satisfactory.

For discretionary awards (so-called "project grants"), it is crucial that granting agencies be aware of the performance implications of grants before funds are allocated. For example, the Department of Education's Adult Education and Literacy program used outcome data to determine which states would re-

ceive monetary incentive awards. State performance on adult
education outcomes partially determines the amount of money
each state receives.[14] The Administration for Children and Families (ACF) uses an instrument, called the Grant Application
and Budget Review Instrument (GABI), along with other information to help identify applicants that have unusually high
administrative costs, teacher/classroom ratios, etc. This assists
ACF in monitoring existing grants and deciding on future grant
funding.[15]

Outsourcing Decisions and Contract Management

Federal agencies have always contracted out a great many services, and this outsourcing trend has increased in recent years.[16]
The services most frequently contracted out include information technology, maintenance services, weapons development,
research and development, evaluation, food service, and specialized technical services (e.g., legal services). Performance and
cost information can be used to inform contracting decisions.

Sometimes the stated justification for outsourcing is that outside
vendors will be able to provide service at a lower cost. These
cost comparisons themselves can be difficult to make, given the
state of many federal and private sector accounting systems.
Even if this problem can be overcome, a reasonable comparison of in-house versus contractual production of a product or
service requires a good understanding of the performance implications of both options. Spending less money for worse performance is not a good deal; spending less money for the same
or better performance is a clear improvement.

Performance considerations also come into play in the contract
management process. The initial contract can specify performance targets and milestones for the agency. Contract management around results (as opposed to technical contract compli-

---

[14]Hatry, Morley, Rossman, and Wholey, pp. 21–22.
[15]U.S. General Accounting Office, "Managing for Results: Efforts to Strengthen
the Link Between Resources and Results at the Administration for Children
and Families," GAO-03-9, December 2002.
[16]Paul C. Light, *The True Size of Government* (Washington, D.C.: Brookings Institution, 1999).

ance, which is traditionally monitored by procurement offices) is currently one of the weaker aspects of federal management. New leaders should examine closely the skills of their contract managers and move quickly to upgrade or replace those who lack sufficient skills, lest resources be wasted and results not achieved. (See Chapter 9 for more information on contracting.)

MONITORING PERFORMANCE DURING BUDGET EXECUTION

It is crucial for managers to engage in constant communication about the relationship between resources and performance during budget execution. Priorities change, as do factors that influence performance, during the budget year. The cost of items important to service delivery may change, as may environmental factors. GAO highlights the importance of performance monitoring during budget execution so that "management has credible, up-to-date information for monitoring and decision-making. Such monitoring should form the basis for decisions that address performance gaps by looking for root causes and, if necessary, adjusting funding allocations to rectify performance problems."[17]

Tracking costs during the fiscal year can have important implications for performance. If the costs of a given activity or program run substantially over or under projections, that clearly affects performance. Further, for many programs, productivity or cost measures are a significant component of performance measurement. GAO notes that the ability to account for direct and indirect costs necessitates an information system that permits all costs to be associated with program goals.

USING PERFORMANCE INFORMATION DURING AUDIT AND EVALUATION

Finally, performance information can be used in important ways in the audit and evaluation stage of the budget process,

---

[17]U.S. General Accounting Office, "Results-Oriented Budget Practices," GAO 0101084SP, August 2001, p. 20.

during which federal programs will be reviewed to determine compliance with laws, management practices, and program performance. (See Part Four for more detailed discussions of evaluation and the roles of your IG, GAO, and OMB in assessing results.)

The results of the audit and evaluation stage should feed into the formulation of the budget during some subsequent fiscal year. This frequently occurs with a significant time lag; by the time audit results are known from one fiscal year, the budget preparation phase my be underway for a fiscal year two (or more) years later. The Bush administration's initiatives share this focus, perhaps particularly manifested in the PART, which requires after-the-fact knowledge of performance and inputs to succeed.

What specific ways, then, can the audit and evaluation process be supportive of performance-informed budgeting? Here are a few:

- *Estimating costs appropriately.* Understanding the connection between resources and results requires the appropriate measurement of each. Audits can assist by providing information on the status of cost accounting and by making recommendations on further developments.

- *Reporting on performance.* The required performance reports under the Government Performance and Results Act and the Chief Financial Officers Act (see Chapter 11) exemplify a performance-informed audit and evaluation process. To the extent that they highlight gaps between expected and actual performance, these reports can be useful tools for future planning.

  Managers need to know that while OMB has exerted extreme pressure on agencies to have timely and accurate financial information, no such pressure has been exerted on agencies regarding performance information, including the costs of achieving results. Managers whose programs have not already done this on their own need to take the initiative here, lest their tenure be marked by inability to manage and report accurately on program performance and costs.

- *Developing "logic models" of the relationship between resources and results.* Understanding costs and performance levels is not enough. A mature performance-informed budgeting system must be able to make connections between the two. Making connections between dollars and performance requires an understanding of how the former affects the latter, meaning that the causal relationships between resources and results must be clearly understood. Since many factors besides the level of funding can affect performance, this is potentially a complex undertaking.

- *Highlighting data limitations and problems.* Finally, audits and evaluations can highlight data limitations and problems in developing a mature performance-informed budgeting system. This can include problems with data reliability, timeliness of collection, timeliness of reporting, or failure to understand causal relationships.

In the end, any sophisticated performance-informed budgeting system requires the ability not only to specify performance before the fact and use performance information in allocating resources at all stages of the process, but the ability to evaluate performance after the fact and make adjustments for the future accordingly. This necessitates an investment in evaluation capacity that has been lacking recently in federal agencies.[18] It also requires that auditors and evaluators ask the right questions and that the information included in these audits be provided to agency staff and leadership, OMB, and Congress in a timely fashion.

---

[18]Kathryn E. Newcomer and Mary Ann Scheirer, "Using Evaluation to Support Performance Management: A Guide for Federal Executives," PriceWaterhouseCoopers Endowment for the Business of Government, January 2001.

Performance information can be used in a variety of ways in the federal budget and program management processes; many agencies are making effective use of such information. Nonetheless, there are significant gaps in our understanding of performance-informed budgeting, and filling these knowledge gaps can contribute to making the budget process at all stages more informed by performance. Substantial progress has been made in the federal government over the past decade in making performance information more widely available. The next step is to move toward the use of performance information at all stages of the budget and management processes.

CHAPTER 13

Communicating Performance Results to Congress and the Public

Carl DeMaio
Ian Koski

"Prior to GPRA, few agencies reported their performance information externally; now it is reported on a regular basis. . . . GPRA also improves the transparency of government results to the American public with more information and new types of information being available."

Patricia Dalton, Director, Strategic Issues,
Government Accountability Office

"Congress must resist the temptation to ignore management reforms. Such efforts are not the most exciting issues, and they rarely make headlines. But in reality, there are few matters more important for Congress to focus on than ensuring that the federal government is well run and results-oriented."

Rep. Todd Platts (R-Pa.), Subcommittee on Government
Efficiency and Financial Management

From Wall Street to Main Street—and all the way to Pennsylvania Avenue—everyone is talking about enhancing transparency. Yet, long before scandals such as Enron made headlines and brought greater transparency of performance for corporate shareholders, the Government Performance and Results Act (GPRA) sought to enhance the transparency of government performance for the taxpayer.

Carl DeMaio *is President and* ***Ian Koski*** *is Director of Public Policy and Communications at The Performance Institute.*

That's why simply measuring your agency's performance is not enough. You must be able to communicate performance results clearly to stakeholders, Congress, and the public at large. Effective communication of performance information will enable leaders and managers to enhance the trust and faith that Congress and the public have in your agency. Moreover, you will educate policymakers and the public on key initiatives that must be undertaken to improve agency performance.

Tips for Leaders and Managers

- Know your audience and tailor your performance data to it.

- Translate performance data into language your audience understands.

- Craft a message that is focused on results and relevant successes.

- Remember that taxpayers care most about how management reform is improving *their* lives.

- Get your external stakeholders involved.

- Invest the effort to get coverage in the news media.

COMMUNICATING PERFORMANCE TO CONGRESS

Getting the attention of a member of Congress is hard on the lightest of days. Amid the barrage of information that floods congressional offices every day are reports and releases on dozens of political issues—many of them issues that will have an impact on the results of their next election. The unfortunate reality is that it is extraordinarily difficult to get the attention of a member of Congress on an issue like program performance.

Ever since GPRA was passed in 1993, federal managers have groused at Congress' apparent lack of interest in performance information. Nevertheless, GPRA has caught on, albeit slowly, as a producer of readily available performance information that members of Congress can draw on in performing oversight and making program budget decisions. Performance measures have been increasingly used in reauthorizations and committee reports, and even to drive sweeping changes in legislation such as the No Child Left Behind Act and Welfare to Work reform.

The trick is to discover *how* Congress is interested in performance and *how* members express that interest in their decisions on legislation, budget, and oversight. A few helpful practices have emerged from agencies that have successfully engaged Congress on performance accountability issues facing their programs and been effective in driving congressional decision-making:

- *Focus on results.* Members of Congress are not interested in the internal management complexities or details of process; they want to hear about progress on national problems and results for Americans. That's why your performance information should be used to "tell the story" of *why* your program is relevant (outcome measures), *what* the policy challenge is to producing greater results (strategy measures), and *how* you are doing at solving those challenges (output and efficiency measures.) In telling this story, it is important that you frame your performance case from the standpoint of *who* will be impacted by improvements in your performance (i.e., individual constituencies).

- *Keep it short.* It is ideal to focus on no more than three to five performance measures per program—and even that might be too much depending on the complexity of the measures. GPRA has produced a *lot* of performance information. Estimates place the annual page total for the GPRA-mandated Performance and Accountability Reports at 16,000—far more than even the most diligent member of Congress and his or her staff can read and process. Inundating members of Congress and committees with data garnered from performance metrics will only serve to overwhelm them. Your performance data must be put into a context that demonstrates where the data fit in, how they impact the budget allocation, and how they affect results.

- *Seek input.* Asking members what performance measures they are most interested in is a key step in getting them to use the information later on. Fortunately, GPRA mandates congressional participation in the formulation of federal agencies' five-year strategic plans, strengthening the oversight relationship early in the process. This requirement should be taken quite seriously, with early and often consultations with members of your congressional committees.

- *Do your homework.* When approaching a member of Congress or responding to a request for information, be certain to provide the data most relevant to that member. This is best done by assessing what issues that member is most concerned about and which stakeholder groups carry the most weight with that individual member.

- *Work with stakeholders.* Nothing gets a member's attention—and time—better than representatives from interest groups. The people and organizations whose policy objectives are impacted by your program can be incredible allies. . .or aggravating enemies. The congressional "outreach" for your program or agency can be dominated by the communication that stakeholders have with members of Congress. Thus, it is vital to cultivate those relationships. Moreover, with federal officials under restrictions on lobbying, stakeholder representatives are sometimes the best vehicles for engaging congressional officials.

- *Focus on authorizers first.* Most agencies make the critical mistake of skipping authorizers and going right to the members with the money: appropriators. The most progress in getting performance information used by Congress and integrated into budget decisions has been made by agencies that start with authorizers.

The goal is to work with authorizers to set clear goals and measures when individual program reauthorizations are made. Committee members are likely to be the most knowledgeable on your program and will almost certainly be the most receptive to the performance information you provide. Work with them to demonstrate what works, what doesn't, why that's the case, and what can be done from a legislative perspective to improve your program's performance.

Inserting the measures into statutes or committee reports at the authorization stage enhances your case when presenting that same information during the budget process. Moreover, if your agency wants to change its budget structure or format to make the performance implications of funding decisions more transparent, that too must begin by changing the program structure from which the budget structure is built. If you change your program structure with the authorizers, the appropriators will likely insist that the budget structure change as well.

- *Engage appropriators.* Ultimately, federal agencies are most interested in getting appropriator "buy-in" for the performance measures being used in the budget—in the hope that good performance will be rewarded with increased budgetary resources. However, managing communications with appropriators is quite a challenge. The most heavily lobbied members of Congress, appropriators are inundated with information.

The biggest challenge is integrating performance information into the budget "justifications of estimates" that are provided to each appropriations committee and serve as the basic decision-making documents of the federal budget process. These voluminous documents are filled with details and object-class breakdowns of all program expenditures. Moreover, the budget account structures used to fund each agency are Byzantine and convoluted; they rarely offer a good structure for aligning performance to individual programs.

The first step in integrating performance into appropriations is to focus on performance information already being provided in the budget justification—working with committee clerks to prioritize and improve the quality of the performance information that the committees find most useful. Then, the agency should seek input on whatever additional results-oriented performance measures might be useful for appropriator decision-making. Once measures are accepted

and in place, then and only then should budget account restructuring and alignment be entertained. This process could
take three to five years to implement fully, so early dialogue
with appropriators is helpful.

- *Ask for what you want.* "If you don't ask, you don't get" is the
  fundamental premise behind effective sales techniques. After
  presenting performance information, identify what specific
  "next steps" Congress can take to help improve agency performance and results.

No doubt, there is a great deal of room for improvement in
the way Congress approaches performance management—as
well as the institutional capacity of Congress to sort through,
interpret, and act on performance information provided by
federal agencies. That's why The Performance Institute has recommended the creation of a Congressional Office of Program
Performance (COPP) to act as the legislative branch's performance watchdog. The COPP would conduct its own program
assessments that fulfill congressionally determined information
needs and peer-review the program assessments published by
the Office of Management and Budget (OMB). The result would
be a more streamlined oversight process that puts performance
measurement front-and-center in the budget process.

COMMUNICATING PERFORMANCE TO STAKEHOLDERS

Too often saddled with the negative connotation associated
with "interest groups," external stakeholders play a vital role
in shaping the success earned by federal agencies. The involvement of non-governmental organizations like associations, trade
groups, think tanks, and academic institutions whose interest
lies in the mission of your agency can influence the politics of
your program, the process of your program, and the product of
your program.

The consultation of stakeholders is actually a statutory requirement. GPRA requires each agency to "solicit and consider the
views and suggestions of those entities potentially affected by
or interested in" its strategic plan. Agencies are finding that beyond GPRA compliance, the involvement of stakeholders has

earned them powerful political allies who already have the ears of Congress, the White House, and the public.

Getting stakeholders on message requires a strategic plan of its own—one designed with the goal of bringing them into the process as tightly as possible. Such a strategy should include:

- *Opening a dialogue.* Simply posting your strategic plan on your agency's website and putting a notice in the *Federal Register* does not constitute stakeholder outreach. Early in the strategic planning process, schedule a series of dialogues designed to generate ideas and build consensus on issues across the agency's strategic plan.

- *Meeting one-on-one.* Get to know your stakeholders individually to determine the specific policy interest of each, as well as to assess their communications and lobbying capabilities. Build relationships with each of your stakeholders to make them feel like part of the team, working *with* you to fulfill your mutual interest.

- *Asking for help.* Don't be afraid to ask your stakeholders to speak up for you on Capitol Hill since you can't lobby. Their credibility can get them meetings with authorizers and appropriators. Armed with accurate information about your agency's performance, they can articulate a clear message of support for your agency's budget request.

- *Reaching the public.* Often, your stakeholders will be in regular contact with the public. Use those contacts. By bringing stakeholders on board, your message can be communicated through their newsletters, mass e-mails, websites, conferences, and mailings.

COMMUNICATING PERFORMANCE TO THE MEDIA AND PUBLIC

Strategic media relations is a pivotal component of communicating performance. Not only is it a cost-efficient strategy for reaching the public, but it can be a highly credible vehicle for reaching policymakers and opinion leaders. The most basic principle of effective media relations is providing the reporters who cover your organization with timely, useful, and accurate information. The reality is that you must cater to them; it is not the other way around. The more useful to a reporter you can be, the better the coverage you will receive.

The trick is to know what your reporters will need from you. What questions will they ask? What data will they want? Make an effort to anticipate and prepare for reporters' informational needs *before* they show up at your press conference to make it easier for them to write about you or your issue.

Imagine for a moment that you've put a large photograph of the engine of a pick-up truck in front of a government press conference in Washington, D.C. What you'd discover is that the different reporters in the room would all find their stories in different parts of the photo. Planning for those different stories—and catering to the reporters' different information needs—is one of the most important aspects of successful media relations. Understanding the different media is also important:

- *Trade press* reporters would look at the mechanics of the engine and consider whether its parts are well-maintained, asking questions like whether the tank has enough gas. They would want to talk about how the engine works.

- *Issue press* reporters would study the photo for smog controls and ask questions about emissions standards. They would want to talk about the engine's impact on the environment.

- *Mainstream* reporters would look at the engine as a whole and ask about the vehicle it propels. They would ask questions like who was driving it, who was paying for it, who was maintaining it, and why it exists. They would want to talk about the truck's impact on people.

They would all see the same photograph but be looking for different things because their audiences have different interests.

As is the case for most industries, the federal government is covered by a group of outlets that primarily cover inside "process stories." They report more on "how" government operates than on "why" government operates. Some, like *Government Executive* and *Federal Times*, cover the range of government management issues, while others, like *Federal HR Week* and *Government Computer News*, focus on smaller niches within the management spectrum.

Communicating performance to these publications is relatively easy. Its reporters are well versed in performance management; given their readerships, program performance is a topic they *must* cover. Few Americans without a GS designation read *GovExec.com* on a daily basis, yet more than 100,000 people receive the daily e-newsletter. The website boasts more than 300,000 unique visitors a month—86 percent of whom are federal employees. Trade media like *GovExec.com* are excellent resources for communicating with your managers, your employees, and other government agencies.

Easily overlooked is the "issue press"—specialty news outlets that cover a specific social or political issue, not necessarily the government's role in that issue. For example, dozens of magazines and websites that are devoted to news about the environment won't necessarily cover the Environmental Protection Agency's (EPA) performance measurement system—but they might cover the improved performance of some EPA programs.

The strength of the issue press is its ability to reach stakeholders. The Sierra Club, which has a strong interest in the EPA, no doubt has a subscription to *Environmental Protection Magazine*. And surely the National Education Association, which speaks directly to 2.7 million educators across the country, has at least one copy of *Education Week* in its lobby. Use the issue press to reach stakeholders and amplify your message.

The trade and issue press is not, however, an appropriate channel for reaching the general public. The difficulty here is getting the mainstream media to make room on its plate for stories about improved program performance and federal employees' commitment to improved results. It seems the only time management performance makes it onto the evening news is in segments with "The Fleecing of America" in the title.

Across the board, the key to communicating performance issues to the mainstream media is showing the impact of performance improvement at an agency on specific constituencies or in addressing national problems. The trick is to make management success relevant to your audience, which is American taxpayers (or a constituency therein). Your message must focus squarely on results, be they savings of tax dollars or better delivery of services.

Such a message can be accomplished through one of two time-tested strategies: (1) communicate how your results impact your audience, and (2) put a human face on your success story.

Consider the 15-year transformation of the Internal Revenue Service (IRS). Tax collection has never been what you'd call "popular" with Americans, but decades of taxpayer mistreatment compounded an already maligned reputation for the IRS.

Years of dry Government Accountability Office (formerly known as the General Accounting Office) reports and testimony warning of widespread taxpayer mistreatment and an IRS culture that made such treatment inevitable had gone largely unheeded. It wasn't until the Senate Finance Committee held a hearing that featured testimony from victimized taxpayers that the issue received the intense national attention needed for real reform. The issue was framed in a way that showed the human face being impacted by the IRS' management problem.

Legislators took action and in 1998 passed the IRS Restructuring and Reform Act. The bill authorized $560 million for technology modernization efforts, but also called for a reassessment of priorities that would make customer service the focus.

A 24-hour hotline was set up and 250 local offices were opened on Saturday mornings. Local offices were reorganized to provide specialization based on regional business development. A new "national taxpayer advocate" office was created with the independence and authority to report directly to Congress on the IRS' customer service performance. Manuals and brochures were rewritten in plain language to try to make paying taxes less confusing.

The message? *The Internal Revenue Service recognizes its reputation and is working hard to serve taxpayers in a more friendly, helpful manner.* The changes centered around the notion of helping taxpayers instead of hunting them, serving them instead of stalking them, and assisting them instead of abusing them.

The overhaul is a management reform initiative whose progress and performance must be communicated effectively to the public to be truly successful. In the short run, taxpayers need to know about the new resources at their disposal. In the long run, a better reputation will lead to more willingness by taxpayers to ask for help, which will in turn lead to higher collections by the IRS.

The announcement of the IRS overhaul was made by then-Vice President Al Gore and received a great deal of media attention. The root of that media success was relevance. Even local newspapers wrote about the campaign, many of them putting a local spin on it by featuring readers who had run-ins with the IRS in the past. The illustration of what was wrong at the IRS actually helped draw attention to what was being done to make it right.

How successful has the image overhaul been? An ABC News poll in February 1998 found that 61 percent of Americans felt the IRS was "too harsh" in its dealings with average Americans. In April 2002, an ABC News poll found that number had dropped to 44 percent. Even though few Americans ever actually deal with IRS collections agents (who are generally seen as the root cause of the agency's image problem), the perception that the IRS has become less harsh and more customer-friendly has improved the agency's reputation nationwide.

News coverage of the protracted creation of the Department of Homeland Security (DHS) has gone similarly to that of the IRS overhaul. The stories generally started on the scope (the extraordinary union of 22 agencies and 170,000 employees) and went straight to the anticipated results (improved tactical coordination, better intelligence-sharing, direct accountability). Mainstream news media stories admitted the management challenge but glossed over the process details.

"Not only do we do our day jobs of guarding the borders, securing the ports and scanning passengers entering the airports, we also are reorganizing the entire department," DHS spokesperson Gordon Johndroe told the *Washington Post* six months after the reorganization began. "The department's roles and missions are still being defined. We're learning what works."

The bottom line on communicating performance—whether to Congress, stakeholders, the news media, or the public—is to tailor the information you present to the appropriate audience while integrating your communications to all audiences using a clear message. The message must be relevant to them, not you. Just as performance measures must be useful to the managers who make day-to-day decisions based on them, they must be useful to Congress if you expect budget decisions to be impacted. They must be useful to stakeholders and the news media if you expect news about your performance success to spread. Take the time to craft a tailored message. The results are well worth the effort.

PART FOUR

Assessing Results

You may be confident that the design and implementation of your programs are producing the intended results. To prove that to yourself, your organization, and outside entities that cast dispassionate eyes on results, however, you need rigorous evaluation. Moreover, you need to know how to work with those entities. Previous chapters have discussed working with Congress on results. In Part Four we help you understand evaluation and explore your relationship with the most prominent agencies that focus on your results.

In Chapter 14, *Dr. Kathryn Newcomer,* Director of the School of Public Policy and Public Administration of The George Washington University, joins *Jonathan Baron,* Executive Director of the Coalition for Evidence-Based Policy, to explain how leaders can better understand, implement, and use high-quality evaluation studies of several kinds.

Chapter 15 covers the two most prominent autonomous entities that review and report on your agency's results: *George Grob,* Assistant Inspector General at the Department of Health and Human Services, discusses agency Offices of Inspector General; and *Dr. Nancy Kingsbury,* Managing Director for Applied Research and Methods at the Government Accountability Office (GAO), discusses GAO. Both acknowledge that these entities are often viewed by agency leaders with trepidation but then show how you can benefit from their insights and reports.

In Chapter 16, *Barry White* draws on his long tenure in the Office of Management and Budget (OMB) as well as service in several agencies to describe how you can be most successful when working with OMB on results issues.

CHAPTER 14

Evaluating Results

Kathryn E. Newcomer, Ph.D.
Jonathan Baron

"Objective evidence trumps subjective opinion every time. This is especially true in the current environment of decreasing budgets and vociferous interest groups. Defending or proposing programmatic initiatives without thorough evaluative support is akin to going to court without having interviewed your witnesses."

—George H. Bohlinger, III, Executive Vice President, Federal Management Systems. Formerly Deputy Associate Attorney General, Department of Justice; Executive Associate Commissioner—Management, Immigration & Naturalization Service

"Good managers need hard data (both programmatic and financial) to be effective advocates of their programs."

—Beth Craig, Deputy Assistant Administrator for Air and Radiation, U.S. Environmental Protection Agency

Demands for evidence that your programs are having the intended results arise first and foremost from your own acceptance of responsibility as program leaders and managers deploying taxpayer resources. Such demands will also be made by a variety of oversight bodies critical to your success in achieving policy objectives. Congressional authorization and appropriation committees will ask to see evidence of results to support their deliberations.

Kathryn E. Newcomer, Ph.D. *is Director of the School of Public Policy and Public Administration at The George Washington University.* ***Jonathan Baron*** *is Executive Director of the Coalition for Evidence-Based Policy.*

The President's Office of Management and Budget (OMB) examiners have always been a major source of demand for results from program managers as part of OMB's role in the budget, policy, and legislative decision-making processes (see Chapter 16). External auditors such as your agency's Office of Inspector General (OIG) and the Government Accountability Office (GAO) will analyze and judge program management (see Chapter 15).

An underlying theme in many of the management laws governing the way your agency operates (as discussed in Chapter 3) is that you should "manage for results." In other words, you are expected to use data on programmatic performance and cost to make internal management improvements and resource allocations in addition to providing the data to support budgetary requests or meet oversight inquiries.

Determining whether or not a program is achieving intended results is an essential task of public management. However, making good evaluation happen is not always easy for career or appointed executives.

In some program areas, interest groups and administration and congressional advocates may not support rigorous evaluation because they do not want to question the value of programs they fought for. They may view the call for evaluation as questioning the importance of addressing what they consider important problems. Program staff may fear evaluation as an assault on their own management. Career executives may sometimes need to bide their time until the atmosphere is receptive for gathering systematic data on program results.

Calling for evaluation of programs may well not be a welcome initiative, and may not make one popular, but it can provide executives with information that may be useful and even vital to the efficient and effective stewardship of taxpayer resources.

Tips for Leaders and Managers

- Identify evaluation resources inside your agency that are available to collect and analyze data on the performance of your programs.

- Review existing performance reports and studies done on your programs to give you some hard data about program operations.

- Work with knowledgeable program managers and budget analysts in your agency to identify good, hard questions to address regarding the implementation and outcomes of your programs—before oversight officials at OMB or on the Hill raise the questions.

- Ask program managers and analytical staff to identify studies that provide persuasive evidence that your programs are achieving their intended results—and the studies that provide persuasive evidence that they are not.

- Keep in mind that well-designed randomized controlled trials are superior to other study designs in measuring a program's true impact; in cases where such trials are not feasible or not yet available, well-matched comparison-group studies and other appropriate techniques may serve the purpose.

WHAT IS PROGRAM EVALUATION?

Program evaluation is the systematic assessment of program implementation and results. Professionals involved in the field of program evaluation provide processes and tools that are useful in obtaining valid, reliable, and credible data to address questions about the performance of your programs. For many complex programs and others that involve special circumstances, the ability of evaluation to make a precise statement of the extent to which the program is the primary source of expected results can be limited. Nonetheless, all managers need to ensure that the best possible evaluation of results is performed for their program to justify its continuation in current form, as well as its resource level.

Evaluation includes ongoing monitoring of programs, typically called performance measurement or outcomes assessment, as well as studies of program implementation processes or program impact. The approaches employed are based on social science research methodologies and professional standards. Program evaluation professional support and tools can help you learn how and when programs are producing the intended results.

Evaluation resources are available in a variety of locations within agencies. For example, policy, planning, and budget shops may have resources. Free-standing central evaluation offices exist in many agencies as well as within bureaus and operative units within larger departments. These evaluation offices often contract out much of the actual evaluation work. The OIGs in the agencies increasingly provide evaluation support as well (see Chapter 15). Marshalling the political will to get evaluation done is usually harder than figuring out how to do it.

HOW DOES EVALUATION SUPPORT GOOD MANAGEMENT?

Executives and managers can use data obtained through evaluation processes and studies to learn about their programs as a means to:

- Provide evidence of program effectiveness (i.e., that their programs are having the intended results)

- Formulate and revise agency and program performance objectives

- Improve program implementation processes and management systems

- Demonstrate to oversight bodies such as OMB and congressional committees that their programs are using resources in compliance with the law and pertinent regulations.

Evaluation processes and tools are available to support each of these uses, as shown in Tables 14-1 and 14-2.

All agencies are required under the Government Performance and Results Act (GPRA) to prepare strategic plans at three to five year intervals, set specific performance goals and targets, and then publish performance reports each year with data on the achievement of goals. GPRA specifies that program evaluation work be cited in the mandated performance reports. Evaluation work may help you justify quantified goals or targets, or explain why goals were not met.

Pending legislation would amend GPRA to require that agency strategic plans be updated at the beginning of each administration, thus allowing each agency leadership team to set its own programmatic performance agenda and objectives. Evaluation work already undertaken can certainly inform these deliberations by helping identify how, where, and why programs work.

While the need to monitor program results has been the GPRA message to management, the Bush administration also introduced a new tool to "hold agencies accountable for accomplishing results" that focuses on assessing program effectiveness. (See www.whitehouse.gov/omb/budget/FY2004/performance.) The Program Assessment Rating Tool (PART) is a questionnaire consisting of approximately 30 questions (the number varies slightly depending on the type of program being evaluated) that federal managers are required to answer about program purpose and design, strategic planning, program management, and program results. Increasingly, agency and OMB staff collaborate on determining the answers.

The PART process has pushed managers to draw upon "independent, objective evaluation of results." The process underscores the need for managers to report on how they assess evaluation studies and apply them to inform program planning and corroborate program results. Attributing results to programs is a layer of analysis that presents much more complex challenges than the more direct measurement of process or short-term outputs and outcomes. Rigorous evaluation studies respond to that challenge. Pending legislation would amend GPRA to require OMB to apply an assessment tool like that introduced as PART.

Table 14-1. Uses of Program Evaluation to Support Program Planning and Management

Different Uses for Program Evaluation

Types of Program Evaluation Support	Support for Strategic and Program Planning	Support for Program Improvements	Evidence to Demonstrate Compliance and Sound Management	Evidence of Program Effectiveness
Conceptual Development	✓	✓		
Evaluation Research Methods	✓	✓		
Process/Implementation Studies	✓	✓	✓	
Outcomes/Impact Evaluations	✓	✓	✓	✓

OMB has used PART to assess 20 percent of the federal government's programs in each of the last three budget rounds. OMB has promised to assess all federal programs in five years. Once a program is assessed, the recommendations from that assessment are revisited each year for progress and problem updates, with a full new assessment for a basically unchanging program not usually done until the next five-year cycle.

A notable aspect of the PART tool for program managers is its explicit focus on program results. A set of questions addressing program results is to be answered with "yes," "large extent," "small extent," or "no." These questions are:

- Has the program demonstrated adequate progress in achieving its long-term performance goals?

- Does the program (including program partners) achieve its annual performance goals?

- Does the program demonstrate improved efficiencies and cost-effectiveness in achieving program goals each year?

Table 14-2. Matching Evaluation Tools to Program Data Needs

Types of Program Evaluation Support	Evaluation Research Tools and Designs
Conceptual Development	Program logic models Literature reviews of program theory in comparable interventions
Evaluation Research Methods	Stakeholder surveys Meta-evaluations Design, collection, and analysis of performance measures Needs assessments Modeling with geographic information systems Evaluability assessments
Process/Implementation Studies	Case studies Multi-site implementation or process studies Comparisons to comparable interventions Cost-benefit and cost-effectiveness studies
Outcomes/Impact Evaluations	Randomized controlled trials Pre- and post-test studies with comparison group designs Multiple time series designs Meta-evaluation of program effects from multiple sites Cost-benefit and cost-effectiveness studies

- Does the performance of this program compare favorably to other programs, including government, private, etc., with similar purpose and goals?

- Do independent and quality evaluations of sufficient scope and quality indicate that the program is effective and is achieving results?

OMB budget examiners assign each program a score based on the answers that they and the program managers and others in the agencies give in the PART questionnaire. Unlike the agency-level reporting requirements under GPRA, PART scores the performance of specific programs. Through use of the PART process, OMB has highlighted the issue of evaluating program effectiveness as a means of focusing upon accountability for program results.

WHAT OTHER SORTS OF QUESTIONS SHOULD BE ASKED ABOUT PROGRAMS?

The evidence about programs produced in GPRA performance reports and through the OMB assessments is clearly only one input into congressional appropriation deliberations. A decade of experience with GPRA has shown that only some congressional appropriation subcommittees pay much attention to the performance data they are provided in systematic formats such as the GPRA and OMB analyses.

However, congressional funders and authorizers do request data about programs—such as whether or not they have been implemented in accordance with relevant federal laws and regulations, to what extent they meet the needs of the targeted recipients, and whether or not they are producing results. Congressional program advocates may request data addressing these sorts of questions, especially if a program is under attack by administration policy proposals. The availability of evaluation analyses will likely be useful when rising deficit-driven considerations of spending become more contentious.

Executives and senior managers can use evaluation work to address a variety of questions that are useful in steering resources internally as well. Table 14-3 arrays the sorts of questions about programs that evaluation studies can address to inform internal agency decision-making. Cost-effectiveness data and analyses demonstrating the comparative advantages of different programmatic strategies can be especially useful both for internal decision-making and for supporting or defending programs at all stages of the budget and policy development processes.

GAO has produced a large number of studies that address exactly these sorts of questions, so a good first step for you is to ask

Table 14-3. Good Questions to Ask about Programs

Purpose of Question	Typical Format	Illustrative Questions
Describe Program Activities or Problem Addressed	What activities are conducted? By whom? How extensive and costly are the programs? Whom do the programs serve? Do activities vary across program components, providers, or subgroups of clients?	How different are schools participating in the Chapter 1 Elementary and Secondary School Act in terms of socioeconomic variables, student performance, and school resources? How do schools receiving Chapter 1 funding differ in instructional strategy and method of delivery and in the added services provided to low-achieving students?
Probe Program Implementation	To what extent is the program implemented in compliance with the law and regulations? Are there feasibility or management problems?	Does evidence suggest significant compliance problems with Community Health Centers' mandate to provide minimally adequate care?
Analyze Program Targeting	Have program activities, services, or products focused on appropriate (mandated) issues or problems? To what extent have programs, services, or products reached appropriate people or organizations? Do current targeting practices leave significant needs (problems) not addressed, clients not reached?	To what extent are Community Health Centers covering their medically underserved populations or areas?
Evaluate Program Impact (Results)	Overall, has the program had results consistent with its purpose (mission)? If impact has not been uniform, how has it varied across program components, approaches, providers, or client subgroups? Which components or providers have consistently failed to show an impact?	To what extent did Comprehensive Child Development Program (CCDP)-funded services improve child development and family self-sufficiency? Under what conditions and with what kinds of service delivery mechanisms has the CCDP program been most or least successful?

Table 14-3. Good Questions to Ask about Programs (continued)

Purpose of Question	Typical Format	Illustrative Questions
Identify Side Effects of Program	Have program activities had important positive or negative side effects for program participants or citizens outside the program?	Have CCDP activities increased provision, quality, and coordination of services to the non-CCDP community?
Assess Competitive Advantage of Program	Is the program strategy more (or less) effective in relation to its costs than other programs serving the same purpose?	Is providing clinics (as opposed to encouraging others to provide services) more successful in increasing access to medical care for the targeted populations?

Source: Adapted from "Program Evaluation: Improving the Flow of Information to the Congress" (GAO/PEMD-95-1), General Accounting Office, January 1995.

for all GAO reports that have been conducted on your programs. The focus and tenor of these reports can give you a sense of the areas in which Congress has shown interest in your programs.

HOW SHOULD YOU JUDGE THE QUALITY OF EVALUATION WORK?

Evaluators follow the professional standards of their specific profession, such as statistical sampling guidelines or principles of survey design. In addition, the American Evaluation Association provides guidance on the implementation of assessments of public and non-profit programs that focuses attention on the interpersonal aspects of the work, such as the involvement of program stakeholders in planning studies and in reality-testing the findings. (See www.eval.org.)

Evaluators regard several concepts as essential touchstones for guiding decisions about project design and data collection to strengthen the validity and reliability of evaluation findings (see Table 14-4). These touchstones reflect different facets of validity and reliability as well as credibility. Good evaluators will discuss each of these six touchstones in their proposals and reports, and clarify how the choices made in conducting the evaluation may potentially strengthen or weaken the findings. The most difficult touchstone is internal validity, or the ability to conclude that a program indeed produced the intended results.

HOW DO WE REALLY KNOW WHEN PROGRAMS WORK?

Evaluators are pressed to take great care when attempting to measure validly a program or intervention's "impact"—that is, the difference between (1) the outcomes when the intervention is in place, and (2) what the outcomes would have been in the absence of the intervention. In a welfare-to-work program, for example, this means measuring the difference between outcomes for program participants (e.g., employment, earnings, welfare dependency) and what their outcomes would have been in the absence of the program.

Table 14-4. Touchstones of Methodological Integrity

Measurement Validity Are we accurately measuring what we intend to measure? Measurement validity is concerned with the accuracy of measurement. The specific criteria for operationalizing concepts, such as program outputs and outcomes, should be logically related to the concepts of interest.

External Validity Are we able to generalize from the study results to the intended population? Evaluation findings are generalizable (or externally valid) if we are able to apply the findings to groups or contexts beyond those being studied.

Internal Validity Are we able to establish definitely whether there is a causal relationship between a specified cause, such as a program, and the intended effect? Attributing program results to a program entails ensuring that changes in program outcomes co-vary with the program activities; that the program was implemented prior to the occurrence of outcomes; and that plausible rival explanations for the outcomes have been ruled out to the extent reasonable.

Statistical Conclusion Validity Do the numbers we generate accurately estimate the size of a relationship between variables or the magnitude of a specific criterion measure? Numerical figures are valid if they are generated with appropriate statistical techniques supported by reasonable assumptions.

Reliability Will the measurement procedures produce similar results on repeated observations of the same condition or event? Measures are reliable to the extent that the criteria or questions consistently measure target behaviors or attitudes. Measurement procedures are reliable to the extent that they are recording data consistently.

Credibility Are the evaluation findings and conclusions believable and legitimate to the intended audience? Evaluation findings are more likely to be accepted if the program stakeholders perceive the evaluation process and data to be legitimate and the recommendations to be feasible.

Because one cannot directly measure what participants' outcomes would have been in the absence of the intervention, many evaluation studies seek to simulate what would have happened by creating a group of individuals that is as similar as possible to the group of participants, but does not receive the intervention. These studies then estimate the intervention's impact by comparing the outcomes for the two groups. The main studies of this type are "randomized controlled trials" and "comparison-group" studies.

Randomized Controlled Trials

Randomized controlled trials are studies that measure an intervention's impact by randomly assigning individuals (or other units, such as schools or police precincts) to an intervention group, which receives the intervention, or to a control group, which does not.

Well-designed and implemented randomized controlled trials are considered the gold standard for measuring an intervention's impact across many diverse fields of human inquiry, such as medicine, welfare and employment, psychology, and education.[1] There is a strong basis for the randomized controlled trial's standing as the gold standard.

First, the unique advantage of random assignment is that it enables you to evaluate whether the intervention itself, as opposed to other factors, causes the observed outcomes. The process of randomly assigning a large number of individuals to either an intervention group or a control group ensures, to a high degree of confidence, that there are no systematic differences between the groups in any characteristics (observed and unobserved) except one: The intervention group participates in the intervention and the control group does not. Therefore, assuming the trial is carried out properly, the resulting difference in outcomes

---

[1]See, for example, the Food and Drug Administration's standard for assessing the effectiveness of pharmaceutical drugs and medical devices, at 21 C.F.R. §314.12; "The Urgent Need to Improve Health Care Quality," Consensus Statement of the Institute of Medicine National Roundtable on Health Care Quality, *Journal of the American Medical Association*, vol. 280, no. 11, September 16, 1998, p. 1003; Office of Management and Budget, *Program Assessment Rating Tool (PART) Guidance for FY 2006 Budget*, p. 24, www.whitehouse.gov/omb/part/2006_part_guidance.pdf; and *Standards of Evidence: Criteria for Efficacy, Effectiveness and Dissemination*, Society for Prevention Research, April 12, 2004, www.preventionresearch.org/sofetext.php. For a dissenting view, see November 4, 2003, statement of the American Evaluation Association, www.eval.org/doestatement.htm.

between the intervention and control groups can confidently be attributed to the intervention and not to other factors.

Second, there is persuasive evidence that the randomized controlled trial, when properly designed and implemented, is superior to other study designs in measuring an intervention's true impact. For example, "pre-post" study designs often produce erroneous results. A pre-post study examines whether participants in an intervention improve or become worse off during the course of the intervention, and then attributes any such improvement or deterioration to the intervention. The problem with this type of study is that, without reference to a randomly assigned control group, it cannot answer whether the participants' improvement or deterioration would have occurred anyway, even without the intervention.

For example, a randomized controlled trial of the Department of Health and Human Services' Comprehensive Child Development Program, which assigned trained case workers to connect poor families with a variety of social services through periodic home visits, found the program to be ineffective—that is, participants fared no better in all major outcomes than the members of the control group. If a pre-post design rather than a randomized design had been used in this study, the study would have concluded erroneously that the program was broadly effective in improving participants' lives. This is because both the families in the program and those in the control group showed significant improvement during the course of the program in the following outcomes: children's vocabulary and achievement scores, mothers' employment and income, families' reliance on welfare and food stamps, and percentage of mothers who were depressed. A pre-post study would have attributed the participants' improvement to the program whereas in fact it was the result of other factors, as evidenced by the equal improvement for families in the control group.[2]

Examples in which the results of randomized controlled trials show that pre-post studies produce erroneous conclusions are

---

[2]Robert G. St. Pierre and Jean I. Layzer, "Using Home Visits for Multiple Purposes: The Comprehensive Child Development Program," *The Future of Children*, vol. 9, no. 1, spring/summer 1999, p. 134.

common; they can be found in almost any area where randomized controlled trials have been carried out.

Comparison-Group Studies

The most common "comparison-group" study designs (also
known as "quasi-experimental" designs) also lead to erroneous
conclusions in many cases.

A comparison-group study compares outcomes for intervention participants with outcomes for a comparison group chosen
through methods other than randomization. For example, comparison-group studies often compare intervention participants
with individuals having similar demographic characteristics
(e.g., age, sex, race, socioeconomic status) who are selected from
state or national survey data.

In social policy, a number of "design replication" studies have
been carried out to examine whether and under what circumstances comparison-group studies can replicate the results of
randomized controlled trials.[3] These investigations have shown
that most comparison-group studies in social policy (e.g., employment, training, welfare-to-work, education) produce inaccurate estimates of an intervention's effects because of unob-
servable differences between the intervention and comparison
groups that differentially affect their outcomes. This is true even
when statistical techniques are used to adjust for observed differences between the two groups. In a sizeable number of cases,
the inaccuracy produced by the comparison-group designs is
large enough to result in erroneous overall conclusions about
whether the intervention is effective, ineffective, or harmful.

For example, over the past 30 years, more than two dozen
comparison-group studies have found hormone replacement

---

[3]For a list of relevant studies in several different fields, see *Identifying and
Implementing Educational Practices Supported by Rigorous Evidence: A User-
Friendly Guide* (www.ed.gov/rschstate/research/pubs/rigorousevid/index.
html), U.S. Education Department, Institute of Education Sciences, December
2003, endnote 12.

therapy for postmenopausal women to be effective in reducing the women's risk of coronary heart disease, typically by 35–50 percent. But when hormone therapy was recently evaluated in two large-scale randomized controlled trials—medicine's gold standard—it was actually found to do the opposite: It *increased* the risk of heart disease, as well as stroke and breast cancer.[4]

When it is not possible to carry out a randomized controlled trial, *well-matched* comparison-group studies may be a good alternative for evaluating an intervention's impact.

Design replication studies generally support the value of comparison-group studies in which the comparison group is very closely matched with the intervention group in (1) demographic characteristics (e.g., age, sex, income level, ethnicity); (2) baseline measures of the characteristics that the intervention is designed to improve (e.g., prior criminal behavior for an intervention designed to prevent criminal activity); (3) time period in which the two groups are studied (e.g., two groups of prison inmates being released from prison in the same year as opposed to sequential years); and (4) methods used to collect outcome data (e.g., the same interview questions asked in the same way to both groups).

Among comparison-group studies, these well-matched studies are the most likely to generate valid conclusions about an intervention's impact. However, their estimates of the *size* of an intervention's impact are often inaccurate, and in some instances they still may produce erroneous overall conclusions about whether the intervention is effective, ineffective, or harmful.

This body of evidence therefore suggests that well-matched comparison-group studies can establish *potential* evidence of an intervention's effectiveness, thereby generating good hypotheses that merit confirmation in randomized controlled trials. In cases where randomized controlled trials are not feasible or not

---

[4]See *Identifying and Implementing Educational Practices Supported by Rigorous Evidence: A User-Friendly Guide* (www.ed.gov/rschstat/research/pubs/rigorousevid/index.html), U.S. Education Department, Institute of Education Sciences, December 2003, endnote 14.

yet available, such well-matched studies may serve as a second-best alternative source of evidence.

Other Evaluation Options

Randomized controlled trials and well-matched comparison-group studies have been carried out in many diverse program areas of human inquiry. However, there are programs in which it is not possible or practical to carry out such studies. For example, one cannot carry out either a randomized trial or a well-matched comparison-group study to evaluate the effectiveness of manned space flight; because we can only afford to carry out one such program, a control or comparison group cannot be created.

In a case like this, when it is impractical to use randomized trials or well-matched comparison-group studies to address a broad program area, it is often possible to use such studies to evaluate the effectiveness of alternative strategies and approaches *within* the program. In the case of manned space travel, for instance, a randomized controlled trial could be used to evaluate the effectiveness of alternative research and development (R&D) strategies to develop the required technology. In such a trial, science and engineering problems could be randomized to the alternative R&D strategies to evaluate their relative effectiveness in developing the needed technologies.

CASE STUDY: U.S. WELFARE POLICY

An example of how rigorous evidence can produce major improvements in the effectiveness of government is U.S. welfare policy.

In the years leading up to the major federal welfare reforms enacted in 1996, the U.S. Department of Health and Human Services (HHS) funded or facilitated a large number of randomized controlled trials of state and local welfare-to-work programs. A central element of this effort, from the Reagan through the Clinton administrations, was HHS' "demonstration waiver" policy. Under this policy, HHS waived certain provisions of federal law to allow state grantees to test new welfare reform approaches, but only if the grantees agreed to evaluate their reforms in randomized trials. This policy directly resulted in more than 20 large-scale randomized trials of welfare reform programs from the mid-1980s through the mid-1990s.

The randomized trials that HHS funded directly, or facilitated with waivers, built valuable, scientifically valid knowledge about what works in moving people from welfare to work. Among the most valuable findings were that:

- Welfare reform programs that emphasized short-term job-search assistance and encouraged participants to find work quickly had larger effects on employment, earnings, and welfare dependence than programs that emphasized basic education. The work-focused programs were also much less costly to operate.

- Welfare-to-work programs often reduced net government expenditures.

- Certain approaches were particularly successful. For example, Portland, Oregon's welfare-to-work program—which encouraged participants to find jobs with the potential for advancement and provided short-term skill-building activities—increased employment by 21 percent and reduced welfare payments by 24 percent over a five-year period compared to the control group.

These valuable findings were key to the political consensus behind the landmark 1996 welfare reform legislation and its strong work requirements, according to leading policymakers.[5] Since passage of the legislation, U.S. welfare rolls have fallen by more than 50 percent, in part because of these law changes. The legislation is widely regarded as one of the most important successes in the history of U.S. social policy.

---

[5]Such policymakers include, most notably, Ron Haskins, who in 1996 was the staff director of the House Ways and Means Subcommittee with jurisdiction over the bill.

Leaders and managers are under great pressure to assess the quality and results of programs stemming from laws such as GPRA as well as internal processes within agencies and OMB. However, a truism in the evaluation profession is that whenever funds are tight, evaluation resources (along with training!) are the first to be cut. Ironically, when resource constraints create pressure to cut back evaluation spending as well as programs themselves, better information on what works would seem to be even more necessary.

Good evaluation work takes resources and, more importantly, the will to place evaluation as a high enough priority within an agency to ensure that it gets done. Executives and senior managers have the opportunity to take the initiative to ensure that managers allocate resources to support high-quality evaluation work to measure the quality and results of their programs. Learning when, where, and why programs work is challenging, but tools and processes are available to support managers in their quest to understand their programs better.

CHAPTER 15

Working with the Review and Oversight Organizations

Each agency's Inspector General (IG) and, for the federal government as a whole, the Government Accountability Office (GAO) (formerly known as the General Accounting Office) have the authority to review and comment, often publicly, on virtually everything a federal agency does, including how well it is achieving results.

Traditionally, this "watchdog" function made these offices as little loved by federal officials as the Internal Revenue Service was by most Americans. In recent years, however, the modern GAO and IG staffs have greatly broadened their focus. They, too, are concerned about achieving results for the American people. While the IGs and GAO have not traded in their investigative functions, agency leaders and managers will find them to be a significant source of objective information about programs and processes; in addition, they often suggest valuable improvements that leaders and managers can implement in their organizations.

How Your Inspector General Can Help You Achieve Results

George F. Grob[1]

> "As a senior level political appointee in two administrations, I know how important it is to establish a good working relationship with the IG's office. In particular, the IG can play an important role in helping to measure program performance. And with the increasing need for accountability, having the IG participate in a collaborative role helps ensure that we are effective stewards of the taxpayers' dollars."
> —Wade Horn, Assistant Secretary for the Administration for Children and Families, Department of Health and Human Services, G.W. Bush administration

Those new to government have probably already formulated the one key principle they need for dealing with the Inspector General (IG) of the federal department or agency where they will be working: "Avoid contact if at all possible." The truth is, if you are a senior executive or a career or political appointee, you probably will have contact with your IG's office—preferably not as the subject of an investigation! Most likely your contact will be in connection with audits or evaluations of programs you will manage. You may even want to request the assistance of your IG to review some matter connected with your agency's programs. Whether you ask for help or get it anyway, your IG can be an invaluable resource to you in achieving program results.

---

[1]This article was written by George F. Grob in his private capacity. No official support or endorsement by the Office of Inspector General, U.S. Department of Health and Human Services, is intended or implied.

George F. Grob is Assistant Inspector General for Evaluation and Inspections at the U.S. Department of Health and Human Services.

Tips for Leaders and Managers

Let your Inspector General's office help you achieve results in the following ways:

- Their body of work—years of reports on your program and others like it—describes lots of ways to make improvements.

- Their institutional knowledge makes them good advice givers.

- They can review proposed laws and rules, helping you avoid problems from the get-go.

- They can help ensure the reliability of your financial records, other internal controls, and IT systems, giving you a solid foundation for performance.

- They can give you independent assessments of progress in meeting program goals.

- They can check into problems and give you independent assessments of deficiencies and performance opportunities.

- Their findings and recommendations are made public, making them easy to get but also enhancing accountability.

WHO ARE THE INSPECTORS GENERAL?

The Inspector General Act of 1978 (www.access.gpo.gov/us-code/title5a/5a_2_.html) was enacted in response to government scandals, such as the then much publicized Billie Sol Estes grain scheme. It establishes the position of IG in most federal agencies, along with special authorities and organizational requirements. The IG's mission is to fight fraud, waste, and abuse. The IGs in the major departments and regulatory agencies are appointed by the President and confirmed by the Senate. Others are appointed by their agency's governing board or Director. By statute, IGs are selected on the basis of their professional experience, not their political affiliation. Usually (by way of practice, not law), they continue in office even during a change of administration from one political party to another.

IGs have unique status with respect to their lines of reporting and supervision. They are obliged to report their findings both to the Secretary of the department or agency in which they reside and to Congress. In addition, they do their work independently. No one may supervise IGs other than the head of their department or agency (or in some cases a Deputy Secretary or similar official). Even then, the agency head may not interfere with the IG in deciding what reviews to conduct. The IGs also have access to all program information within their agency. In short, they are expected to exercise a remarkable level of independence in carrying out their duties.

The concepts of independence and open reporting have been extended in practice in recent years through the broad publication of Office of Inspector General (OIG) audits, evaluations, investigative results, advisories, and other documents. Most IGs put all their products on the Internet. Even if they don't, the information can generally be obtained under the Freedom of Information Act. As a result, IG products serve as a kind of public report card on the effectiveness of federal programs and how well they are being managed.

The core work of the IGs is their audits and investigations. The IG Act makes this their number one responsibility and mandates that they establish offices and appoint senior officials to perform these two functions. The IG Act also requires them to examine the economy, efficiency, and effectiveness of programs, to prevent fraud, to advise the agency head and Congress of program vulnerabilities and deficiencies, and to provide advice on proposed laws and regulations. These latter responsibilities, in combination with the experience and institutional knowledge of the IG staff and the perspectives they have from reviewing many different programs, make the IGs an asset that can be a real plus for leaders and managers who are interested in taking advantage of them.

A growing part of the audit profession is performance audits. Unlike traditional financial audits, performance audits focus on how well programs are managed. They size up programs against statutory or regulatory criteria, or against the commonly recognized standards or practices of comparable programs in the public or private sector, and assess whether the programs are producing their intended results. They also examine systems and structures to determine if the programs are being managed with results in mind, such as whether performance goals are established and tracked and management actions are taken to address shortfalls.

Practices vary considerably among IG offices in terms of how much they use performance audits and their focus. Some good examples are the Department of Housing and Urban Development (HUD) IG's reports on vulnerabilities and performance tracking systems in public housing programs and the Department of Health and Human Services (HHS) IG's audits of quality assurance of donated blood.

Although not required by statute, some IGs have also established offices that perform inspections and evaluations. Inspections are highly focused reviews of some aspect of a program's operations; evaluations are broad program reviews often focusing on effectiveness. The distinction between these functions is somewhat blurred. Together they encompass a much wider family of studies that rely on an amalgam of analytical methods to gather and analyze information. They complement audits and investigations in carrying out broad IG missions. (For a broader discussion of evaluation, see Chapter 14.)

The IG mission is also carried out through advisories issued by the IGs in the form of special reports or brief publications written to help program officials avoid problems encountered in IG audits and investigations.

IG websites provide a wealth of information. Two organizations can also help: the President's Council on Integrity and Efficiency (PCIE), which is composed of the President-appointed IGs, and the Executive Council on Integrity and Efficiency (ECIE), a comparable organization for the other IGs. Their common website provides valuable information about what the IGs do (www.ignet.gov/pcieecie1.html).

HOW CAN THE IG HELP?

Your IG can help you get the most out of your programs in at least three ways: You can learn from the body of work the IG's office has done in your program area; you can ask for help in reviewing programs under your cognizance; and you can exploit the experience of being audited or evaluated even if you haven't asked to be.

Learning from the IG's Body of Work

The quickest way to get help from your IG's office is to find out what it has been saying about your office's programs. This can be especially valuable if you are entering a program area for the first time. You can find out what information the IG's office has been gathering about the program for years. You can also see what it and other IG offices are saying about similar or related programs.

Getting an overall sense of issues and performance problems related to your program and similar programs can be very valuable. You can learn the most if you survey the IG's work when you first report on board. Then wait a bit and do it again. The first look will enable you to see the big picture and to learn about major vulnerabilities. You will soon get wrapped up in countless issues of your own as you try to control and give new direction to your program. As you do, you will also become more sophisticated in terms of assessing your program's vulnerabilities. A second look at the IG's body of work will give you new insights after you become more familiar with the mechanics and inner workings of your program.

Most IGs publish everything they do on their websites. Here's what to look for.

- *Top management issues.* IGs are required by statute to annually identify what they believe are the top management issues confronting their agencies. Their agencies are required to comment on the IG's assessment, and both the IG's assessment and the agency's comments are included in the agency's annual Performance and Accountability report (PAR). This top management report naturally focuses on large issues, many of which are hard to correct in one year's time. Looking at several years' worth of PARs will help you understand what the enduring problems are, not only in your own program but throughout your agency. (See Chapter 11.)

- *Semiannual reports.* By law, each IG must publish semiannual reports. These reports describe recent audits, other studies, and major investigations completed, along with the number of recommendations made and whether they have been accepted, not accepted, or are under consideration by management. The reports also list convictions, dollars recovered, and funds that can be put to better use. Because they are published every six months, these reports will give you a good overview of what your IG is looking at. In addition to the detailed information about particular audits and investigations, you will be able to spot trends and perennial vulnerabilities. For this reason, it would probably be useful to read the semiannual reports from the last five years or so.

- *Audit and evaluation reports.* Once you have a general picture about the vulnerabilities in your program and its related program areas, you can learn even more by reading the audit and evaluation reports. This is not as daunting as it may sound. Most contain executive summaries or cover letters that explain their major findings and recommendations. If you need more detail, you can delve deeper into the reports. You will probably find all the reports on your IG's website. If not, call the IG office and ask for copies. Almost all of these reports are available to the public under the Freedom of Information Act, so there is no reason why you should not get copies.

- *Work plans.* Most IGs publish annual work plans describing the audits and inspections they plan to work on during the year. In many cases, these work plans are on the IG's website. They will give you a more focused understanding of the current problems that your IG office sees in your program area. You can call your IG office if you want even more specific information to understand its concerns.

- *Program advisories.* Some IGs publish special fraud alerts or other advisories about problems they have encountered in their audits and investigations. The purpose of these advisories is to prevent fraud, waste, and abuse and to help program officials and other stakeholders stay out of trouble.

- *CFO audits.* The Chief Financial Officers (CFO) Act requires each major federal department or agency to produce an annual financial statement describing the income and expenditure of financial resources available to the agency. The statement is somewhat akin to the financial statements of publicly traded companies. Like those of their private sector counterparts, the federal agencies' financial statements are required to be audited to ensure their reliability as well as to ensure that accounting for agency funds has been executed correctly. The CFO audit also assesses the internal control systems and compliance of agencies' programs with rules and regulations. The agency's IG conducts or oversees these audits and reviews.

- *Federal Information Security Management Act audits.* The worlds of public administration, management, and accounting have become almost completely automated. Information technology is pervasive, offering economy, reliability, and effectiveness of previously unimagined scope. However, this new technology has also brought its own set of vulnerabilities: It may provide access by unauthorized individuals to private information, open programs to theft and mischief, and subject major management systems and program infrastructure to damage and destruction. To guard against this, the Federal Information Security Management Act prescribes safeguards relating to hardware, software, data, operation, access, and physical security. Critical automated systems are subject to audit to ensure that these standards are met.

Some IG products, such as evaluations and performance audits, may provide information targeted specifically to program effectiveness and efficiency. However, almost all IG products relate directly or indirectly to program performance. An awareness of IG findings and recommendations is essential to your success.

Reliable financial information, secure IT systems, effective internal controls, and program operations that comply with federal rules won't guarantee positive program results, but their absence will almost certainly forestall their achievement. Consider how difficult it will be to achieve remarkable program impact if you cannot rely on the financial information and reports or on your computer systems. The last thing you want to do is to spend your time in office explaining why your agency is disregarding the very rules that are intended to make programs successful. And you certainly don't want to lose valuable resources through fraud and waste. The body of IG work available about your program will help you fix anything that is wrong fast and help you fine tune the management systems that are essential to success.

Asking for Help

IGs are required to act independently in performing their audits, investigations, and evaluations. But that doesn't mean they cannot or will not respond to requests for help. Secretaries, other senior agency officials, and congressional committees do in fact request and receive assistance from IGs. This help may be essential, for example, if your agency receives allegations of fraud or abuse. Your IG's office can perform an independent and professional investigation to determine the truth of the matter and refer it for appropriate action if wrongdoing is discovered. Even outside the realm of willful wrongdoing, your IG can be helpful. Here are some examples:

- *Advice on proposed laws and regulations.* This IG function is required by statute. Your IG's advice can be valuable in preventing fraud, waste, and abuse by identifying vulnerabilities in draft rules and legislation and by making suggestions on how to achieve controls and accountability.

- *Advice on and monitoring of program implementation.* Getting a new program off the ground is always a daunting task. Sometimes there is considerable pressure to speed things up just to get the ball rolling, even to "get the money out there quickly." At such times, asking the IG to keep an eye out for trouble may seem like one more roadblock to getting results fast. However, it is during the exciting period of starting something new that the expertise of the IG's office can be most useful. The newness of programs and the pressure to meet ambitious schedules can leave the organization without even the most rudimentary financial systems or internal controls. It is a lot better to do it right than to waste money and shortchange program goals in the name of proving how quickly something can be done. The IG staff know what to look for and can give lots of good advice on how to set the controls in place while the program is being implemented.

- *Verification of program compliance.* Senior program officials sometimes need to be sure their initiatives are going as planned, particularly when the initiatives rely on numerous partners, such as multiple agencies, state and local governments, or other grantees. A recent example was the tackling of the Year 2000 (Y2K) computer bug. Some federal agency executives asked their IGs to verify that each program office within the agency had taken the steps mandated by the initiative and that their IT systems were Y2K-compliant. This hand-in-hand partnership between agency heads and their IGs was one important factor in the success of that initiative. A current example is the on-the-fly oversight of new and developing anti-terrorism initiatives authorized in the wake of the 9/11 disasters.

- *Special concerns.* If you become aware of a program vulnerability and you want to get out in front of it, you can ask the IG for help. This could involve something serious like loss of accounting control, waste, danger to program beneficiaries, or a festering management problem. The IG will have to weigh your concerns against all other priorities, but often is glad to be of assistance. Usually IG staff will work with senior executives to "scope out" the review to meet their needs. Be aware, though, that the eventual scope and focus of the review will be decided by the IG's office. Of course, you should not hesitate to report any potential criminal matter and to cooperate in any investigation.

- *Comments on draft IG work plan.* When IGs are preparing annual audit and evaluation work plans, many seek the comments of program offices on early drafts of the plan. While IGs are truly independent and must decide for themselves what reviews to conduct, they generally appreciate the advice and insights of officials whose programs they will study.

- *Briefings.* You can always request a briefing from IG staff on what they know about your programs. They have probably been looking at those programs, or ones similar to them, for many years and likely have insights about them that an incoming executive will appreciate hearing about. Because of their independence, they might be able to offer advice and insights that are not forthcoming from program management staff. This may be especially valuable to you before you appear before a congressional oversight hearing or an OMB budget hearing on your program.

- *Special reviews.* Again, because of their institutional knowledge, IG staff can be very helpful as members or even leaders of broad management or program reviews. For example, shortly after taking office, the new Secretary of Education in the Bush administration asked the then career Deputy IG to lead a cross-agency team of senior career staff to address and recommend fixes for long-standing management problems. The result was a blueprint for management improvement and the capability to manage progress implementing it. During the Clinton administration, the HHS IG was asked to review health care reform proposals with an eye toward "designing the fraud out" them.

Just how close should you get to your IG office? There is no simple answer to this question. Much depends on the personalities, interests, and practices of both parties. IGs and federal executives report mixed results in working together. Potentially, you can get so close that the IG is no longer independent or is too intrusive. Or you can encounter the opposite problem, where IG staff are writing reports on one set of issues while program officials are interested in others.

The greatest value the IG brings to its reviews is its independence. You can count on an unbiased study. You also get experience and professionalism in the bargain. The trick is for both parties to exploit the independence, experience, and professionalism of the IG staff. At the same time, don't forget that most IG reports become public property. Program deficiencies will become well known, as will the interests and efforts of the program agency to address them.

Exploiting the Experience of Being Audited or Evaluated

Chances are good that your program will be audited or evaluated while you are in office. Sometimes, the scope of an audit is dictated by law, such as the CFO audits. Other times, an audit or evaluation is conducted because the IG's office is concerned about a vulnerability that has come to its attention. Still other times, the review is simply part of a cycle whereby the IG staff ensures that all programs are audited or evaluated periodically.

In the latter cases, the IG staff may be interested in your view of the program. In fact, all audits and evaluations usually begin with a formal entrance conference during which the scope, methods, schedule, and any special conditions or logistical needs are discussed. You can advise the IG team of any issues of particular interest to you or explain why you believe other issues are less important.

Once an audit or evaluation begins, be sure to avoid certain classic mistakes that will either get you into trouble or make the review more difficult. In particular, do not try to direct the study, do not withhold information, and do not interfere with the study in any way. Your agency probably has an office dedicated to facilitating IG and GAO reviews. They will be able to explain the process to you and help coordinate meetings and information exchanges. All programs eventually get reviewed, and your audit liaison staff will know how to guide you through this not-uncommon experience.

When the field work and preliminary analysis of results are available, you will be invited to an exit conference. Here you will have a chance to comment on any potential misunderstanding and again discuss the relative importance of the study results.

The next step is the IG office's issuance of a formal draft audit or evaluation draft report. You will be asked to submit formal written comments—which will typically be published verbatim in the final report. This is your chance to tell the world your side of the story. You can emphasize the overall goals of your program, describe what you have been doing to make improvements in it, and highlight the results you have achieved.

While the audit and evaluation processes may sometimes make you uncomfortable and force your attention on things you'd prefer not to engage in right now, they also provide an opportunity to focus on some aspects of your program that may not going as well as you thought or intended.

WHAT ROLE DO IGS PLAY IN GPRA AND EXECUTIVE BRANCH MANAGEMENT INITIATIVES?

IGs are becoming increasingly involved with the Government Performance and Results Act (GPRA), but the type and amount of their involvement varies considerably. IG resources are limited, and much of their work is done in response to statutory mandates. Of course, they must give priority to the prevention, detection, and response to fraud, waste, and abuse.

The IGs' role in GPRA is evolving. Some of their more common activities include analyzing the reliability of agency performance data, reviewing the systems from which the data are generated, and assessing the value of the measures themselves. To various degrees, the IGs consult with agencies on the development of performance measures, conduct audits or reviews of program results, and provide information helpful in setting baselines.

Similarly, IGs are usually asked to play their part in the management initiatives of various administrations. In the Bush administration, for example, management goals and assessments are formalized in the President's Management Agenda and OMB's Program Assessment Rating Tool (see Chapters 4 and 14). In all such programs, IGs can provide oversight, independent assessments of progress, and evaluation studies to enrich program managers' understandings of the underlying conditions and processes that can impede or enhance program success.

IGs can help you achieve results. You can learn much from their body of work on your agency's programs. Their routine audits can help you ensure that you have a reliable infrastructure of financial systems, internal controls, IT services, and compliant operations without which program results will be impossible to achieve. Their performance audits and evaluations can provide information and insights on how successful your programs are and what needs to be done to make them more so. They can help you by reviewing legislative and regulatory proposals, monitoring and avoiding vulnerabilities while implementing programs, assessing and certifying compliance with important program requirements, checking out special concerns you may have, and advising you on the development of performance measures and the reliability of the data and systems that support them.

How much help you can get will depend on IG workloads and priorities. The value of your IG's help will be affected by the nature of your relationship. The relationship works best if it is based on mutual trust and respect as well as a cautious balance of partnership and independence. The IGs' most valuable assets are their independence, institutional knowledge, and professionalism.

How the Government Accountability Office Can Help You Achieve Results

Nancy Kingsbury, Ph.D.[1]

Even if you are new to government, you have likely seen press reports about the findings and recommendations of the Government Accountability Office (GAO). Its recommendations are an important source of ideas about how to improve the effectiveness of government programs and their results. GAO performs its work largely in response to inquiries from Congress, but almost all its reports are available to the public.

Tips for Leaders and Managers

- Be aware that GAO can audit or evaluate virtually every activity of government. You may not want GAO in your agency but its work can help you improve results.

- Read GAO reports on your agency and program to learn what's been said to Congress and the public.

- Know the GAO staff who look at your agency and ask for briefings on studies, especially if your agency or program is on the "high-risk list" or alternatively has been featured in a "GAO best practices" report.

---

[1]This article was written by Dr. Nancy Kingsbury in her private capacity. No official support or endorsement by the Government Accountability Office is intended or implied.

Nancy Kingsbury Ph.D., is Managing Director for Applied Research and Methods at the Government Accountability Office.

AN INTRODUCTION TO GAO

GAO is an independent, nonpartisan agency in the legislative branch. It was created in 1921 by the Budget and Accounting Act to improve federal financial management after World War I, but its role has evolved considerably. Congress has expanded GAO's statutory authority, calling on GAO with increasing frequency in carrying out its legislative and oversight responsibilities. In the 1950s and 1960s, after World War II, GAO's emphasis shifted toward examining the economy and efficiency of government operations. Through the early 1970s, GAO broadened its work into program evaluation. Also in the 1970s, GAO started recruiting physical scientists, computer professionals, economists, social scientists, and experts in health care, public policy, information management, and diverse other fields. In the 1980s, GAO reclassified most of its auditors and management analysts as evaluators and later analysts to reflect the agency's varied work. Over the next two decades, GAO turned to high-risk areas in government operations.

GAO was known for more than 80 years as the U.S. General Accounting Office. In July 2004, President Bush signed legislation changing its name to the Government Accountability Office to reflect more accurately the breadth of its responsibilities and work. GAO's engagements today include evaluations of federal programs and performance, financial and management audits, policy analyses, legal opinions, bid protest adjudications, and investigations. Its work is complementary to, but often broader than, the work of Inspectors General (IGs); the legislation establishing IGs requires that IGs and GAO avoid overlapping work.

GAO's 3,300 staff have offices in Washington, D.C., and 11 cities around the country (Atlanta, Boston, Chicago, Dallas, Denver, Los Angeles, San Francisco, Seattle; Norfolk, Virginia; Dayton, Ohio; and Huntsville, Alabama). They are responsible for auditing or evaluating almost all the activities of the federal government, from the Internal Revenue Service's abatements of tax assessments to the Environmental Protection Agency's cleanup of zinc smelters at hazardous waste sites. The agency's organization largely reflects activities distributed across the federal agencies in natural resources and the environment; physical infrastructure; defense capabilities and management; health care;

education, workforce, and income security; homeland security and justice; and financial markets and community investment. GAO also focuses on issues that cut across the government, such as financial management, acquisition management, human capital, strategic issues, budget execution, and information technology. GAO issues legal decisions on such matters as appropriations law and adjudicates bid protest claims in agency acquisitions.

The result of most of GAO's work is printed in its trademark blue cover reports, but GAO's staff also testify before congressional committees more than 200 times a year. The agency regularly briefs Congress, both during its audits and evaluations and after it has completed these engagements. Since GAO's goal is to be a model federal agency, it has also been open and transparent in the organizational improvement initiatives it has begun and it has invested considerable energy in improving its operations. As a result, GAO staff often assist other agencies in their efforts to achieve similar improvements, especially in such areas as human capital management.

You can get a good overall view of the scope of GAO's work from its strategic plan and its Performance and Accountability Report (PAR). Like almost all GAO reports and other products, both the plan and the report are available on GAO's website at www.gao.gov. For agency officials, GAO has developed a publication on agency protocols.[2] This publication summarizes GAO's expectations of agencies—such as providing documents and arranging meetings with their officials for GAO staff—as well as what agency officials can expect of GAO during the course of an engagement.

One way to see how GAO can help you as a newly appointed agency official is to search its website (www.gao.gov) for reports on topics related to your agency or program. The website has recently been upgraded, and all reports since 1975 can be found online by report number, keyword, date, topic, or agency. For example, typing "Gulf War illnesses" in the search box on the home page at the upper right will take you to a page that links

---

[2]U.S. General Accounting Office, "GAO's Agency Protocols," GAO-03-232SP, December 2, 2002. www.gao.gov/new.items/d03232sp.pdf.

to several reports on this topic. One of these is GAO-04-159, GAO's June 1, 2004, report to congressional requesters entitled "Gulf War Illnesses: DOD's Conclusions about U.S. Troops' Exposure Cannot Be Adequately Supported."

If you click on the link to this report, you will find a relatively new feature of GAO's reports—the "Highlights" page, which appears directly after the cover. Highlights succinctly summarizes why GAO did the study, what GAO found, and what GAO recommended. This page may tell you all you want to know about the report topic or it may draw you in to the rest of the report. Some reports provide a link to the report and a separate link just to the Highlights page.

When you want to search for what GAO has said specifically about your agency, go back to the home page (www.gao.gov) and click on "Reports and Testimony." Here you will see a page of the current week's reports; on the right are links to ways to search for reports by date, topic, and agency. For example, clicking on "Agency" will call up a page listing 27 departments and agencies; you can select one or more, plus a range of dates. Alternatively, you can call up a list of reports by typing keywords in agencies' names.

If you would like to know who is most likely to head up the section in GAO that might review your agency's work, you can find this information from GAO's home page by clicking on "About GAO" at the right and then on "GAO's Organization Chart" at the left. Along the bottom of the chart, you will see the names of GAO's 13 audit and evaluation teams. Clicking on any one team's name will open up a set of pages describing that team's work and listing its accomplishments and key projects. The first page also lists the team's principal staff, beginning with the Managing Director, and gives the telephone number of the Managing Director's executive assistant as well as the team's address.

New agency managers, whether career or appointed, are always welcome to call and ask for a general briefing on the GAO team's programs, relevant staff, and recent reports. If you feel you want to come prepared, you should know that the last appendix in almost every GAO report lists the staff who made major contributions to that engagement.

WORKING WITH GAO

Most GAO work begins with a mandate in legislation, a committee report, or a request from a congressional committee chair or ranking member. GAO also undertakes work on the Comptroller General's initiative, especially when the issues are of widespread interest to Congress and the public. Notwithstanding GAO's role in serving Congress, it is committed to maintaining constructive and continuing communications with agency officials.

The Comptroller General meets regularly with agency heads, and GAO's executives meet regularly with senior agency officials on their areas of responsibility to discuss mutual interests and concerns. Most GAO executives have extensive experience from their several years of reviewing agency activities. They are therefore in a good position to provide context and perspective on a large range of program activities. In addition to discussing recently completed and ongoing work, they can share their expectations about future work as reflected in GAO's strategic plan.[3]

When GAO initiates work at an agency, GAO designates an official as the primary point of contact to be available throughout the engagement. This GAO contact responds to requests for information on the status of the work and discusses any concerns about the work's scope or approach. In turn, GAO expects the agency to designate a knowledgeable official who can help GAO obtain information and complete its work in a timely manner. While an engagement is underway, GAO provides people who are not involved in the engagement with information only about its objectives, scope, and methodology, the source of the work (for example, whether it was a mandate or a request), and the expected completion date.

---

[3]U.S. General Accounting Office, "Strategic Plan 2004–2009," March 2004. www.gao.gov/sp/d04534sp.pdf.

Most agency officials prefer (understandably) that GAO not look into their programs. But a review of an agency or its programs is often an opportunity to learn new information and develop strategies for improvement that might not otherwise be available. This was an observation GAO made, for example, in a review two years ago of the Administration for Children and Families, the Coast Guard, the National Highway Traffic Safety Administration, the National Science Foundation, and the Office of Community Planning and Development within the Department of Housing and Urban Development:

> The five agencies we reviewed employed various strategies to obtain useful evaluations of program effectiveness. Just as the programs differed from one another, so did the look and content of the evaluations and so did the types of challenges faced by agencies. . . .Whether evaluation activities were an intrinsic part of the agency's history or a response to new external forces, learning from evaluation allowed for continuous improvements in operations and programs, and the advancement of a knowledge base. . . ."[4]

WHAT IT MEANS TO BE ON GAO'S "HIGH-RISK" LIST

For more than a decade, GAO has issued a biennial series of reports that discuss major government programs that it describes as "high risk." GAO may identify a program as high risk if the program or its mission has national significance, involves a management function that is key to performance and accountability, is in need of broad-based transformation, or its nature represents an inherent risk for fraud or waste or a systemic risk because of ineffective management systems or internal controls. Other factors GAO takes into account are whether the risk is detrimental to major national initiatives (such as health, safety, or national security) or whether the risk could result in major program failure or injury or loss of life. Table 15-1 provides a few examples of the high-risk areas GAO has identified and reported on.

---

[4]U.S. General Accounting Office, "Program Evaluation: An Evaluation Culture and Collaborative Partnerships Help Build Agency Capacity," GAO-03-454, May 2, 2003. www.gao.gov/new.items/d03454.pdf.

Table 15-1. Examples of Federal Programs GAO Has Identified As High Risk

Programs Cutting across Government	• Federal real property • Modernizing federal disability programs • Protecting information systems supporting the nation's critical infrastructure • Strategic human capital management
Agency Programs	• Collection of unpaid taxes • Financial accountability (DOD, FAA, IRS, Forest Service) • Information systems modernizations (DOD, FAA, IRS) • Medicaid, Medicare • Postal Service transformation efforts and long-term outlook

---

GAO also considers an agency's attention to corrective measures and their status and effectiveness.[5] When legislative and agency actions result in significant progress toward resolving a high-risk problem, GAO removes the designation. GAO has removed several programs from the high-risk list since the initiative began in 1990. For example, in 1991 GAO designated the Bank Insurance Fund high risk because an unprecedented number of bank failures and insurance losses in the late 1980s and early 1990s depleted the fund's reserves. After legislative action to rebuild the reserves and agency actions to improve program governance, regulation, and accounting in the early 1990s, GAO removed the program from the high-risk list in 1995.

GAO'S "BEST PRACTICES" WORK

Another line of GAO work that should be of special interest to new agency officials is detailed on the web page called "Select-

---

[5]For additional information on GAO's high-risk criteria, see "Determining Performance and Accountability Challenges and High Risks," GAO-01-159SP, November 2000. www.gao.gov/special.pubs/d01159sp.pdf. For additional information on the high-risk list itself, see "GAO: High Risk Series," GAO-03-119, January 2003.

ed GAO Best Practices Work" (www.gao.gov/bestpractices). Here you can read the results of GAO's analyses of other public and private sector organizations widely recognized for major improvements in their performance in a specific area, such as financial management, human capital, information technology, or performance measurement. Identified as best practices, these organizations' processes, practices, and systems provide models for agencies with a similar function or mission.

GAO also makes available comparative benchmarking products, primarily reports whose findings compare the processes or practices of a government agency with those of other leading organizations. Finally, GAO provides a number of guides to best practices methodology. These offer a framework for assessing programs, operations, or functions similar to those at the agencies that you are most familiar with or are that you are currently working with. Table 15-2 lists a few of these three types of GAO's best practices products.

GAO AT LARGE

The congressional intent in establishing GAO was to improve federal financial management by providing Congress with better information and control over expenditures. The Budget and Accounting Act made GAO independent of the executive branch, giving it a broad mandate to investigate how federal funds are spent. Over the years, GAO has done more than point out shortcomings in government operations, however. It works with executive branch agencies to recommend ways to modernize outmoded financial systems, prepare yearly financial statements, and submit them for audit. The passage of the Chief Financial Officers Act and the establishment of a Federal Accounting Standards Advisory Board resulted from GAO's emphasis on strengthening federal financial management.

More recently, as the federal government has faced new challenges, diffuse security threats, greater interconnectedness between global economies, and rapid technological change, one of GAO's goals has been to help Congress reexamine what government does, how it does business, and in some instances who does it. It appears that to achieve results, the federal govern-

Table 15-2. Examples of GAO's Best Practices Reports

Best Practices Reviews	*Executive Guide: Strategies to Manage Improper Payments: Learning from Public and Private Sector Organizations*, GAO-02-69G (Oct. 2001)
	Human Capital: Effective Use of Flexibilities Can Assist Agencies in Managing Their Workforces, GAO-03-2 (Dec. 6, 2002)
	Information Technology: Leading Commercial Practices for Outsourcing, GAO-02-214 (Nov. 30, 2001)
	Managing Results: Emerging Benefits from Selected Agencies' Use of Performance Agreements, GAO-01-115 (Oct. 30, 2000)
	Results-Oriented Cultures: Creating a Clear Linkage between Individual Performance and Organizational Success, GAO-03-488 (Mar. 14, 2003)
Comparative Benchmarking	*2000 Census: Review of Partnership Program Highlights Best Practices for Future Operations*, GAO-01-579 (Aug. 20, 2001)
	Defense Management: Industry Practices Can Help Military Exchanges Better Assure That Their Goods Are Not Made by Child or Forced Labor, GAO-02-256 (Jan. 31, 2002)
Best Practices Methdology	*Determining Performance and Accountability Challenges and High Risks*, GAO-01-159SP (Nov. 2000)
	Human Capital: A Self-Assessment Checklist for Agency Leaders, GAO/OCG-00-14G, v. 1 (Sept. 2000)
	Program Evaluation: Studies Helped Agencies Measure or Explain Program Performance, GGD-00-204 (Sept. 29, 2000)

ment needs to work more closely, both at home and abroad, with other governments, nongovernmental organizations, and the private sector. Analyzing the entire mix of policy tools available for addressing the nation's objectives has become a priority. In this regard, GAO continues to apply its well-known capacity for examining existing programs and operations for potential cost savings to create the fiscal flexibility required to address emerging needs.

Among GAO's engagements in fiscal year 2003, for example, were reports that drew on the agency's already extensive body of work on homeland security. GAO identified specific vulnerabilities and areas for improvement to protect aviation and surface transportation, chemical facilities, sea and land ports, financial markets, and radioactive sealed sources. In other work, GAO analyzed the U.S. visa-issuing process, showing that the Department of State's visa operations were more focused on preventing illegal immigrants from obtaining nonimmigrant visas than on detecting potential terrorists. After GAO recommended that the State Department reassess its policies, consular staffing procedures, and training program, the department adjusted policies and regulations related to screening visa applicants and staffing and training consular officers.

Table 15-3 lists a sample of products relating to such issues. More can be found under "Featured Issues" on GAO's website or by searching for specific topics.

GAO also plays a key role in improving government audits around the world through its work with the International Organization of Supreme Audit Institutions (INTOSAI). INTOSAI is the professional organization of the national audit offices of 184 countries. In fiscal year 2004, GAO led a task force of 10 nations to develop a five-year strategic plan for INTOSAI—the first in its 50-year history. The final plan was submitted to INTOSAI's membership and was approved at the triennial conference in Budapest in October 2004.

The Comptroller General also leads the Auditor General Global Working Group. In this group, the heads of the national audit offices of 16 countries representing more than 70 percent of the world's economic resources meet annually to discuss mutual challenges, share experiences, and identify opportunities for collaboration.

GAO, STANDARDS, AND INDEPENDENCE

One of GAO's key functions is publishing what is familiarly called "the yellow book," more formally entitled *Government*

Table 15-3. Examples of GAO Products Cutting across Domestic and International Issues

Homeland Security	*Anthrax Vaccine: Changes to the Manufacturing Process,* GAO-02-181T (Oct. 23, 2001) *Technology Assessment: Using Biometrics for Border Security,* GAO-03-174 (Nov. 15, 2002) *Overstay Tracking: A Key Component of Homeland Security and a Layered Defense,* GAO-04-82 (May 21, 2004) *September 11: Overview of Federal Disaster Assistance to the New York City Area,* GAO-04-72 (Oct. 31, 2003)
Airport Security	*Aviation Security: Further Steps Needed to Strengthen the Security of Commercial Airport Perimeters and Access Controls,* GAO-04-728 (June 4, 2004) *Aviation Security: Vulnerabilities and Potential Improvements for the Air Cargo System,* GAO-03-344 (Dec. 20, 2002)
Terrorism	*Central and Southwest Asian Countries: Trends in U.S. Assistance and Key Economic, Governance, and Demographic Characteristics,* GAO-03-634R (May 9, 2003) *Combating Terrorism: DOD Efforts to Improve Installation Preparedness Can Be Enhanced with Clarified Responsibilities and Comprehensive Planning,* GAO-04-855 (Aug. 12, 2004)

Auditing Standards.[6] The yellow book contains standards for audits of government organizations, programs, activities, and functions, as well as standards for audits of government assistance that contractors, nonprofit organizations, and other nongovernment organizations receive. Often referred to as "generally accepted government auditing standards," these standards must be followed by auditors and audit organizations when

---

[6]U. S. General Accounting Office, Comptroller General of the United States, "Government Auditing Standards, 2003 Revision," GAO-03-673G, June 2003. www.gao.gov/govaud/yb2003.pdf.

required by law, regulation, agreement, contract, or policy. The standards pertain to auditors' professional qualifications, the quality of their work, and the characteristics of their reports.

One of the more important standards the yellow book spells out is the standard for independence:

> In all matters relating to the audit work, the audit organization and the individual auditor, whether government or public, should be free both in fact and appearance from personal, external, and organizational impairments to independence.[7]

What you as a new agency official may come to regard as most significant about this standard is that GAO staff themselves adhere to it rigorously. This means that they do not perform an agency's management functions or make management decisions.

The standard makes a distinction between an audit function and a nonaudit function. At some length, it explains that since an auditor who is performing a nonaudit function may have an understanding of an audited agency's internal controls, that auditor is at liberty to share the information if it appears to be useful. However, even the auditor who is not performing an audit function is regarded as being impaired with respect to the audit, or lacking in independence, if he or she has a direct, significant, or material indirect financial interest in programs or activities related to the agency being audited. In such cases, the auditor is to withdraw from the engagement. GAO has considerable safeguards in place to ensure that its staff meet the independence standard.[8]

---

[7]U. S. General Accounting Office, Comptroller General of the United States, "Government Auditing Standards, 2003 Revision," GAO-03-673G, June 2003, pp. 27–28. www.gao.gov/govaud/yb2003.pdf.
[8]More information on this and other yellow book standards is available on GAO's website at www.gao.gov/govaud/ybk01.htm.

GAO'S INTERNAL AND EXTERNAL EXPERTISE

In the 1980s GAO began to call its professional staff "evaluators." This was to reflect the fact that the agency was hiring fewer auditors and more people with postgraduate degrees in public administration, public policy, law, business, computer science, economics, and the social sciences. One result of this recruiting policy is that GAO has long had a pool of talented and skilled experts who are able to investigate in depth such issues as national defense, international affairs, education, the environment, health care, transportation, financial management, and information technology. They work not just with the federal agencies that manage programs in these areas but also with local and state governments and with agents of foreign governments.

When a GAO engagement team finds itself lacking knowledge in some particular area, the agency has in place a contract with the National Research Council that allows the team to draw on the wealth of expertise available through the National Academies and its member organizations. The National Academies can find experts from academia, industry, the private sector, and government in technology, science, medicine, and other specialties. It draws experts from inside and outside the National Academies' 4,000 members, which include many of the nation's top scientists, engineers, and other professionals.

The National Academies identifies and selects experts to provide technical assistance at meetings with GAO staff (usually moderated panel discussions) on engagement topics that GAO specifies. The persons selected are known experts in their subject areas based on their background in policy, research, or practice and because collectively they represent a wide range of perspectives on the questions GAO asks them to discuss.

The Board on Agriculture and Natural Resources, Board on Radiation Effects Research, and Natural Disasters Roundtable are three among the many possible boards, committees, and other groups the National Academies can draw experts from on GAO's behalf. The range of agency concerns that GAO is capable of addressing with the help of such experts is indicated by just three projects completed in the past—one on the adequacy of the U.S. surface transportation infrastructure to meet future travel levels, another on improvements needed for the safe and secure shipment of hazardous materials by rail after September 11, 2001, and a third on federal real property acquisition, management, and disposal.

It is a standing joke in GAO that we like to approach our work in the spirit of "we're here to help" when we announce a review of agency activities or programs, but that agency officials usually laugh at the idea. Another joke is that all of our report titles imply "agency activities are improving but more needs to be done." There is a thread of truth in both clichés: We do try to be helpful, sometimes entering into what we call "constructive engagements" to assist agencies in making important improvements while we are conducting our work.

While there have been times in the past when we might not have reported the positive things we find, we work hard today to ensure that agency accomplishments are accurately reported; our best practices work often serves as a vehicle for reporting on agency activities that are important models. Many agency officials have been able to implement significant improvements in their programs because of the weight of GAO's findings and recommendations.

CHAPTER 16

Working with the Office of Management and Budget on Results

Barry White

"Numbers are the keys to the doors of everything. Spending for the arts, the sciences, foreign policy and defense, health and welfare, education, agriculture, the environment, everything— and revenues from every source—are all reflected, recorded, and battled over in numbers. Because [you in OMB] are responsible for advising the President about numbers, you are, de facto, in the stream of every policy decision made by the federal government. . . .We are doomed to repeat the mistakes of the past if we lack a trusted cadre of experts who can span the issues of partisan politics and survive the transition between parties in power. That is the role that is the raison d'etre of the Office of Management and Budget."
— Paul H. O'Neill, former OMB Deputy Director,
Chairman and CEO of ALCOA,
Secretary of the Treasury

In every administration, the Office of Management and Budget (OMB) is the institution that is most consistently focused on the results that programs and program managers achieve; consideration of those results is a required ingredient in the budget and policy decision-making processes. Thus, interaction with OMB, directly or through staff or superiors, is an inevitable aspect of senior career and appointed program management. A program leader may be able to succeed without a good relationship with OMB, but doing so will be much more difficult.

Barry White is Director of Government Performance Projects at the Council for Excellence in Government.

Agency leaders and managers can engage with OMB on results in a number of ways. With a little forethought, you can work toward making that engagement less like a contact sport and more like a shared approach to achieving the results the administration, the laws, and the public expect.

Tips for Leaders and Managers

- Learn OMB's role in the budget, policy, regulatory, management, and legislative development processes.

- Establish good working relationships early on, directly or through staff or superiors, with appointed and career OMB staff.

- Exploit the many ambiguities in the OMB process and structure to your advantage, working as a well-informed agency leader with a well thought-out strategy.

- Be aware that although OMB always uses results data in its decision processes, it also incorporates administration policy and preference and therefore cannot be driven solely by those data.

- Know and coordinate with your peers in other agencies with similar programs, lest you leave to OMB the task of coming up with solutions to perceived overlap and inefficiency as resources get tighter.

HOW DOES OMB USE RESULTS DATA?

OMB's principal uses of results, most in place since its creation as the Bureau of the Budget in 1921, are carried out primarily through its resource management offices (RMOs) or budget divisions:

- Managing the process and participating in the decisions for developing the annual President's budget, including making specific recommendations to the OMB Director on program funding levels and policy direction

- Clearing—prior to transmittal to Congress—agency testimony, legislation, letters, and reports for consistency with the President's program, and arbitrating the frequent differences among agencies on legislative issues to try to ensure everyone is singing from the same songbook (functions formalized in the Truman administration)

- Depending on the styles of a particular White House and the individual OMB political and career executives (there are no set rules for this), leading or playing a strong role in developing legislative proposals, participating in or leading legislative negotiations on authorizations, appropriations, and tax expenditures, and possibly even testifying on individual bills

- Engaging each agency on program and policy management and implementation, factoring quality of management into the resource decision-making process.

The other ways managers work with OMB, most of more recent vintage, are through OMB leadership in implementing the series of separate government-wide management laws laid out in Chapter 3.[1] Most of those laws are overseen by an appointee with a career staff. Each interacts with the budget and policy decision processes led by the RMOs. An agency leader can hope that all parts of OMB are working together, but none of the management laws establishes a framework for that.

The OMB Director, Deputy Director, and Deputy Director for Management have to set the tone of cooperation and make the system work. They always try, but experience is mixed in every administration. Agency leaders may have to get involved in those relationships if they want their proposals to move ahead relatively smoothly through all parts of OMB.

---

[1]The other offices and officials that agencies work with most frequently include the Office of Federal Financial Management, the Office of Federal Procurement Policy, the Office of Information and Regulatory Affairs, the Office of E-government and Information Technology, the Legislative Reference Division, the Chief Economist, and the Budget Review Division.

WHAT IS THE OMB STRUCTURE FOR PROGRAM RESULTS ISSUES?

Navigating successfully through the sometimes Byzantine halls of OMB requires some familiarity with its structure. Here are the players most agencies need to know for *primary* contact on results issues. About half of the 500 OMB staff is in this structure:

- Director—PAS (presidential appointee, Senate-confirmed) appointee
- Deputy Director—PAS appointee
- Deputy Director for Management—PAS appointee
- Program Associate Director (PAD)—appointed by the Director
  - —There are four, each with responsibility for a set of agencies.
  - —Each PAD heads a resource management office (RMO)
- Budget divisions—each RMO has two, each headed by a career senior executive (SES)
- Budget branches—two or more per division, each headed by a career SES
- Program examiners—career civil servants, 225 in total: 20–30 per division; 6–8 per branch.

Administrations sometimes rearrange the structure and reporting relationships to suit their management style or policy focus. For example, during the Clinton administration there was a fifth PAD to increase focus on health care reform. This structure is not as rigidly hierarchical as it looks. OMB is a small agency whose career staff routinely interact directly with each level of SES and political leader.

Each RMO oversees a group of departments and agencies with roughly related missions, so that most agency leaders will normally deal with only one PAD, one budget division, and one budget branch. For example, one PAD has the division that works with State and other international affairs agencies, plus the division that works with Defense and other national security agencies. The largest departments, such as Defense, can have several branches under one division devoted to their operations and programs.

However, as might be expected given how diverse agency program portfolios can be, several departments deal with multiple PADs, divisions, and branches. For example, Agriculture relates to one PAD, division, and branch on farm and natural resources issues; that PAD also deals with Interior, the Environmental Protection Agency, and other natural resources agencies. Agriculture also relates to a second PAD, division, and branch on its food stamps and school lunch responsibilities; this second PAD also has welfare and children's programs that are in the Departments of Health and Human Services, Education, and Labor. While programmatically logical, these split relationships make getting agreement with OMB on agency priorities much more complex, sometimes putting agency leaders in the position of brokering agreements between PADs.

The program examiners are the basic point of contact for agency staff. They have a wide range of backgrounds, work history, training, and preferences. Each examiner typically reviews a part of a Cabinet department or large agency and often multiple small agencies. Most examiners have relatively short tenure (3 to 5 years), though tenures of 10 to 20 years are not uncommon. The SES branch and division chiefs usually have much longer OMB tenure, some holding their positions for decades. The most effective examiners and SES are deeply knowledgeable of their agencies, have been through many budget and legislative cycles, know the issues from the Hill and interest group perspectives, know the most pertinent research on results, and understand the traditions within the agency.

WHOM DO YOU TALK TO ABOUT RESULTS?

There are two answers to this question: the "textbook" answer and the pragmatic answer. The textbook would tell you that:

- An agency Deputy Secretary, Program Assistant Secretary, or Assistant Secretary for Budget deals with appointee peers at OMB: the Director, the Deputies, and the PADs.

- Agency career budget officers deal with OMB career division and branch chiefs.

- Contact between RMO staff and agency program managers and staff is arranged through and monitored by the agency budget office.

In the real, fast-paced, and rarely orderly world of agency-OMB interaction, there are no such firm rules. Smart agency program managers at all levels get to know their OMB division and branch chiefs and examiners as well as the OMB appointees. They learn how these people think about agency issues, which programs are high priority for them personally (which is not always the same as administration priorities), and how much they know about program evaluation, reporting systems, management systems, staff quality, congressional and interest group involvement, and all the rest of what goes into leading and managing programs successfully.

HOW IMPORTANT ARE PERSONAL RELATIONSHIPS WITH OMB STAFF?

In general, political and career managers whose programs do best with OMB in the long run are those who make the effort to achieve a good working relationship with OMB staff, either personally or through their staff. Personally, I served in OMB for more than two decades, as well as in three Cabinet departments. As OMB examiner, branch chief, and division chief, I had a host of personal interactions with agency career managers, Assistant Secretaries, and Deputy Secretaries (on occasion even the Secretary), which were more or less successful because of the personal relationships built up over time.

Some years ago I was at the OMB Director's side for a Cabinet agency's budget appeal meeting. The agency Secretary opened with a statement of his total desired increase. The OMB Director countered with a much lower number. The Secretary promptly agreed to the lower number, throwing the OMB contingent, which was anticipating a tense negotiation, off balance. The Director suggested that they move on to discussing the distribution of both the base and incremental resources across programs. The Secretary waved at his chief appointed and career budget aides and me, all of whom had been working closely for years, and said, "No, let's let these fellows figure all that out." The meeting adjourned. And we did figure all that out.

Because many career managers serve across administrations, and many new political managers may well serve in future administrations, personal relationships established between OMB staff and agency leaders in one administration affect agency relationships in future administrations. Much time was saved in establishing OMB-agency relationships when officials experienced in dealing with OMB and who knew some of the OMB staff from their service under President Carter arrived in the Clinton administration, when officials from the Nixon-Ford years came in with President Reagan, and when officials from the Reagan administration came in with both Bush presidencies. Occasionally, old animosities were rekindled; more often, though, prior knowledge of people and process greatly aided both agency officials and OMB.

WILL OMB ALWAYS REWARD THE AGENCY PROGRAMS THAT SHOW THE BEST RESULTS?

OMB recommendations to the White House also have to take into account administration policy and preference, as well as knowledge of the relative strengths of interest groups and members of Congress. Thus, OMB cannot always reward the agency programs that show the best results. OMB cannot function effectively if it operates entirely as if it were in an ivory tower, able to consider only objective evidence of results.

However, you should know that in the budget and policy development processes, OMB is responsible for presenting agency and other views fairly among the decision options put forward. The career staff are trained to focus closely on ensuring that what is known about results is a key input to decisions. But OMB's priority in the end is to support and help develop administration priorities. Usually that means supporting programs with good results—but not always and not routinely in any administration under any results-based management initiative.

It should not, then, be surprising that:

- A program with proven positive results but which the administration does not believe is an appropriate federal responsibility will not usually fare well in final executive branch budget and policy decisions—even though it may do very well in Congress.

- A program with poor results may fare much better than it deserves on the basis of those results if administration policy favors supporting it. In that circumstance, however, OMB will generally try to negotiate agency commitments to improve program design or management to enhance results.

- A program with poor results but powerful interest group or political support may also fare much better in the process, in both OMB and Congress, than it deserves on the merits when a political judgment is made not to take on those forces.

WHAT IS OMB'S ROLE IN AN ADMINISTRATION'S RESULTS-FOCUSED MANAGEMENT INITIATIVE?

Since its creation (as the Bureau of the Budget) over 80 years ago, OMB has traditionally centered its work on the government achieving positive results for the taxpayer. Thus, OMB is the natural focal point for results-focused management reform. As discussed in Chapter 4, using OMB as the focal point was especially reinforced during the G.W. Bush administration. Implementation of the President's Management Agenda was led by the OMB Deputy Director for Management, RMO staff were directly engaged in PMA implementation, and the Program Assessment Rating Tool (PART) was developed to guide RMO assessments of programs.

The Bush administration's program assessment process marked two significant departures from OMB tradition.

First, OMB's program assessments began a move toward being consistent and systematic across all RMOs. Traditionally budget divisions have enjoyed substantial autonomy on how each analyzes programs. A consistent, systematic approach to program assessment cuts across this tradition (and causes some discomfort to some career staff). Although collaboration with agencies on each assessment is increasing, the final conclusions are OMB conclusions and the assessments are generally perceived as "OMB assessments."

Second, OMB began publishing its program assessments. When OMB's system works well, the *internal* decision-making processes are highly candid and open to all options. Even when administration policy is well-established, OMB staff has the leeway internally to expose that policy to analysis of results achieved and, when appropriate, to recommend alternatives. The products of that process have never routinely been made public, notwithstanding occasional leaks to the media.

Even when OMB questioning of agency leaders turns on significant perceived flaws in the program, agency leaders have been able to take some comfort in knowing that the discussions, because they are part of the "pre-decisional" presidential decision-making process, are legally not open to the public. This can be especially important because once a final policy decision is made, OMB turns to working with the agency to develop and publish the best possible supporting justification for that decision, even when the internal process revealed flaws in the program.

Now a significant element in OMB's analysis, the PART program assessments are published for Congress, the media, and the public to see and react to. While publishing the assessments of program design, management, and results that are done well upstream of final decisions is not tantamount to publishing actual options papers, analyses, and final decisions, doing so still puts more information in the public record than has ever been there before.

WHY SHOULD A SYSTEMATIC APPROACH AND PUBLICATION OF ASSESSMENTS MATTER TO AGENCY LEADERS?

The two changes offer important potential benefits—and pose important potential risks—for agency leaders.

On the benefits side, agency leaders can know in advance the core of the questioning they will get from OMB and thus are able to assemble the best data on programs and policies, initiate high-quality evaluations and data collections when needed, and respond effectively to initial OMB questioning. Over time, they can build up an accepted base of common knowledge and program understanding with OMB. This can reduce the time spent every year trying to figure out what OMB wants and add to the time available for more important discussions of policy direction and management improvement.

The risks are equally important. Program leaders and managers may well have a program that cannot respond effectively to the systematic questioning. Substantial numbers of programs each year receive a "results not demonstrated" rating. As media and congressional awareness of published assessments grows, leaders can find themselves responding in public to critiques that in past years were confined to the internal administration decision-making process. Where previously they could defer mounting rigorous evaluations of programs, now they will be taken to task for the lack of such evidence. (See Chapter 14 for a more complete discussion of evaluation.)

Responding to such questioning for programs that have powerful backing and whose elimination or reduction—regardless of program results—is politically inconceivable can seem a waste of time to agency leaders. In the long run, however, most should realize that the process works in favor of improving the results achieved with scarce taxpayer dollars, and should therefore support the process.

DOES OMB COMPARE SIMILAR PROGRAMS IN DIFFERENT AGENCIES?

A truism of federal programs is that there is almost no issue of any consequence of which only one agency and one program have sole ownership. Traditionally, the rigidities of agency, congressional committee, and OMB structure, coupled with the efforts of interest groups and program advocates, work against systematically comparing the results of similar programs in different agencies. That could change, however, especially in this era of predicted declining resource availability and systematic public assessments.

For example, early childhood education and child care are addressed by several multi-hundred million or billion dollar funding streams in HHS, Agriculture, Education, and Treasury (via a tax credit). Each has its own history, rationale, and advocates. Consistent assessment of each of these programs would facilitate objective comparison of design, management, and evidence of results for children and families. If such assessments did not demonstrate sound programmatic reasons for maintaining each program and program funding level when considered alongside the others, then OMB, Congress, the media, and the public would be better able to question the need for multiple funding streams.

If this change occurs, and there are indications in recent Presidents' budgets that it may, it would signal to agency program leaders and managers that they cannot start too soon learning about programs like their own in other agencies, forging good working relationships with their peers in those agencies, and taking the lead in assessing the need for change. Such change may be politically perilous and may frighten powerful interest groups, members of Congress, and their own administration's advocates. Regardless of the peril, however, it is usually better for a leader to be out ahead of thinking about major change than to be swept up in the wake of others' priorities.

In no way should the relationship with OMB occupy any career or appointed program leader's every waking moment. You have an enormous range of leadership and management responsibilities; dealing with OMB is only one. Nonetheless, it is a very important one, intimately linked to the results you achieve and the resources you have to work with, and therefore one that deserves your ongoing, thoughtful attention.

Getting Results: Will You Find the Time to Measure Up?

Kathryn E. Newcomer, Ph.D.

As with most things in life, getting results in your programs and polices is subject to the vagaries of time. Time matters in terms of the effort it takes to work through issues, obstacles, or potential obstacles and to secure agreement on program and policy objectives, strategy, and tactics.

Time is a critical factor for both career executives and appointed executives. Career executives are pressed on all sides by demands related not only to achieving results, but also to dealing with institutional issues vertically from above and below and horizontally among peers. Long-term strategies, agency relationships with interest groups and Congress, and administrative imperatives demand careful and thoughtful balance. Appointed executives have limited terms that force them to triage tasks and goals and to determine which ones to focus on.

So how can executives with limited time achieve their objectives? Prioritizing, coordinating, and learning about the policy or program history are key to getting things done. Brute force rarely results in genuine, long-term, sustainable change.

FOCUS ON A FEW MEASURABLE ACHIEVEMENTS

In view of the limited time horizon for all leaders and managers, prioritizing select objectives to accomplish is key. It is es-

Kathryn E. Newcomer, Ph.D., *is Director of the School of Public Policy and Public Administration at The George Washington University.*

sential to focus on a limited number of policy or programmatic objectives that appear doable, measurable, and likely to produce valuable and observable results. While stretch goals may represent the management philosophy *de jour*, you need to recognize that most of those goals have already been set.

In an era when strategic planning and performance targeting are not only accepted but expected managerial responsibilities, focusing on a limited number of strategic objectives that fit in with your agency's mission and broad strategic goals is prudent. Given the time it typically takes to secure the needed agreements and perform the required coordination with the diverse stakeholders in our intergovernmental policy system, identifying a limited number of programmatic areas for improvement or innovation will enhance the likelihood of achieving those objectives.

FORGE PARTNERSHIPS BETWEEN POLITICAL APPOINTEES AND TOP CAREER EXECUTIVES

Coordinating with the critical stakeholders starts at home. Top career executives are necessary partners for political appointees who want to plan and implement change. Conversely, career executives rarely succeed for long without a strong partnership or at least a mutually supportive working relationship with political executives. As Davis and Smith noted in Chapter 7 about managing change, leaders need to motivate and convince others of the likely benefits of change in policies or programs.

Consultation with the top career executives who possess institutional knowledge about programs, organizational culture, and processes that can help or hinder efforts to innovate and create change will prove invaluable to political appointees. Top career executives will be dependent on working with their political appointee counterparts to coordinate and facilitate the achievement of policy or program change. Thus, career executives and political appointees seeking change are natural partners for success.

LEARN ABOUT THE POLITICAL AND PROGRAM HISTORY

Where to start? Learning about the political and program history in your area is a first step toward setting performance targets for innovation. Learning about what has worked—and what has not worked—is extremely useful. Learning who took which sides on issues helps identify who might lend support or who needs to be persuaded or neutralized to achieve sought-after results.

Understanding the background of the debate and the history of opposition as well as support for "new" ideas or strategies in the past is key to developing your own strategy and targets. Many innovative program strategies bounced around for years before they were finally implemented by savvy leaders. For example, user fees are widely accepted in many program areas now, but were the subject of multiple administrative initiatives by both parties before they were actually implemented. In the Coast Guard they were deliberated on and off for over 25 years before they were finally adopted for use in licensing merchant mariners in the early 1980s. The successful innovators learned from studying the history of the arguments offered by both promoters and detractors.

TIME YOUR MOVE WELL

Once you master the lessons that program and organizational history can teach, and have thought through your strategy, you need to judge when the time is right to make your move with an initiative. There are no hard-and-fast rules about when to make that move. During the learning process, you will talk to a range of knowledgeable people both within and outside your agency, many of whom will offer their own advice on timing.

Here are some reasons for deciding the time is right to act:

- You want to move in time to capitalize on the "honeymoon" period of a new administration.

- You want to take the initiative because a consensus is emerging that will support your approach.

- You want to try to shake up the traditional way of doing business now because the results from that approach aren't good enough.

- You believe your approach can be the catalyst that the community will rally around, even though consensus is not apparent.

- The administration needs you to challenge the status quo even if you aren't likely to succeed this time around. (There are some charges you need to lead regardless of the outcome.)

Whatever your reason, be sure you have a sound basis for it and have lined up the necessary support from within your organization and, when feasible, outside parties. A good decision on when to move—defined retrospectively as a decision that leads toward achievement of your goals—is one of the tests of leadership at any level.

Getting results, in terms of programmatic improvements and innovation, is a valuable legacy for all leaders. Keeping focused on a limited number of priorities, forging partnerships between political appointees and career counterparts, learning about the policy and program history, and timing initiatives well will all help you produce results. You only have a finite time frame in which to achieve measurable change; don't squander it by attempting to solve the management equivalent of world hunger.

About the Editors and Authors

THE EDITORS

Barry White is Director of Government Performance Projects at the Council for Excellence in Government and an independent consultant. He had a 31-year federal career, primarily at the Office of Management and Budget, finishing his service as Deputy Associate Director heading the Education, Income Maintenance, and Labor Division. He also coordinates the work of the Government Performance Coalition. He is a Fellow of the National Academy of Public Administration and a Judge for the Arthur S. Flemming Awards for Outstanding Federal Employees. He is the author of "Budgeting for Chief Executives" in *Handbook of Government Budgeting*, and "Will Policy Makers Use Long-Range Forecasts?" in *Government Foresight: Myth, Dream, or Reality?*

Kathryn E. Newcomer, Ph.D., is Director of the School of Public Policy and Public Administration at The George Washington University, where she teaches public and nonprofit program evaluation, research design, and applied statistics. She conducts research and training for federal and local government agencies on performance measurement and program evaluation. She has published *Improving Government Performance*, *The Handbook of Practical Program Evaluation*, *Using Performance Measurement to Improve Public and Nonprofit Programs*, and *Meeting the Challenges of Performance-Oriented Government*. She is a Fellow of the National Academy of Public Administration.

THE AUTHORS

Thad W. Allen, Vice Admiral, is Chief of Staff of the U.S. Coast Guard and Commanding Officer of Coast Guard Headquarters in Washington, D.C. He graduated from the Coast Guard Academy in 1971 and has served continuously since then. Among previous positions, he served as Commander, Coast Guard Atlantic Area, Fifth Coast Guard District, and was operational commander for all Coast Guard Districts, spanning 14 million square miles and involving 26,000 military and civilian employees and 27,900 auxiliarists. He was Transition Director for the relocation of the Coast Guard from the Department of Transportation to the Department of Homeland Security and is Chair of the Department of Homeland Security Joint Requirements Council.

Jonathan Baron is Executive Director of the nonprofit Coalition for Evidence-Based Policy, which he founded in 2001 under the sponsorship of the Council for Excellence in Government. The Coalition works with executive branch and congressional policymakers to advance evidence-based reforms in major U.S. social programs. He has been nominated by the President and confirmed by the Senate to serve on the National Board for Education Sciences. Previously, he served as Executive Director of the Presidential Commission on Offsets in International Trade, Program Manager of the Department of Defense Small Business Innovation Research program, and Counsel to the House of Representatives Committee on Small Business.

Jonathan D. Breul is a Senior Fellow at the IBM Center for The Business of Government and formerly served as Senior Advisor to the Deputy Director for Management in the Office of Management and Budget in the Executive Office of the President. He is a Fellow of the National Academy for Public Administration and an adjunct faculty member at Georgetown University's Graduate Public Policy Institute.

Brent Bushey is a Research Assistant in the Center for Innovation in Public Service (CIPS), a collaborative venture between The George Washington University's School of Public Policy and Public Administration and BearingPoint, the global consulting company. His interests are in federal management issues and challenges posed by third-party government. He is co-author of "Human Capital Management: A Research Prospectus" and is currently working on another CIPS publication concerning human capital management in the federal government.

Mike Davis is Executive Director of the Center for Innovation in Public Service (CIPS), a collaborative venture between The George Washington University School of Public Policy and Public Administration and BearingPoint, the global consulting company. CIPS brings together thought leaders from the private, public, and academic sectors to address pressing public management challenges. He has served in leadership positions in the federal government, nonprofit agencies, and the private sector, and has been a consultant to government organizations engaged in organizational transformation at the local, state, and federal levels.

Carl DeMaio is President and founder of The Performance Institute, a non-partisan, private think tank dedicated to reforming government through the principles of performance, transparency, competition, and accountability. He is recognized as a national leader in government reform and taxpayer protection initiatives. Elected and career officials from both political parties routinely seek his advice on how to hold government programs accountable for delivering tangible results to the taxpayer.

Mortimer L. Downey is Chairman of PB Consult, Inc., where he has provided executive strategic advice to state and regional agencies engaged in achieving important transportation goals. He was Deputy Secretary and Chief Operating Officer for the Transportation Department in the Clinton administration, and before that, Assistant Secretary for Budget and Programs. Previously he was with the Port Authority of New York and New Jersey and then Executive Director and Chief Financial Officer for the New York Metropolitan Transportation Authority.

Thomas F. Dungan is President of Management Concepts, a 31-year-old integrated consulting, training, and publications company dedicated to improving workplace performance in the federal government. Previously, he worked for Arthur Andersen. He serves on the Board of Directors of Potomac Bank of Virginia and the Professional Services Council.

George F. Grob is Assistant Inspector General for Evaluation and Inspections at the U.S. Department of Health and Human Services (HHS). He has served for 36 years as a program analyst in the federal government, almost all of it at HHS, half with the Office of the Assistant Secretary for Planning and Evaluation and half with the Office of Inspector General. His office conducts reviews of the entire spectrum of health and human services programs, with a special emphasis on Medicare fraud, waste, and abuse.

Philip G. Joyce, Ph.D., is Professor of Public Policy and Public Administration at The George Washington University. He has published widely on the federal budget process and the use of performance information in government budget processes. He has 12 years of public sector work experience, including five years with the U.S. Congressional Budget Office.

John M. Kamensky is a Senior Fellow at the IBM Center for The Business of Government. He previously served as Deputy Director of the National Partnership for Reinventing Government under Vice President Al Gore. He also served in the Office of Management and Budget as well as the U. S. General Accounting Office.

Richard F. Keevey is Director of the Performance Consortium and Director of State Operations for the National Academy of Public Administration. He is Visiting Professor at Princeton University, teaching state and local finance. He has also served as Chief Financial Officer for the Department of Housing and Urban Development and Deputy Under Secretary for Financial Management and then Director of the Finance and Accounting Agency for the Department of Defense. He was previously Budget Director and Comptroller for New Jersey, a Practice Director for Arthur Andersen, LLP, and a Director at Unisys Corporation.

Nancy Kingsbury, Ph.D., is Managing Director for Applied Research and Methods with the Government Accountability Office. She is responsible for managing GAO's advanced technical staff. She has held many other positions at GAO and, prior to 1984, held management positions at the Office of Personnel Management, the Peace Corps, and the Department of Commerce. She is a Fellow of the National Academy of Public Administration.

Rosslyn Kleeman is currently Distinguished Executive in Residence at the School of Public Policy and Public Administration of The George Washington University. She is also the Chair of the Coalition for Effective Change (CEC), a coalition of 30 managerial, executive, and professional associations whose mission is to improve government operations and ensure sound management of the civil service. For this purpose, CEC contributes the ideas, knowledge, skills, experience, and points of view of member organizations. She is a Fellow of the National Academy of Public Administration (NAPA) and Chair of the NAPA Public Service Panel.

Ian Koski is Director of Public Policy and Communications at The Performance Institute, a private, nonpartisan government reform think tank. He directs congressional outreach, media relations, and branding and research activities, and also maintains the Institute's strategic relationships with top-level agency leadership and non-governmental stakeholders. Prior to joining the Institute, he was the managing editor of the Highbridge Horizon newspaper in New York and a reporter with the *Daily Times* in suburban Philadelphia.

David McClure, Ph.D., is Vice President for E-Government/ Technology at the Council for Excellence in Government. He is the strategic leader of the Council's e-government information technology programs, developing collaborative strategies with public and private sector leaders to use information and communication technology to improve the performance of government and engage citizens. He created the Council's Chief Information Officer (CIO) Senior Advisors to Government Executives (SAGE) group, comprised of noteworthy former public sector CIOs who serve as strategic advisors and mentors to CIOs and other senior executives primarily in state and local government. Prior to joining the Council, he was the Director for Information Technology Management Issues at the General Accounting Office.

Patricia McGinnis is President and CEO of the nonpartisan, nonprofit Council for Excellence in Government. The Council's mission is to improve the performance of government at all levels and to increase citizen confidence and participation in governance. Before coming to the Council, she was a co-founder and Principal of the FMR Group and a member of the strategic planning and government practices of Cresap, McCormick & Paget. In government, she served as Deputy Associate Director of the Office of Management and Budget during the Carter administration, where she led the effort to establish a Cabinet-level Department of Education. She has also held posts at the Senate Budget Committee and the Departments of Commerce and Health and Human Services.

Maurice McTigue is Director of the Government Accountability Project and Vice President for Outreach at the Mercatus Center at George Mason University. He came to the United States in 1997 after completing his term as New Zealand's Ambassador to Canada. Previously, as a Cabinet Minister and a Member of Parliament, he led an ambitious and extremely successful effort to restructure New Zealand's public sector and to revitalize its stagnant economy in the 1980s and 1990s. Queen Elizabeth II bestowed upon Mr. McTigue the Queen's Service Order in 1999. He works with members of Congress, executives, the White House, and scores of federal agencies on applying the principles of results-based management in the public sector. He frequently speaks at conferences on performance issues and testifies before congressional committees on issues of government reform.

Pete Smith is President of the Private Sector Council and the former President and CEO of Watson Wyatt Worldwide, a human resources consulting firm. He has extensive experience leading change in both the private and public sectors, and has worked directly with many federal agencies. He is also active in civic affairs and serves on a number of not-for-profit boards.

Harold I. Steinberg was the first Deputy Controller/Acting Controller, Office of Federal Financial Management, at the Office of Management and Budget. He was with KPMG LLP for 30 years, heading the firm's government practice. He has been involved with performance reporting since co-authoring the Financial Accounting Standards Board's 1980 publication, *Reporting Service Efforts and Accomplishments,* and helping the City of Sunnyvale, California, adopt a performance measurement system for its public safety function. He currently is the Technical Director of the Association of Government Accountants' Certificate of Excellence in Accountability Reporting program and a similar program for evaluating and improving state and local governments' performance reports.

Robert M. Tobias is a Professor of Public Administration at American University, where he also heads the Institute for the Study of Public Policy Implementation. In addition, he has been appointed by the President and confirmed by the Senate to be a member of the Internal Revenue Service Oversight Board. Previously, he served for 31 years with the National Treasury Employees Union (as its President from 1983–1999), where he worked to establish collaborative labor management relationships with the goal of creating a workplace that is more satisfying and productive and delivers better service to the public.

Hugh Walkup, Ph.D., directs strategic planning, performance reporting, and strategic plan implementation for the U.S. Department of Education and leads efforts to align and automate education information systems, including the Performance-Based Data Management Initiative. He previously led Washington State's school reform planning process and has served as administrator, counselor, researcher and instructor in schools, universities, and state and local agencies.

Members of the Government Performance Coalition

The American Society for Public Administration (ASPA)
www.aspanet.org
Founded in 1939, ASPA is the only broad-based, nationally focused organization supporting public administrators. ASPA's mission is to: advance the art, science, teaching, and practice of public and nonprofit administration; promote the value of joining and elevating the public service profession; build bridges among all who pursue public purposes; provide networking and professional development opportunities to those committed to public service values; and achieve innovative solutions to the challenges of governance.

The Association of Government Accountants (AGA)
www.agacgfm.org
AGA serves government accountability professionals by providing quality education, fostering professional development and certification, and supporting standards and research to advance government accountability. Signature programs include the Certificate of Excellence in Accountability Reporting Program and the Certified Government Financial Manager professional designation.

The Coalition for Effective Change (CEC)
www.effective-change.org
CEC was formed in 1993 as a non-partisan alliance of 30 associations representing current and former federal managers, executives, and professionals. CEC provides a channel for these public employees to contribute to the success of government management. CEC works with representatives of the Office of Management and Budget, the Office of Personnel Management, congressional committee staffs, members of Congress, and others to discuss efforts to improve government.

The Committee for Economic Development (CED)
www.ced.org
CED is an independent, nonpartisan organization of business and education leaders dedicated to policy research on the major economic and social issues of our time and the implementation of its recommendations by the public and private sectors. CED has supported research and implementation of long-term improvements to government for more than 60 years. CED's 1999 landmark report, "Investing in the People's Business: A Business Report for Campaign Finance Reform," has played an important role in the effort to reform the campaign finance system in this country.

The Council for Excellence in Government (CEG)
www.excelgov.org
CEG works to improve the performance of government at all levels and government's place in the lives and esteem of American citizens. With its experienced staff, network of experts and members ("Principals"), and diverse partners, CEG helps strengthen public sector leadership and management, driven by innovation and focused on results, and increase citizen confidence and participation in government through better understanding of government and its role. Among its initiatives are its leadership programs for presidential appointees and White House staff, organized at the request of the Clinton and G.W. Bush administrations; a public-private Technology Leadership Consortium, which produced a blueprint for harnessing information and communications technology in the public interest ("E-Government: The Next American Revolution"); and a collaborative effort with leaders in government, the private sector, and citizens across the country to produce an agenda and recommendations for our nation's homeland security enterprise from the citizen's perspective.

The George Washington University School of Public Policy and Public Administration (SPPPA) and the **Center for Innovation in Public Service** (CIPS)
www.gwu.edu/~spppa
www.centerinnovation.net
The School of Public Policy and Public Administration provides a recognized research and education center in the areas of public policy, public administration, public service, and public affairs. The school maintains close ties with the George Wash-

ington Institute of Public Policy (GWIPP). SPPPA is closely affiliated with other research and public service institutes, including: the Center for Excellence in Public Leadership; the Center for Washington Area Studies, and the Center for Innovation in Public Service (CIPS).

CIPS is a research collaborative of the School of Public Policy and Public Administration and BearingPoint. The Center's goal is to promote excellence in public service through collaboration with premier public service thought leaders across academia, business, and government for the purpose of identifying and synthesizing diverse perspectives in the public management community. CIPS activities include research, publications, discussion forums, and other collaborative public service initiatives.

The Heritage Foundation
www.heritage.org
Founded in 1973, The Heritage Foundation is a research and educational institute—a think tank—whose mission is to formulate and promote conservative public policies based on the principles of free enterprise, limited government, individual freedom, traditional American values, and a strong national defense. The Foundation's vision is to build an America where freedom, opportunity, prosperity, and civil society flourish.

The IBM Center for The Business of Government
www.businessofgovernment.org
Through research stipends and events, the IBM Center for The Business of Government stimulates research and facilitates discussion of new approaches to improving the effectiveness of government at the federal, state, local, and international levels. The Center is one of the ways IBM seeks to advance knowledge on how to improve public sector effectiveness. The IBM Center focuses on the future of the operation and management of the public sector.

The Institute for the Study of Public Policy Implementation at American University
http//spa.american.edu/isppi/
The Institute has created a non-partisan forum for stakeholders in the public policy implementation system (members of Congress, political appointees, career government executives, mid-level manager association leaders, union leaders, academ-

ics, and the consulting and technology community). This forum provides a place to: meet in a safe, facilitated environment to discuss policy implementation; explore root causes for policy implementation breakdowns and to develop theories on how an agency can create an organizational structure, organize its human resources, and develop the technology necessary to achieve agency implementation goals and objectives; discuss how the root causes of policy implementation breakdowns can be eliminated; and report the results to the public on a regular basis.

The Institute sponsors the Leadership Forum and the Center for Strategic Training and Development as well as a non-credit program, the Leadership for Public Policy Implementation Certificate Program, which enhances leadership skills and abilities and prepares federal managers for leadership and Senior Executive Service roles.

Professor Donald F. Kettl
dkettl@sas.upenn.edu
Donald F. Kettl is the Stanley I. Sheerr Endowed Term Professor in the Social Sciences at the University of Pennsylvania, where he is Professor of Political Science. He is also Nonresident Senior Fellow in Washington's Brookings Institution. He specializes in the design and performance of public organizations. Professor Kettl contributes a regular column to *Governing* magazine, is Executive Director of the Century Foundation's Working Group on Federalism and Homeland Security, and is the author of *System under Stress: Homeland Security and American Politics*; *Team Bush: Leadership Lessons from the Bush White House*; *The Transformation of Governance: Public Administration for the 21st Century*; and *Deficit Politics*. He chaired the Wisconsin Governor's Blue Ribbon Commission on State-Local Partnerships for the 21st Century. He has also taught at the University of Wisconsin-Madison, Vanderbilt University, the University of Virginia, and Columbia University. He is a fellow of the National Academy of Public Administration.

Management Concepts
www.managementconcepts.com
For more than a quarter of a century, Management Concepts has provided quality training and performance improvement solutions for the mind at work. Management Concepts partners

with individuals and organizations to improve performance through consulting solutions, high-impact training courses, certificate programs for career development, onsite and customized training, and publications.

The Mercatus Center at George Mason University
www.mercatus.org
The Mercatus Center is a research, education, and outreach organization that works with scholars, policy experts, and government officials to connect academic learning and real world practice. The Center's mission is to promote sound interdisciplinary research and application in the humane sciences that integrates theory and practice to produce solutions that sustainably advance a free, prosperous, and civil society. The Mercatus Center's research and outreach programs—Capitol Hill Campus, Government Accountability Project, Regulatory Studies Program, and Global Prosperity Initiative—support this mission.

The National Academy of Public Administration (NAPA)
www.napawash.org
NAPA is an independent, nonpartisan organization chartered by Congress to assist federal, state, and local governments in improving their effectiveness, efficiency, and accountability. The unique source of the Academy's expertise is its membership of Fellows, who are elected based on their distinguished contributions to the field of public administration through their government service, scholarship, or civic activism. The Fellows of the Academy include more than 500 current and former Cabinet officers, members of Congress, governors, mayors, state and local administrators, legislators, business executives, and scholars.

The Performance Institute
www.performanceweb.org
The Performance Institute is a private, nonpartisan think tank improving government results through the principles of performance, competition, transparency, and accountability. Based in Washington, D.C., and San Diego, the Institute serves as the nation's leading authority and repository on performance-based management practices for government. Through national conferences on pressing issues, interactive executive training programs, best practice research, and strategic consulting services, the Institute provides cutting-edge expertise in the design, im-

plementation, and evaluation of strategies to solve operational challenges, improve customer service, and enhance organizational performance.

The Progressive Policy Institute
www.ppionline.org
The Progressive Policy Institute is a research and education institute that is a project of the Third Way Foundation Inc. and is affiliated with the Democratic Leadership Council. PPI's mission is to define and promote a new progressive politics for America in the 21st century. Through its research, policies, and perspectives, the Institute is fashioning a new governing philosophy and an agenda for public innovation geared to the information age.

The Rockefeller Institute
www.rockinst.org
The Nelson A. Rockefeller Institute of Government, the public policy research arm of the State University of New York (SUNY), was established in 1982 to bring the resources of the 64-campus SUNY system to bear on public policy issues. The Institute is active nationally in research and special projects on the role of state governments in American federalism and the management and finances of both state and local governments in major areas of domestic public affairs.

The Senior Executives Association (SEA)
www.seniorexecs.org
The Senior Executives Association is a nonprofit professional association that promotes ethical and dynamic public service by fostering an outstanding career executive corps, advocates the interests of career federal executives (both active and retired), and provides information and services to SEA members. Since its founding, SEA's mission has been to: improve the efficiency, effectiveness, and productivity of the federal government; advance the professionalism of career executives; advocate the interests of career federal executives, especially members of SEA; and enhance public recognition of the contributions of federal career executives.